WORK OF HER OWN

A Woman's Guide to Success
Off the Career Track

Susan Wittig Albert, Ph.D.

Foreword by
DIANE FASSEL

A JEREMY P. TARCHER/PUTNAM BOOK
published by
G. P. Putnam's Sons
New York

A Jeremy P. Tarcher/Putnam Book
Published by G. P. Putnam's Sons
Publishers Since 1838
200 Madison Avenue
New York, NY 10016

Jeremy P. Tarcher, Inc.
5858 Wilshire Blvd., Suite 200
Los Angeles, CA 90036

Published simultaneously in Canada.

Library of Congress Cataloging-in-Publication Data

Albert, Susan Wittig.
    Work of her own : a woman's guide to success off the career track /
Susan Wittig Albert ; foreword by Diane Fassel. —1st Trade Paperback ed.
        p.   cm.
    Includes bibliographical references and index.
    ISBN 0-87477-767-4
    1. Self-employed women.   2. Career changes.   I. Title.
HD6072.5.A43   1994   93-28850   CIP
650.14′082—dc20

Design by Tanya Maiboroda

Printed in the United States of America
1   2   3   4   5   6   7   8   9   10

This book is printed on acid-free paper.

To my mother, who showed me how to work

CONTENTS

ACKNOWLEDGMENTS

I owe a great debt of gratitude to many wonderful people: the women who generously shared the stories of their career leaving with me; my agent, Anita McClellan, whose expert guidance and enthusiastic support helped me to turn the research project into a book; my editor, Connie Zweig, whose warmth and patience made writing the book a genuine joy; my husband and partner, Bill Albert, whose unfailing emotional support keeps me going and whose challenges keep the going interesting.

FOREWORD

$\mathcal{R}$eading Susan Albert's book *Work of Her Own* gave me the opportunity to review my life around the issues she raises. I recalled that for the past three years I've had conversations with women that begin with the line, "I know a woman who . . ." Then the speaker relates a story about someone who left her career, became an entrepreneur, made a radical change of work and/or personal relationship (they often go together), earns money as a waitress while pursuing her real work as an artist, and on and on the stories go. I, too, know many such women. Two who come to mind are talented, nay, brilliant physicians, who left hectic medical practices to live in Hawaii. Now they grow Sharwell avocados (the Cadillac of avocados, in case you haven't tasted them), raise Jersey cows, and grow exotic plants. One practices internal medicine two days a week; the other runs the farm and oversees the construction of a new home. Do they regret leaving medicine? No way. Are they happy, productive, and at peace? Obviously.

My physician friends are only recent history. I also remember 1974, when I was finishing a graduate degree at Harvard and embarking on my work as an organizational consultant. I had the good fortune to conduct a small study for a book by Rosabeth Moss Kanter called *Men and Women of the Corporation*. Our main concern was to understand the blocks preventing women from reaching full status in large corporations. We soon saw that the blocks were not in the individual psychology of the women. The blocks were in the structure of the organization itself. The organization was not disposed to allow equal access in terms of opportunity, power, and numbers. This situation was so severe that women who made it into the ranks of executive life were assigned certain "roles" in the minds and behaviors of the male executives. Women executives found themselves to be either sex objects, mascots, or, if they were assertive, iron maidens.

Nevertheless, many commentators on women's issues in the workplace underestimated the power, drive, and sheer creativity of women in all walks of life. And they underestimated the economics of the country, which would result in the inevitable pressures on women to earn income if families were to survive. So women entered the work force in ever-increasing numbers. In my consulting practice, it was not long before I was meeting hard-working, hard-talking, dress-for-success women, who were making it in the corporate, service, and academic worlds; but even so, something was wrong.

Many women complained that although they got to suit up, and some got to sit on the bench, few actually got to play. Enter the glass ceiling. Enter working harder and smarter than men. Enter alarming amounts of workaholism, chronic-fatigue syndrome, and burnout. It always has puzzled me to observe that many of us who are concerned with women's issues, who resolutely clean up our health through nutrition, exercise, and meditation, never raise an outcry against women's workaholism. I believe that workaholism has given us the ticket into the white male organizational system, a system whose approval we have sought even against our better instincts.

Now comes Susan Albert's fine book. She documents yet another trend among women regarding their work: Increasing numbers of women are leaving their chosen careers for work of their own. Such work may or may not be rewarded monetarily, but it is highly lucrative in spiritual currency and an enhanced quality of life.

Susan Albert's book emerges in a new genre of writing about women and their work. *Work of Her Own* is rooted in a style congruent with women's lives. It is experiential, particular, and specific to women. In an unspoken yet dramatic way, *Work of Her Own* challenges a mechanistic, reductionistic worldview and all of the disciplines such a worldview has spawned. Medicine and psychology, organizational theory and career counseling—these and other ways of knowing are no longer able to offer us effective processes for addressing the complexities of our current realities as women and as citizens of the planet. Susan Albert shows us women who seek unique solutions to their personal yearnings as well as to our global problems. As Vaclav Havel, president of Czechoslovakia, says, "The way forward is not in the mere construction of universal systemic solutions, to be applied to reality from the outside; it is also in getting to the heart of reality through personal experience."

Beginning with spirituality, individual longing, and responsiveness to the smallest internal voices, the women of *Work of Her Own* promise us another way to fulfillment. It is the harder way, the way of indirection, trusting our intuition, our bodies, and our inner promptings. Seeking a work of one's own is not without its hazards, however, for one does not opt out of the dominant culture without some considerable loss of perceived rewards, however ephemeral. Yet for some women there is no other choice. Their very lives depend on finding another way.

Like all small social rumblings, the women in this book portend a growing trend: Some women have had it all in organizational life and found it wanting. Not surprisingly, they have found that the "all" was defined by institutional, largely male values, which focus on power and status. Power and status are decidedly hollow measures of fulfillment for those who desire a wholeness born of relationship and integrity. So once again some women courageously set out on their own, down a path that they chart in the going.

Curiously, I wondered if the reduced standard of living embraced by many of the women in this book in exchange for greater quality of life would be seen as advantageous by women who have never made it in corporate America, or who don't have careers and who comprise the majority of the working poor. While such considerations are not within the scope of *Work of Her Own*, I felt an alliance among these women in the natural attraction to values other than prestige and power. I finished *Work of Her Own* with a desire to forge new bonds with women across all economic strata, convinced that we have much in common and that our divisions across class lines have been an unnecessary impediment. It strikes me that whether we made it into the board room and found it shallow or we never got there at all, the corporate structure is simply not home to us. We are all strangers in that land because there we become strangers to ourselves.

I have Susan Albert to thank for stirring these realizations in me. I also looked back in gratitude to a juncture in my own life, when I decided that who I am was more important than what I did. I arrived at a place of internal ease with myself and knew that I would take that ease with me into whatever work I chose. I would not look outside myself for external validation. I recall the relief accompanying that decision. This inner resolve led me into more excitement, challenge, and serenity than I could ever have planned. May we all have such gifts, and may *Work of Her Own* nurture our commitments, however halting, to follow our inner knowing, for it is a creative book about courageous women and their choices.

Diane Fassel, Ph.D.
author, *The Addictive Organization*
and *Working Ourselves to Death*

PREFACE:
WORK OF MY OWN

*I*n 1982, at the age of forty-two, I became the first female vice-president of one of the fastest-growing universities in the country. I was on an escalator headed for the peak of achievement in higher education and expected to move to a presidency in another few years. I had the proper credentials: a Ph.D. from Berkeley; fifteen years of teaching, research, and administration; and extensive experience in managing organizations, including my own small business, which grossed nearly a quarter of a million dollars in the year before I sold it. As vice-president, I earned seventy thousand dollars a year in salary and benefits. I managed a forty-million-dollar annual budget and a faculty and staff of more than one thousand people. I served on numerous boards and national committees, and I played a leadership role in the development of state and national educational programs. Someone looking at my life from the outside would have said that I had everything a professional woman was supposed to want.

But looking at my career and my life from the inside, I had the disquieting sense that I did not have what I wanted. I had become increasingly disillusioned with the competitive politics of higher education. I had entered college teaching with the idea that the business of professors was to generate new knowledge through their research and to teach what they knew to their students; I had believed that the goals of higher education were accomplished in an environment that was relatively free of the power politics characteristic of commercial business. Neither of these perceptions, however, proved to be accurate. I began to question the ethical integrity of the industry to which I had committed my life and felt unable to make any changes other than superficial, cosmetic changes in it. Although I tried, I could no longer empathize with its purposes or its people. My professional life had become empty of real meaning, filled with nothing but the tense, frantic gestures of busyness.

There were other difficulties. At the same time that I was experiencing a sense of separation from my work, I began to realize that I had allowed that work to become the most important influence in my life. It was not hard to understand the reason for this imbalance. I was the oldest of two children in a lower-middle-class family. My father was a blue-collar worker. My mother worked as a clerk to help support the family. Neither of my parents graduated from high school. For me, achieving in school was a way to distinguish myself and to earn my father's approval. I had excellent grades when I graduated from high school, but few women in my rural community went to college during the fifties. I married instead of continuing my education and by the age of twenty-one had borne three children.

After five years of being a wife and mother, I felt the need to do something more with my life. Emboldened by Betty Friedan's *The Feminine Mystique* and assured by Ayn Rand's *The Virtue of Selfishness* that I needed to blaze my own trail, I entered the university. There, I felt I had found myself and decided to become a professor. The goal seemed impossible: I did not have a single female professor as a role model. My undergraduate grades, however, brought me a Danforth Graduate Fellowship, and I moved my family to Berkeley, California, so I could attend graduate school. I completed my doctoral program in the near-record time of four years even though my husband and I were divorced a week before my oral examinations. I began my teaching career at the University of Texas and within four years had earned tenure and promotion, started a business, and married an architect who was also heavily committed to his career. Ten years after receiving my doctorate, I accepted the vice-presidency of Southwest Texas State University.

I had climbed fast and hard and loved the feeling of being accepted, of being *chosen*, that marked each promotion. More and more, I felt like a member of the inner circle. But I was paying a high price for my career gains. I regularly worked sixty to seventy hours a week, and I had little energy for a personal life. The year I accepted the vice-presidency, my second husband and I divorced. My three children were in their twenties and busy with their lives. My father and I were estranged; I felt uneasy with my mother, who seemed to represent the very feminine passivity that I had rejected. I had visited them only twice in five years. I had seen my brother, who had become a vice-president of a Fortune 100 company and was as committed to his work as I, only once in the same period. Friendships with other women were measured over lunch in crowded restaurants. I had no hobbies and no time for personal reading, movies, or television. The unremitting stress at work brought backaches, headaches, chronic fatigue, and insomnia. I ate too many restaurant meals, drank too much at parties, smoked too much, and spent too much money with too little to show for it. Relationships, begun uneasily, were abruptly broken off. In rare moments of honesty with myself, I admitted that I was lonely, with a deep, disturbing loneliness that I could not bury even in work. I was empty, with no inner life, no spark of meaning to vitalize my actions. What I was suffering, I learned later, was what Jungian psychologist June Singer has called "the sadness of the successful woman"[1] (in her essay by that name, in *The Goddess Re-Awakening*, edited by Shirley Nicholson).

Finally, after a great deal of anguished debate with myself, I asked for a year's unpaid leave of absence. I expected to finish the research for a book I had been planning to write, rest, visit my parents, reconnect with my children, and make some friends. When I returned to the job, I would be re-energized, re-committed, ready to slug it out again. Since vice-presidents rarely take leaves my request was an odd one, but it was granted.

The leave gave me time—the very first extended free time in my entire adult life—to reflect. My reflections were not comfortable ones. Instead of research on eighteenth-century novels, I found myself engaged in a study of quite a different sort: a close and searching study of my *self*. With the help of a therapist, I began to ask myself how—and more importantly, why—I had chosen to sacrifice so much of my personal life to my work. I began to ask if there might be a different way to work. What would it be like to work in a less cutthroat environment? To be less driven about what I did for a living? To create, rather than to replicate, administer, and maintain? Not only to think in my work, but also to feel?

But feelings hurt. They hurt, especially, because I had never before in my life allowed myself to feel so-called bad feelings for more than a moment. When I stopped intellectualizing and just let myself feel, my deepest feelings were of fear and pain. I was afraid of a formless, structureless future. I felt the pain of having no one with whom to share my fear. Most of all, I felt the fear and the pain of having failed. During the first weeks of my leave, I feared that somebody would ask why I was not at work. I suffered terrible guilt, like a little girl with all F's on her report card, playing hooky from school. The feeling seemed justified. I had literally and figuratively stopped going to school because I had obviously failed at my school work. Other academics stood up to the unremitting pressure and stress; why had I caved in? Playing politics was part of the job; why couldn't I simply accept that? Why couldn't I just tough it out?

Convinced that I had failed—anguished, depressed, and ashamed—I retreated from my previous activities as thoroughly as I could. I resigned from the boards and committees to which I belonged; I looked the other way when I ran into university people in the small college town where I lived; I eventually rented out my house and moved to the anonymity of a nearby city. I stopped using the academic title *doctor*, which meant nothing at all outside of academia.

Giving up the academic title was a symbolic gesture that made my central question more intense, more agonizing: Who was I? Without external credentials, I felt that my life had no meaning. Without the work that filled up my days, I was empty; I was not *real*. I had no interests beyond work and had little clothing other than the dress-for-success suits I wore to work— my school clothes. I had so fully defined myself in the context of my successful career that I had no other self. How do I say in words how terrified I was, how shattered by these discoveries? How I longed for a new self, one that belonged, truly and deeply, to me—whoever I was?

How do I say how lonely I was in those months, especially for other women? Lacking role models, I had copied my professional behavior and my commitment to work from male faculty and administrators in the male-dominated university. Now I needed to hear how other women made space for personal lives in the midst of their work lives. I needed to know how they had achieved the balance I had failed to find. The women I counted as my friends at the university, however, were too busy with their work to tell me. What pained me even more was their view of me as a traitor to the feminist cause: a woman who had made it summa cum laude but who now wanted out.

I began to understand in a profoundly personal way a term used by feminists: male-identified. I noticed that my female colleagues (not all, but most) were indeed male-identified—so closely allied to the masculine viewpoint that they had abandoned their own perspective. I saw that I, too, had surrendered whatever feminine soul I might once have possessed. My achievements had conferred on me a confident self, certified through degrees, rank, and tenure, but she was the armored Athena that Jean Shinoda Bolen describes in *Goddesses in Everywoman*, sprung fully formed from the forehead of her godfather, Zeus. That self—that planning, managing, achieving Athena within me—had become enormously hungry for more achievements, more power. It was a hunger that literally could not be satiated, because more accomplishments only heightened the desire, only fed the compulsive need to be approved. Left to her own achievement-seeking devices, Athena had gained the upper hand. She had become the only self I was.

Understanding these things at once terrified me and brought me an odd relief. Through all the pain of giving up the person I had become, of releasing my dependency on work, I felt I was somehow growing up, growing away from the institution that had granted me, as if handing me a degree, my self-definition, my self-worth, my power. Leaving the career, transforming my Athena self, now seemed to me a sign of my surest, most individual achievement. I felt I had graduated at last.

The self-knowledge I gained during my leave of absence made it possible to walk into the president's office and hand him my resignation letter. "I knew we were going to lose you," he said with what seemed like genuine sadness. "But I thought it would be to a presidency—not to . . . this."

I knew what he meant by "this." In his eyes, leaving a promising career because of a trivial discomfort with politics was an act of utter madness, the act of someone who had lost her mind. Yes, I had lost my mind—the old Athena mind, the mind that needed to manage and control and order my world and everyone in it. "This" was an act of glorious madness. I felt as if I had dropped an enormous burden from my shoulders, and I cried out of sheer happiness.

After I resigned my vice-presidency, I was buoyed for weeks by a new sense of being finally and irrevocably responsible only for and to myself. Still, I had to make a living. I knew that if I went back to my tenured position as a full-time faculty member, Athena would be reborn before long. Instead, I turned to freelance writing. It was creative, energizing work that I enjoyed— work I felt I had a talent for, work I hoped would support me without consuming me.

I was right. During the next year, I found enough work to support myself with a moderate effort. I was by no means making seventy thousand dollars a year, but I was able to pay my bills and had a wonderfully flexible schedule. Without a guaranteed income I had to free myself from my dependence on credit and spend my cash more carefully. Instead of looking for outside entertainment, I stayed home and discovered to my surprise that home is a warm, sustaining place to be. I changed my diet, ate at restaurants far less often, and gave up alcohol and tobacco. Free from job stress as well, I began to feel and look healthy. It was a health that was growing from the inside out, from transforming wholeness, from a deep healing of the rift between the male-oriented identity that I had assumed to meet the world and the feminine self that I truly was.

Indeed, the most transforming aspect of the change involved reconnecting with my feminine self. When I took off the tough, defensive mask I had worn on the job, I saw a soft and vulnerable woman, and being soft and vulnerable felt good. When I stopped being a perennial candidate for the next promotion, I discovered I could be content with who I was at the moment. When I began to honor the part of me that needed to nurture and be nurtured, I rediscovered meaningful connections to my sons and my daughter. My brother and I began to talk regularly on the telephone, trying to understand together the forces that had compelled each of us to give so much of our lives to our work. Most importantly, I began to feel a close connection with my mother. I saw her as a valuable source of wisdom and experience. Later that year, I had the following dream:

I am with my mother, who stands in the middle of a circle of her sisters, my aunts. Mother is young and pretty, and there is a halo around her head. She looks like a goddess. "I am graduating from the university," she announces. Her sisters embrace her. We all embrace. I am weeping.

I woke from the dream with a feeling of joy and wonder and the clear sense that my deepest feminine self, which was the only source of true wisdom for me, was beginning to find a new expression in my life.

Opening to myself and to my family, I found it less frightening to risk opening to another person. I met a man who offered me a healing relationship, and we were married. Although for the past decade I had limited my romantic interest to high-powered professional men who put their work first just as I did, the man I chose now was willing to commit his energies to a life we could build together. He was willing to be the full partner I was ready to want.

The year following our marriage, my husband, Bill (by then also a career leaver), and I moved to the Texas Hill Country and began to collaborate as writers. Our earnings during the first year were only 20 percent of our combined former salaries and have not grown a great deal higher. We earn enough, however, to support the lifestyle we have chosen. We work six hours a day on our writing, not sixteen. We decide what work we will do, and we shape our work environment to suit our needs. As artisans, we take pride in our work, deriving our status from our competence, rather than from the manipulation of others or of bureaucratic systems.

We also make time for other work that we feel good about: woodworking, wreath making, gardening, tending chickens and geese, clearing the woods by the creek, volunteering in the local community, teaching adults in informal settings. Our health has miraculously improved: Bill's blood pressure dropped twenty points during the first year, and my backaches and headaches have vanished. We love what we do, and that love reveals itself in our healthier, happier lives. There are disappointments, to be sure, and sometimes I still overcommit myself. We have, however, found our work, our place, ourselves, and we are home to stay.

In the changing combination of the varied tasks I do—writing, working on the land, volunteering, teaching informally—I believe I have found what the Buddhists call right livelihood: work that is an expression of my truest, deepest self; work that not only affirms me but also confirms my care for others in the community and for the planet on which we all live; work done mindfully and joyfully as an expression of love. I have found what Virginia Woolf encouraged women to look for in *A Room of One's Own*.

I have found work of my own.

About This Book

As I reflected on the experience of leaving my career and read what others had written about women's work, I began to feel that my personal experience of leaving my career had a larger cultural dimension. I began to ask why—given the long, slow, painful entry of women into the career culture and the passionate, almost religious commitment that many women make to the idea of becoming somebody through paid work—some of us reach the point where we are not happy with the person we have become. I wanted to learn why some female achievers say no to the continued promise of a high-powered career and make changes in the way they work. I wanted to find out what kinds of changes they make and what those changes show us about contemporary women and their needs.

This book grew out of my study of the experiences of other women. It is built on the stories of eighty women who said no, who made changes in their lives. They were doctors, certified public accountants, geologists, botanists, lawyers, sales managers, systems analysts, teachers, nurses, health-care administrators, public relations executives, bank officers, vice-presidents, presidents. All of them left successful careers to find, as I did, their right livelihood. Some have permanently downshifted to part-time jobs in order to make time in the day for other interests, such as art, volunteer work, self-development, spiritual interests and travel. A number of others have created their own small businesses: Two own bookstores; one runs a sheep farm; three operate day-care centers; one has her own elder-care center; one runs a rehabilitation program; one operates a community lending program; one does massage therapy; two work with new mothers; and one counsels older parents. They have opened such home-based businesses as accounting, graphic arts, nanny placement, real estate, and tutoring. Some have become consultants; others, writers. One has become a literary agent. One turned to managing a spiritual community; another heads a women's spiritual program and edits a nationwide newspaper devoted to women's spiritual interests. Some have committed themselves to the work of full-time mothering. A number are retraining themselves for new work. All have given to the word *success* a very personal definition.

Not all the stories have happy endings. Many of the women I talked with still struggle with the central questions. What is my right livelihood? What balance between work and the rest of my life is best for me? Despite their continued questioning, however, most feel that they have grown psychologically through their painful efforts to recompose their lives around something other than a marketplace career. They believe that this process has resulted in greater personal authenticity. They agree that the changes they have made in their work lives have been of crucial importance to a new sense of self. *Work of Her Own* is about the challenging inner effort that has transformed the grief and the loss each woman felt when she left her career and moved toward a larger and more powerful sense of feminine self and self-in-the-world. It is the story of women who confronted what Judith Viorst calls the necessary loss of a way of life and transformed it through insight and imagination into necessary growth

TO THE READER

Since you are reading this book, you obviously have a strong interest in the experiences of women who left their careers. Perhaps you are considering leaving your own career; or perhaps you have a sister or a friend who has already taken this radical step. If you are reading this book because you are worried about the direction your career seems to be taking you, you will quickly see from what is described here that you are not alone. You are part of a new and very exciting trend, for the community of female career leavers is growing every day, every week, every year. Knowing that others have lived through this difficult experience may give you the courage to face your own feelings honestly and openly and to acknowledge them for what they are—anxieties and fears about playing a work role according to someone else's script. Reading other women's real-life stories and experiencing *their* painful experiences may enable you to better understand where *you* are in the process of choosing your future. You may be inspired by women whose lives are studies in courage—the courage to find their own way on a path that women have never before taken. You may learn—in a very practical sense—how they responded to what often seemed like unsolvable problems and insurmountable challenges and how you can put their experience to work in your own life.

Courage, understanding, inspiration, and practical advice on how to do it—that is what I hope you will gain from *Work of Her Own*. If fifty women, or five women, or even one woman can create whole, balanced, challenging, successful lives outside of the world of all-consuming careers, commuting, and fifteen-hour days, the rest of us can do it too.

Part

| 1 |

THE PROCESS
OF CAREER
LEAVING

No movement has ever been more than an accumulation of small motions of people acting within their own spheres. In rearranging our lives, we participate in rearranging the life of society.

MARILYN FRENCH

CAREER LEAVING: TRAGEDY OR TRIUMPH?

*T*he word *career* is commonly used to mean any kind of work we do for a considerable period of time. The dictionary, however, defines *career* as "consecutive progressive advancement especially in public, professional, or business life." That is how I use the term. When you have a career, you look for a position in an organization or industry that offers the possibility of advancement up the rungs of the so-called career ladder. You want each promotion to lead to greater responsibility, broader powers, and wider recognition within the hierarchy established by your employer. You expect that each successive position will reflect your upward movement by carrying a more impressive title and a larger salary than did the one before it. As a careerist, your goal is to climb to the top of the career ladder as fast as possible.

It is true, of course, that not all people who have careers are careerists. A careerist is someone who behaves as if the career has a greater priority than any other life activity, and who gives more time, more attention, and more energy to the career than to anything else. It is far more healthy to keep the career emphasis in balance with other aspects of life, to give forty hours a week to earning a living and to devote the rest of the hours to living itself. As Juliet Schor has shown in her impressive study of *The Overworked American*, however, our worktime has expanded into our living time, and our careers have grown to the point where they overshadow the landscape of our lives. According to Schor's estimates, the average person employed today works 163 hours more each year than he or she did twenty years ago—the equivalent of a whole extra month. Because many women work at two careers (a professional career and mothering), women's work has expanded even more dramatically: by 305 hours a year or almost

3

two extra months.[1] It is a sad fact of American life that most professions, corporations, and businesses demand more than forty hours a week and behave as if the professional or corporate career has a higher priority than anything else people do. They insist that those who wish to have significant careers must become careerists, an insistence that is difficult to defy.

In the United States today, almost everybody wants a career. In fact, what I call the *career culture* has come to dominate the lives of more and more Americans. This culture, oriented around the business organizations in which careers are shaped, is the framework for their dreams of social and economic empowerment and personal prosperity. The career culture controls people's decisions not only about where and how to work, but also about where and how to live, how to spend money and leisure time, and how to bear, raise, and educate children.

Through the fifties, sixties, and seventies, a career seemed to be a lifetime commitment. Careerists expected to spend their work lives with a single company or with two or three companies in a single industry. That is no longer the case. Today, given the rapid growth of new technologies and the turbulence of the economic climate, both men and women are more likely to change their career fields, to step off one career ladder and onto another: To move from the field of engineering, say, to law or medicine, or from technical to managerial work. Often, a career changer obtains formal training in a new field and then starts over again, climbing another career ladder.

When I stepped off my career ladder, however, I did not step onto another. My work as a free-lance writer does not involve consecutive progressive advancement, except in the sense of choosing more personally challenging projects. I am not loyal to an organization that confers rank, title, and salary upon me. I do not expect to climb up the higher rungs of anything. As a career leaver, I work on the margin of the career culture, with all the associated risks and challenges—some of them very frightening. I made the radical trade of institutionalized work in formal business organizations for self-generated work. I left the career culture.

Leaving the career culture isn't the only way to modify a career commitment. The popular contemporary term *downshifter* refers to somebody who has temporarily cut back time and effort but remains committed to a career. For instance, the author of an article in the *New York Times* entitled "Saying No to the Mommy Track" (January 28, 1990) describes an engineer who got a promotion even though she spent half of the day at home with her children. When her children are grown, she expects to shift back into high gear and go back to full-time work at the corporation that promoted her.

But *career downshifting* involves a more radical step. Career downshifters reduce not only their time commitment to their work but also their lifetime commitment to a particular career. Take Carla, for instance. A computer systems analyst, she decided after much soul-searching to reject her company's offer of a management position and to take a part-time programming job. Her choice closed off the option of career advancement, but it gave her time to pursue her passion: the study of art. Or look at the experience of Elizabeth. At forty-two, she began to remove herself from her high-paying career in public relations management because it did not give her enough opportunity to express her creativity. Over a period of time, she reduced her work load to thirty hours per week and eventually took a leave of absence. The downshifting phase helped her protect her income while she built up an independent client base in the graphic arts. Both Carla and Elizabeth have moved to the margin of the career culture. They are still involved in mainstream, institutionalized work, but both are more committed to work of their own.

MEN AS CAREER LEAVERS

Men, too, can be career leavers and career downshifters. Two psychologists have written about the process: Donald Kranz wrote *Radical Career Changers,* and Samuel Osherson wrote *Holding On or Letting Go.* Reading these books about male career leavers and talking with my husband and other career leavers, I asked myself whether the experience is significantly different for women and men.

My answer is yes: Although there are many instructive similarities, the experience is not the same. Men and women come to their careers from very different historical, social, economic, and psychological perspectives. This fact creates at least two significant differences in the process of career leaving for women and for men.

The first difference has to do with the nature of a woman's investment in her career. Women, late entrants into the career culture, have only in the last few decades and at the cost of tremendous emotional effort even approached the status of so-called insiders. It is not surprising, then, that we receive a different kind of return on our career investments than men do. From the culture surrounding our mothers, grandmothers, and great-grandmothers, we have inherited a devalued sense of self. We are only one or two generations away from the belief that a woman's place is, or ought to be, in the private sphere of the domestic culture, where her work (at least since the Industrial Revolution) was invisible, unpaid or underpaid, and undervalued. Only in the last generation have significant numbers of us moved out of the female-dominated domestic culture and into visible, paid work in the public sphere of the male-dominated career culture. In fact, it is only through career achievement that we have enhanced our gender identity and commanded respect in the public sphere. It is only when we become as good as men that we gain respect and are granted authority. Those of us who stay home are still considered, like our mothers, second-class citizens.

The decision to leave a visible, highly paid, and prestigious position in the career culture, then, holds consequences for women that it does not hold for men. A successful man who leaves his career certainly risks lowering his standard of living, and he may feel alienated from friends and colleagues who continue to define themselves through the career culture. His action, however, raises little question about the cultural value of his identity. He may have voluntarily canceled his membership in the old-boys' club, but there is no disputing the fact that he remains, in our gender-based and gender-biased society, a member of the more privileged and powerful sex.

In contrast, a successful woman who chooses to leave her career risks trading her work-enhanced identity for one that is worth a great deal less on the social-status market. This is especially true if she goes back to the domestic culture or if she turns to work that has been traditionally identified as women's work, such as nurturing, volunteering, teaching, working with children or with the aged. In the eyes of the culture at large, she has given up her first-class ticket and returned to second-class status.

The second difference between women and men who leave their careers involves the right to an opportunity for equal employment, an opportunity for which women—not men—have had to fight. Many of us believe that a successful career woman who has enjoyed these opportunities has a special obligation to other women. Her presence in the executive office sends a strong signal to other women: I got here, you can get here, too. She might serve as a mentor as well, actively helping other female careerists. When this woman leaves her career, she often feels guilty about abandoning the women she leaves behind. Further, she worries about disappointing the men and women who went out of their way to boost her to the top.

Further, she may also face outright disapproval. Deborah Arron, in her book *Running from the Law: Why Good Lawyers Are Getting Out of the Legal Profession*, tells about Mary Kay, a deputy prosecuting attorney and law instructor who left her work soon after she was promoted to chief criminal prosecutor:

> I took on enormous guilt for wanting to reject my promotion. . . . I felt guilty because the people I confided in said things like, You can't quit. It wouldn't be fair to your boss who stuck his neck out when he gave you the job; or, It's incredible that a woman is in this job. You have to stay there. . . . It was as if all the rulemakers in my life, the people who told me to succeed, were standing around me saying, You're going to do *what*? . . . I felt like it was, I don't know, like it was a sin to quit my job.[2]

You're going to do *what*? The question is often spoken in a tone of horrified disbelief and disapproval by a career leaver's feminist friends, colleagues, and mentors. In her book *In Transition*, psychologist Judith Bardwick reports a comment made by her mother about a friend who left her psychiatric practice to stay home with her baby. "That is a disgrace!" Bardwick's mother burst out in anger. "She has no right not to work, not when she has taken up so many of society's resources, not when women are struggling to get into medicine! Not when women are struggling for their rights!"[3]

Sometimes this disapproval is dramatically exaggerated. In *Power Failure,* a polemic against women who turn down top management positions, Barbra Bools and Lydia Swan write about a career leaver named Catherine. Her decision not to continue the upward swing of her career, Bools and Swan believe, holds dire consequences for all women. Catherine, they write, could have been a "pinnacle of hope, a legendary pioneer for generations of American businesswomen to follow."[4] The way they tell the story, Catherine was a heroine capable of epic triumphs in women's struggle to gain entry to top management. Her decision to quit before she reached the office of chief executive officer was considered by these authors, at least, a tragedy of epic proportions.

Male career leavers are not burdened with the idea that they are pinnacles of hope or legendary pioneers who are breaking the way for others of their gender. They are not made to feel any moral obligation to the men they leave behind in the office. No one tells them that they have no right to quit their jobs simply because they are successful and visible men.

Successful women are models of achievement not only for women but also for men. "Because I am a woman," Clare Boothe Luce is reported to have said: "I must make unusual efforts to succeed. If I fail, someone will say, She doesn't have what it takes. When a man leaves his career, no one says, It's exactly as I expected all along. Men just don't have what it takes. They don't measure up."[5]

PROFESSIONAL TRAGEDY OR PERSONAL TRIUMPH?

Given a woman's special obligation to succeed in work, it is easy to understand why her abandonment of her career is described by committed women careerists—and by many feminists—as a professional tragedy, not only for the woman herself but also for all women. "We are all affected by their Power Failure," Bools and Swan assert.[6]

Sarah Hardesty and Nehama Jacobs make the same charge in *Success and Betrayal: The Crisis of Women in Corporate America.* Career leavers are self-betrayed martyrs to their own "self-limiting attitudes," these writers say.[7] They are sad victims of their own self-sabotage, examples of arrested professional development, of failed personal growth. Leavers are losers who have fallen from grace. They have cut themselves off from the source of real power in the world.

But my personal experience runs counter to what these writers tell me. I do not define my career leaving as a tragedy. When I left my work, I discovered a new kind of grace. I was freed from the limited self that my narrow concentration on work had created. I learned why and to what degree I had adapted my beliefs and my behaviors to the expectations of others, almost exclusively men, who were in a position to reward me. I learned how to measure my skills and my abilities and chose new ways to use them in work of my own choosing. The process of creating work of my own was a process of growth, unfolding, and self-empowerment, fundamental to the development of my full potential as a female human being. The learning period was full of anguish and torment and fear, as significant growth often is. Through it, however, I achieved a radically new independence from others' expectations. I moved beyond the limits that my culture placed on my imagination of myself to make transforming choices that my culture actively discouraged me from making.

Women who are career leavers tell me that they share this sense of self-liberation. Leaving is agonizing, but they experience a clear sense of personal growth as they struggle through it. By the time they reach the final stages of the leaving process and begin to create new kinds of work—work better suited to their feminine selves—they feel in charge of their lives and more confident of their beliefs, more capable, more powerful. They feel that they know more about themselves, have examined their commitments to work, have assessed their strengths and weaknesses, and have put their strengths to the test in new work environments. They feel more whole, more real, more truly themselves. At the same time, they feel more committed to connection with others and more open to intimacy.

Barbra Bools may be right when she says that we experience a power failure—in the sense of giving up the power that we once had *over* other people. But career leavers assert emphatically that they have never before felt more powerful in their lives. They feel energized by a new kind of power from sources deep within: true self-empowerment, not power conferred through title, position, or salary. This is what some feminists call power with, rather than power over. It involves power shared among equals, rather than power hierarchically distributed to people on the top and denied to people on the bottom.

Not all female career leavers have arrived at a point where they feel in charge of their lives, free to make significant changes, unconflicted, and self-confident. If they have not shed the career culture's values and expectations, they will continue to measure their current accomplishments against their former achievements and against the judgments of others. They may not feel comfortable with the outcome. For them, there is still little evidence in their lives of personal triumph or personal growth.

ADULT GROWTH AND DEVELOPMENT

What is growth, in psychological terms? What do psychologists mean when they talk about personal growth?

Only recently have we come to understand that when physical growth slows, adults continue to grow inwardly. In the early 1900s, Sigmund Freud taught that by the end of adolescence, people are as mature as they ever will be. Adults, he said, basically continue to reenact the conflicts they could not resolve during childhood. Adult life is simply a repetition of unfinished childhood business. We spend our lives as grown-ups rehearsing the drama of our early years.

Later humanistic psychologists criticize the Freudian model because it focuses only on the rehearsal of old conflicts, rather than describing people who continue to grow as they confront and acknowledge new possibilities for their lives. Karen Horney used the term *other-directed* to describe people who let their lives be shaped by the demands of others. In contrast, Horney said, people who follow their own inner direction are self-realized and true to the fundamental needs of the self. Self-realization, however we achieve it, is essential to true adult growth.[8]

Charlotte Buhler's term for a creative, self-realized life was *self-determination*. We lead self-determined lives, she said, when we become personally authentic, when our choices reflect our

10

own personal values. Buhler felt that the ego—that part of ourselves that meets the demands of our social world—is not all, or even the best part, of us. Out to make its mark on the world, the ego often pursues superficial ambitions or values to which the whole self does not subscribe. According to Buhler, true growth comes from what she calls the core of the self, not from the shell-like external ego, which is easily influenced to imitate the power structures around it.[9]

Interestingly, it was a former student and close associate of Freud who focused most intently and productively on adult growth. The Swiss psychologist Carl Jung used the term *individuation* to describe the developmental quest that begins at mid-life—a quest, he said, that is both psychological and spiritual. As adults, the main purpose of our growth is freedom: setting ourselves free from the models and patterns by which, as younger people, we are taught to live. As long as we act and believe, consciously or unconsciously, according to the dictates of others, we are not truly individuals, nor are we truly mature. Our task in adulthood, Jung suggested, is to find our own freedom, to liberate ourselves from the power others hold over us and to become who we really are.[10]

Most psychologists agree that adults continue to grow emotionally. Growth occurs when an existing psychological structure—an old way of seeing, an old set of convictions, an old prescription for action—no longer fits us and we are forced to let it go. In its place, we must gift ourselves with a new structure—a new vision, new convictions, a new course of action—that answers to our individual and maturing needs.

Growth involves learning who we really are. Growth challenges us to stop acting out somebody else's ideas—often somebody we respect, admire, love, or fear—about who we ought to be.

Growth means opening ourselves to messages from the deep core of our selves and letting those messages inform and reform our conscious, ego-built life.

Growth comes through crisis. Growth comes through pain. It is quite likely that growth will not come unless we experience crisis and pain.

Growth leads us to self-realization, self-determination, and independence.

Growth takes us farther and deeper, toward our true selves—even beyond ourselves, to caring for others.

GROWTH BEYOND AUTONOMY

Until very recently, most of the detailed studies of adult growth have been studies of men, and when psychologists talk about growth, they generally mean men's growth. An exception is Harvard psychologist Carol Gilligan, whose study of women's psychological development, *In a Different Voice,* has made an invigorating and enlightening contribution to the discussion of how adults grow.

Gilligan points out that women and men grow in different ways. A boy's first task is to separate himself from his mother, from that which is feminine. An adolescent boy continues this basic work of separation as he grows into an adult, creating his autonomous selfhood through his independence from other selves. Separation, autonomy, independence—these are the milestones of men's growth, as our Western culture has defined it.[11]

Measured against these masculine milestones, women until recently have been found to be different. From a masculine point of view, this difference looks like a lack. As girls, we understand early in our lives that we are fundamentally like our mothers; we do not have to learn to be something other or to break off our connection with our mothers. In adolescence and adult life our task is to maintain our relationships with others at the same time that we are working to establish an authentically independent identity. To the male researchers whose definitions have shaped developmental psychology, our relationships to others look and feel like liabilities. Our caring seems to hinder us from achieving a fully separate, autonomous, and independent identity. When psychologists posit individual achievement and personal autonomy as the indicators of human maturity, our commitment to others appears as a handicap; it condemns us to a lifetime of lack, psychological immaturity, and unrealized growth.

Another critic of stereotypically male models of the way we grow is psychologist Robert Kegan. Kegan believes that the current model of adult growth, which he calls hypermasculine, gives us a completely inadequate picture of the potential of human development. In *The Evolving Self,* he suggests that male-sanctioned autonomy and individuality do not constitute the parameters of our potential.[12] Kegan pictures adult growth as an ascending spiral. As we grow, we progress through psychological stages that emphasize relationship (feminine stages) and those that emphasize independence (masculine stages).

The three highest levels in Kegan's spiral are the interpersonal, institutional, and interindividual. At the interpersonal level, our individual power is based on our personal relationships. We are who we are—daughters, lovers, wives, mothers—chiefly in terms of our emotional connections with other people. In preindustrial society, of course, people of both genders defined themselves in interpersonal terms. In an industrialized society, Kegan says, women are far more likely than men to operate primarily at the interpersonal level and to derive their power from those with whom they have close emotional bonds. This level is thought of stereotypically as a feminine phase of growth. People (mostly women) who operate at this level are seen as dependent and immature.

The next stage of Kegan's spiral of growth is the institutional level. (This corresponds to what I have called the career culture.) At this level, we are less connected to other people and more connected to institutions. Our power and authority derive from the institutions that confer on us our identities. We are who we are—lawyers, accountants, teachers, managers—specifically in terms of the organizations we work for and belong to. Because institutional affiliations are limited, they are granted to a limited number of individuals selected according to criteria that the institutions themselves establish. To succeed at this level, we have to be willing to tailor ourselves to the institutional mold; we have to elbow ourselves into position for recognition and advancement; and we have to be willing to sacrifice personal aims for institutional goals. In most societies throughout history, men have created the institutional level and the rules governing it; women who want to be accepted into it must behave like men. People who operate at this level (until the last two decades, mostly male) are seen as independent, autonomous, and mature.

But there is an interesting paradox at the institutional level of growth: Our culture depicts people who do not depend on personal relationships for power and authority as being truly independent and autonomous. When we look at the situation objectively, however, we see that people at the institutional level have simply traded a dependence on personal relationships for a dependence on institutional affiliations. A male manager who feels strong and powerful because he works for a strong and powerful corporation is equally as dependent (and therefore as readily labeled immature) as is a woman who derives her personal authority from her father or her husband. Neither is truly autonomous or truly independent. Neither is capable of vesting personal authority in an authoritative self. Both are confined within a closed, self-reinforcing system.

Although our culture honors the institutional level as the highest level of growth, there is growth beyond, Kegan says. He calls this more highly evolved stage of personal growth the inter-individual level. At this level, we have given up our dependency on institutions. We think and act as true individuals, deriving our power from ourselves rather than from some powerful other.

At the same time that we think and act as individuals, however, we also think and act as members of a community. We are not separated or alienated. We accept our connections to others within a responsible network of interaction. We are for ourselves, but we are also for others. Each person is an integral, co-operative member of a noncompetitive community and accepts responsibility for the welfare of that community. Because all work together, blending their capabilities, gender differences are viewed as strengths, rather than as liabilities. At this level, the self-in-community has a new and more inclusive identity. Once alienated from other selves and wholly dependent on institutions for our definition, we are now a part of a society within which all others are deeply and irrevocably interconnected. We are part of a society about which we all deeply care and to which we each contribute as we are able.

Our idea of human growth, both Gilligan and Kegan suggest, has been seriously limited by our traditional perspectives on gender and by industrialized society's model of competitive production and consumption. In order to grow beyond these limiting parameters, we must see ourselves as individuals and as members of communities. In this book, I will suggest that such an come when we view our work in a new way.

Strong Women Can Say No

We easily recognize a woman at the pinnacle of her career. She is a self-realized, self-determined, stand-alone person. She has an autonomous, independent identity, the major components of which include her work, her title, and the status and prestige that come with the title—all conferred by the work institution to which she belongs. She has successfully climbed the masculine staircase of adult growth and development to the institutional level: the highest level of achievement in our culture.

As she moves up through the work world, the successful woman is required to repudiate most of what makes her a woman: her feminine viewpoint, her feminine values of nurturing and caring. In order to succeed, she develops a strongly male-oriented bias and a tendency to uphold and defend the masculine culture of ideas and ideals. She has become what psychologist Maureen Murdock, in *The Heroine's Journey*, calls "a spiritual daughter of the patriarchy."[13]

For a woman, career leaving often involves the rejection of this male-scripted success story and the reclaiming of her feminine self. It means redefining success. It means saying no to the male success story. This is a painful, anxious rejection, for creating her institutional self was neither easy nor painless. It is a rejection that requires great strength, a rejection that builds strength. "Strong women can say no," Maureen Murdock observes. Even for a strong woman, however, saying no is painful and costly, for it requires her to say no to parts of herself that her colleagues, mentors, and friends admire and respect. It hurts because, as Murdock remarks, "it feels so good to be chosen, especially by the king."[14]

For the women I interviewed, saying no was a process that involved six stages. Each of these stages has its own particular triumph and its own special pain. Each stage ultimately results in clear, positive growth. This growth begins with the task of releasing the old, narrow identity and ends with the development of a new and more inclusive one. This is the pattern of growth that we will trace out in chapters 2 through 7.

THE FIRST STAGE:
DOUBTING

*A*s members of the career culture, most of us work for companies that demand our sustained allegiance to industry standards, corporate policy, and company rules. The game plan is very simple: If you value your career, if you want to improve your position and chances for advancement, you adapt to your organization. You may have to work at this adaptation in the beginning, but after a while, acceptable organizational behavior comes to seem like your own behavior. You may sometimes disagree with and complain about the way things are done, but you probably accept the organization's basic purposes and philosophy. They come to seem normal.

COMMITTING OURSELVES

Adapting to the organization is thought to be fundamental to career success: hence, a prerequisite to material success in our culture. In fact, many psychologists consider organizational adaptation as a sign of mental health. In general, people who adapt to the work situation are believed by others to be fulfilled and sane, according to Douglas LaBier, psychologist and author of *Modern Madness: The Emotional Fallout of Success.* He adds that both the typical careerist and the typical psychologist believe that people who experience work-related conflicts are weaker and more neurotic than those who adapt. These conflicts are seen as "simply a reflection of some internal weakness or deficit, which prevents us from becoming winners," LaBier says. Those who advocate adaptation suggest, often cynically, that our best strategy is to develop defense mechanisms that will enable us to take advantage of the system: "Their solution is to develop a hardened shell, become more adept at self-promotion and putting down others, and finely hone our techniques for gaining control over the situations which make us feel weak, frightened, and angry. In short, their message is get yours before the Bomb drops, the economy collapses, or you become too old."[1]

Initially almost everyone makes a determined effort to adapt, to play by the rules of the corporation. Sooner or later, some of us cease to find much comfort in the get-yours-first philosophy. We begin to wonder whether our adaptation to the work world, although it seems perfectly normal in the workplace, is sufficiently rewarding, entirely healthy, or even altogether sane.

These wonderings and questionings—vague and uncomfortable and almost never expressed in the beginning—gradually become clearer and sharper and more painful. They are painful because they prompt us to question the rightness of what we are doing and have been doing for some years, and to wonder how long we can continue doing it. They are painful because they isolate us from those around us who continue to work unquestioningly. They are painful because they force us to feel, when we may have stifled our feelings for a very long time. When we begin to let ourselves feel, we realize that we are like the incredulous child who watches the naked emperor parading through the streets, wondering if she is the only one who sees what she thinks she sees, wondering if she is the only one who is able to ask What's really real? Eventually, the questions can become so painful that we can no longer ignore them or push them away.

In this chapter, I want to explore the first stage of the process of finding work of our own. It is the time when we first sense that we are growing disillusioned with our work and discontented with the narrowing of our life choices. Like every stage of the process, it has its own special pain and its own particular growth.

DISILLUSIONMENT: IS THIS THE REAL THING?

In her sociological study *Becoming an Ex*, Dr. Helen Ebaugh interviewed a large group of women and men who had stopped doing whatever they had been doing—doctors, lawyers, policemen, prostitutes, and others who left their work, nuns who left the convent, spouses who left marriages. *Role exit* is the term Dr. Ebaugh uses to describe the painful process of voluntarily leaving a role we have shaped ourselves to fit. The process begins, she says, with first doubts about whether the role we assumed, often at great sacrifice of time and effort and of other things we wanted to do, is the right role for us. "The doubting stage is essentially one of reinterpreting and redefining a situation that was previously taken for granted. Events and expectations that had been defined as acceptable begin to take on new meanings. First doubts involve a reinterpretation of reality, a realization that things are not what they had seemed."[2]

Doubting, Ebaugh says, means beginning to suspect that things are not what we thought they were. It means reinterpreting reality and seeing our career investment in a new and different way, asking ourselves whether that investment is worth the cost of maintaining and protecting it. If this is all there is, we might say, I am not sure it is worth what I am paying for it.

Doubting is a psychological process that may or may not drive us to do something. We can continue to doubt and question, sometimes for years, while we go on acting as if we have no doubts. Or we can doubt for a time, then feel that we have resolved our doubts and stop doubting. Or we can doubt, then act on our doubts, making dramatic changes in our behaviors within a few months.

We usually feel our first doubts about our career commitment in a nagging discomfort with the work situation: something about our work feels wrong, or out of kilter, or just not enough. Sometimes this discomfort grows out of stressful working situations. Often, it is focused on what we experience as a deeply felt moral dilemma.

Karen is a highly educated, highly trained scientist with a deep concern for the environment. She majored in forestry as an undergraduate because she wanted, as she says, to help save the planet. Forestry jobs were impossible to get, however, so she earned a master's degree in geology and went to work for the oil industry. Throughout her eight years of work in oil exploration, she felt an increasingly worrisome dissonance between her fears for the environment and what she had to do to keep her job. Finally, the dissonance became so great that she could no longer ignore it.

My values were out of sync with theirs—and with what I was doing. I felt I was caught in an ethical dilemma. Every day, in big and little ways, I saw that *I* was responsible for the rape of the planet, just as much as the company I worked for. The dilemma became so painful that I simply couldn't go on working in my field any longer.

Lisa is a thirty-year-old black woman with undergraduate and master's degrees from excellent universities—and deep anti-war feelings. After graduation she was offered a promising position as a manager in a major corporation that produced (among other things) military hardware. Although her strong convictions about the immorality of war made her think twice before she took the job, the salary was an important signal of status and acceptance into the mainstream career culture—strong incentives for a woman of color who felt she had an obligation to others to get ahead.

For a while, Lisa's regular salary increases and quick promotions made the job acceptable, and her satisfaction with her progress toward her goal of personal and economic independence outweighed her moral distaste for her work. Her concerns about the company's products, however, eventually became so unsettling that they undermined her commitment to getting ahead in her career. "It's true that everyone has a price," Lisa says now, several years after she left her work. "The price paid to me was my salary." In the long run, she decided, her integrity was more valuable than economic security.

> Every day, I compromised my morals and ethics—what I believed in. There I was, an advocate of peace, and I was involved in promoting war! My actions were in direct contradition to my beliefs. For a while, I could ignore the conflict. But after a while, I felt so bad about what I was doing that it almost made me sick to go to work. I had to leave. I *had* to—I didn't have any other choice.

Karen and Lisa are what we might call opportunistic careerists—women who move into a field not because it is their first choice, or even their second, but because it offers the greatest opportunities. Their eventual sense of lack of fit and growing disillusionment with work that is badly out of sync with their values might have been predicted when they entered their careers.

Of course, all of us would fare much better if we carefully assessed our beliefs and values and compared them to the beliefs and values held in a potential career field. Such information, however, is not always available, and when it is, it may not be accurate. "I understood the professed ethical/value system of my career field," one woman told me, "but not the actual ethical/value system. I didn't see the real thing until I was thoroughly hooked." Another woman said: "They never say what really goes on in the executive office. And even if they did, people wouldn't believe them. You don't believe it until you find out that somebody's been indicted." What is more, many careerists do not have a wide range of choice, especially in a declining economy, where job seekers are more numerous than jobs.

Even when we have the freedom to deliberately choose our careers and our first jobs, and even when our choices reflect our basic values, we may eventually come to believe that our choice was a mistake. This is often true when we base it upon an unrealistic, ideal sense of what the profession or organization is about and is especially true for the service professions—education, health care, and religion.

Nancy chose a career in health care out of a desire to help people. At thirty-three, she had achieved her personal goal: she was the administrator of a nursing home, responsible for the lives, health, and welfare of many elders. The owners of the for-profit nursing home had less altruistic goals for their business. They constantly insisted on higher and higher profit levels, and Nancy began to feel that she was compromising her patients' needs and her own professional and ethical convictions to meet the owners' demands. When they required that she reduce staff to a minimum, her workload increased. She began to feel swallowed by the massive amount of paperwork that the regulatory agencies required. "Twenty-four hours a day weren't enough to do what I considered to be a halfway decent job," she says. "I wasn't in control of my own mental, physical, or emotional well-being any longer. I felt more and more like a victim of the system, of other people's greed, of everything." Her forty-thousand-dollar annual salary, she felt, was not adequate compensation for the loss of her beliefs about the importance of good health care.

Another health-care professional saw the same problem from a slightly different angle. At forty, Jan gave up her position as the chief of a department in a southern hospital even though it paid three hundred thousand dollars a year. A significant part of her reason for leaving was the agonizing conflict she experienced between her work as a healer and the standard of care she was expected to provide. "The government is making it more and more difficult to care for people," she says.

> Physicians are forced into a double bind. As a doctor, you feel you have to do everything humanly possible for the patient. That's what you want to do, that's what you believe in. On the other hand, the hospital often has to kick them out before they are ready. I felt sad, I felt hurt, I felt disillusioned—but most of all I felt terribly angry. I wanted to be a healer, but the system won't let me do that.

The more disillusioned Jan became with the realities of the career to which she had committed her total life, the more exhausted she felt, emotionally and physically, and the less able she was to cope with the escalating demands of her work. Finally, she developed breast cancer—one of the diseases she was trained to treat and committed to heal.

Like most young people entering medical-related fields, both Nancy and Jan had high expectations, compelling ideals, and strong other-oriented values. For both of them, in different ways, increasing bureaucratization and the need to make health care more profitable meant that the level of service they were permitted to give fell below what they knew to be needed. Eventually they were no longer able to pretend to themselves that they were caring for people the way they wanted to.

Kerry, who held a doctorate in veterinary medicine and had practiced for twenty years, felt the same way.

> I became a vet because I love working with animals. But things began to change in the late seventies. It got harder and harder to keep up with government requirements. And people's attitudes changed too. They stopped looking at the vet as a fellow human being trained to treat their animals. They make unreasonable demands, and there's always the threat of litigation lurking in the background. This creates a tremendous background anxiety. How could I keep working in a situation like that?

Michelle was as idealistic as Nancy, Jan, and Kerry. She turned to agronomy education as a career field because she felt that improved agricultural practices could help reduce hunger. "I was convinced that what I was doing could make a contribution to the world food supply," she says about her work as a teacher and research associate in a university laboratory. Ironically, she was working on a research project involving drought-tolerant beans during the famine that killed hundreds of thousands in Africa. "The beans could have relieved hunger," she says. But the project that seemed so promising was compromised by academic politics. Disillusioned with what she saw as cutthroat competition and power struggles among the researchers, ultimately unable to believe that her work was making a significant contribution to reducing world hunger, Michelle emotionally detached herself from the research and a year later left the field.

Sometimes the disillusionment we experience has its source in our career relationships with other women. Elaine enjoyed her position as sales manager in a large women's retail clothing chain, until a new vice-president, a woman, was named.

> This woman got the job by undercutting another woman in a way that was really very brutal. The whole thing made me feel terribly uncomfortable, and I began to question other things about the job—the constant travel, the incredible hours, the competition in the industry. But most of all, I wondered if I'd have to be the way she was in order to get ahead. People in the corporation said she was a feminist and admired her for being tough. Well, if being a feminist means stepping on other people's heads on your way up the ladder, you can count me out. Maybe I'm naive, but I think women should be above using other women.

Career leavers frequently criticize the power-grabbing tactics they see other women—some of them so-called feminists—using to get ahead in the male-directed business world, and they sometimes refuse to allow themselves to be described as feminists because they reject the every-woman-for-herself attitude.

Other career leavers argue that the problem is not with tough women, but with the patriarchal system that makes everybody—women and men—heartless and competitive. Judith makes this point emphatically. She invested thirteen years in her successful library career, earning a position as the head of the reference department in a major public library system. Even though she loved books and enjoyed working with the library's patrons, however, she grew more and more unhappy with her career. "It was the old-style, dictatorial, patriarchal administration of the library," she told me. "It totally disheartened me."

> The library bureaucracy gave me almost no freedom to run my department the way I wanted. They made all my decisions for me. I wasn't enjoying my job, because it had very little to do with what I thought we were there for—to help people. Most of the time I was really very angry at the male administration, the male power structure. A lot of my staff felt the same way. I'm afraid we took it out on our patrons.

Chris, a former minister of a large midwestern church, found herself in a similar situation. As she became more aware of issues centering on women's spirituality, she began to challenge the church policies and practices she had once accepted unquestioningly and to doubt the vocation to which she felt she had been called. Over the course of a year, her doubts about her vocation and about the church grew stronger and stronger, until she was able to articulate very clearly how she felt:

> All existing institutions, including the church and higher education, are male. That is, they're linear, hierarchical, patriarchal. In addition, the traditional definition of work is a male one—one that's fragmented in many ways. Work takes place away from home, disconnected from human relationships, and separated from the rest of life. As I began to understand this, I began to feel disconnected from my work in the church. My disconnection made me feel enormously sad—after all, I'd given years and years of my life to the church. I had lost something I believed in very much, and I felt as if there was nothing I could hold on to. It was a terrible, lost feeling. I felt betrayed.

While Chris speaks sadly of her disillusionment and betrayal, Marlene speaks quite angrily. She left her eighty-thousand-dollar annual salary as senior vice-president in a large communications agency because, she says, "I got tired of cleaning up men's messes." She has strong feelings about the effect of the business environment on women and men alike. "The male competitive win-lose mentality of business is destructive to all concerned, inside and outside the company," she says with firm conviction.

> I was repelled by business as war, one-upmanship, and male measures of business and personal success. I couldn't do a slapdash job or "roll with the punches," one of the many repellent macho business phrases. Although my work was respected and rewarded, it was for the wrong reasons. I felt isolated in my need for meaning in the process as well as the purpose of work.

Marlene's need for meaning is endorsed by a large number of women. "I was unhappy living the values of the corporate, for-profit world which conflicted with my personal life as a women's rights and peace activist," says Jeanne, who left a thirty-thousand-dollar-a-year position as a computer programmer-analyst for a job in a community women's center at half the salary. "I needed to find some meaning in what I did."

Nicole is a former public relations executive who left her career when she understood that she did fit into the corporate value system—too well. Looking back from a healthier perspective, she speaks with wry humor about her earlier self:

> I hate to say it, but I belonged. If I had a gift, it was to be able to figure out immediately what role I had to play to survive and thrive, and then play it. I could be one of the guys, I could be tough, I could be helpless, but always I would be in, in, in! There might have been barriers if I had had any ethics, but I didn't. Not then. I do now, and my life has become incredibly difficult as a result.

At stage one in the career-leaving process, women begin to feel that they have been laboring under illusions about their work. They feel that there is not a good fit between themselves and their work environment and that they do not share the values of their workplace. They begin to see marked differences between the career-self they wear to work and the self they perceive themselves to be or want to be. These are not early warning signals of a terminal disease called "failure to adapt." They are the seeds of psychological growth.

Not Worth the Price

The unhappiness that stage-one career leavers feel cannot be attributed entirely to their work environments. "My real problem came from somewhere deeper," Dee told me, thinking back on the events that led her to leave her successful career in commercial real estate.

> I had everything I ever wanted—a terrific condo with a view of the lake, lovely furniture, a nice car, plenty of money, clothes, travel. But it wasn't enough. The more money I had, the more things I could buy, the less satisfied I was.

Divorced, her children in college, unable to find a satisfying relationship that lasted more than a few chaotic months, Dee felt that her work was all that was keeping her afloat, and, she says, "it was a pretty leaky lifeboat." Nothing seemed to matter to her, and she could not avoid the idea that at some point along the line, she was the one who had robbed herself.

> Something inside of me felt all shriveled up. Maybe I once had a soul but not any longer. I decided that maybe I'd traded it in on a commercial development.

Jungian analyst June Singer wrote that she has counseled numerous women who fear, like Dee, that they have traded their souls for career achievement. She describes a typical client: the woman who got what she thought she wanted but realizes that her success can never fulfill her. In her depression she suffers, Singer says, from "the sadness of the successful woman." Often, she tries to deal with her sadness in a rational way—"the same rational way that men do," Singer observes. Her feelings are so deep and so far-reaching, however, that no amount of logical, analytic examination can help her to deal with them: "There was nothing rational about [her sadness]. Something rose up in her psyche, something so deep, so elemental, that there are no words for it. It was felt bodily, it was felt in the unconscious, and only gradually did it seep into consciousness to color the very fabric of her life, so that there was no mistaking it."[3]

Hilary Cosell, in *Woman on a Seesaw*, quotes at length her conversation with an analyst who, like Singer, sees clients whose successful professional lives are pervaded by a deep disappointment. "Many women, in order to achieve real success in their professional lives, are forced to deny large parts of themselves," the analyst says.

> I see a great deal of frustration in these women because it's popular right now to say that these conflicts don't exist anymore, and my patients are living lives that are proof that the conflicts are very real. They have had to deny or repress many aspects of being female, and they have no personal life where they can act their femininity out. I also hear a lot about emptiness and isolation, women saying they feel isolated from other women as well as men, and describing their success as empty or hollow. This is especially true with women who have grown up believing that they must achieve, where success is fundamental to self-esteem and self-worth, where anything less means they have failed. When women grow up in this atmosphere and then have this reinforced by the women's movement, they often wind up in a situation that feels like the worst kind of trap imaginable, and it feels as if there is no way out.[4]

The sense of almost indescribable loss that Singer and Cosell report, the sense that something significant is missing from an outwardly successful life, appears as a major opening theme in the stories of women career leavers. Their unhappiness has two sources. The first is the frustration and anger they feel as they think back on how they have tried to adapt themselves to their external work world. The second is the inner disquiet, the deep apprehension that they have somehow, somewhere in that process of adaptation, given away or traded away or abandoned an essential part of themselves. The successful self they gained in return is not enough to compensate them for what is gone.

Andrea is a clear example of the sadness of the successful woman. Her work as executive editor for a midsize publishing house brought her a yearly salary of fifty thousand dollars and the urban lifestyle of a young, upwardly mobile professional woman. She was nagged, however, by the persistently uneasy feeling that her essential self was changing under the pressures of her work. "I found myself becoming more and more a person I did not like," she says. "I rushed too much. I put aside people that I did not have time to be bothered with. I endured people I disliked. I could see myself changing." It was, Andrea says, a terribly saddening experience.

Anne, whose master's degree in marketing led to a successful career in public relations, found herself deeply torn between what she wanted to be and what she felt she had to be:

> Not only did I have a conflict with values in my work, but I had a conflict in my soul. I'm basically an honest, straightforward, loving person, not manipulative, competitive, and greedy. But that's what I had become. I was denying myself the pleasure of being myself. I was sick to death of being someone else's image of me.

In my own life and career, the sadness of the successful woman was hidden under a constantly accelerating drivenness. I had the compelling idea that if I ran faster and smarter I could catch up to the elusive happiness and contentment that had so far eluded me—and if I did not, I would be so exhausted that I would not miss what I did not have. If people accused me of being a workaholic, I denied it. Work is what I do for fun, I remember saying, as I would race off for another Saturday at the office. But it was not true. Work was what my career self did to stifle the feelings of sadness and emptiness that were growing inside me.

Other women also report that they try to hide the sense of a lost inner self under a poised and confident outer self. Mary-Alice, whose story we will hear in greater detail in a later chapter, earned over one hundred thousand dollars a year in salary and commission as the general sales manager of a radio station in the Pacific Northwest. In spite of her success, she felt herself to be an imposter. "Deep inside, I kept feeling like a big piece of me was missing," she says. "I wasn't the person everybody thought I was."

> I'm a great actress, and I could put on a terrific act. But when I started questioning my priorities and really feeling the lack of balance in my life, I realized it was all an act. I had no real me to know, love, respect, improve, or change. I couldn't find myself amid all the roles and other-directed facets of my existence. I felt that I had

looked into a frightening void inside myself and realized my worst fear: there was nothing of my own there. It scared the shit out of me.

Women often speak of their careers as a play and themselves as performers playing a role. For Nicole, maintaining the outer self was a full-time acting job that took all of her public-relations energy. "I had no personal identity back in my career days," she reflects, with a quiet self-irony:

> My identity was based solely on my professional *persona du jour.* But being artificial, manipulating, charming, and phony take a great deal of energy, and I finally just ran out of gas. I couldn't act any longer.

The sense of emptiness is often experienced as psychological depression or as anger. "The pain of a denied self, a buried self, finally came to a head," Marlene says, describing what happened in the year before she left the marketing firm where she was vice-president.

> It burst out in emotional explosions at home, where I took out my buried frustrations. I knew if I didn't get out of the business world, my work would deteriorate and I'd have a breakdown.

Many women do experience physical and psychological breakdowns of various sorts: migraines, backaches, ulcers, chronic fatigue, eating disorders, depression. Although not all of the physical symptoms can be definitely traced to pain and emotional emptiness, the sufferers often suspect that their illnesses are caused by career-related stress. An insurance executive quoted in the book *Women Leading: Making Tough Decisions on the Fast Track,* comments on the increasing number of job-stress claims: "We are being swamped with claims relating to job stress—this includes burnout, anxiety, nervous breakdowns, manic depression, to just plain mental fatigue. These claims have doubled in the past several years and are rising. If it is worth it, why are women now in positions of increasing authority filing so many claims?"[5]

Many of the women I talked with reported health problems. "For years, I suffered migraine headaches and panic attacks," says fifty-five-year-old Rita, who worked in the computer software industry. "I know it was because my high-stress work left me with no time or energy for personal fulfillment. I could never be me, and it was making me sick. I firmly believe that if I hadn't gotten out, I wouldn't be talking to you right now."

Virginia, a wife with two children and a successful career as a college professor, contracted cancer. "My life felt too fast, too harried," she says. "I'm not sure of the connection between that and my cancer, but I certainly question it."

Jan, the doctor who developed cancer, is more emphatic about the connection between her physical disease and her psychological and spiritual dis-ease. "I was empty," she says. "My work totally drained my spirit. The cancer filled me up. In a sense, it was all I had."

For many women, however, it is not a sense of emptiness that creates their unhappiness, but a terrible sense of conflicting commitments, a feeling of being torn between two obligations. The cost of career success can be very high. Tom Peters, widely respected business consultant and author of two best-sellers, *In Search of Excellence* and *Passion for Excellence*, spells out the dilemma:

> We are frequently asked if it is possible to 'have it all'—a full and satisfying personal life and a full and satisfying professional one. Our answer is: No. The price of excellence is time, energy, attention and focus, at the very same time that energy, attention and focus could have gone toward enjoying your daughter's soccer game. Excellence is a high-cost item. As David Ogilvy observed in *Confessions of an Advertising Man*: 'If you prefer to spend all your spare time growing roses or playing with your children, I like you better, but do not complain that you are not being promoted fast enough.'[6]

In the career culture, there is no room for wavering commitment between competing obligations. The cost of career success—excellence, in Peters' words—is high for both men and women. Women bear the cost with much greater difficulty than do men. "I knew I needed to be home with my child," says Sonya, whose demanding job as a manager of a service business earned her forty thousand dollars a year.

> My work took more and more time and responsibility and left no time for family relationships. When I was on the job, I felt a pull to be with my little boy. But when I was home, I had a guilty conscience because I was neglecting my work.

This theme is echoed over and over as women with both family and career commitments try to deal with the difficult task of being two people at the same time. "I felt split between my personal and professional selves," Rachel says. Her work in a biology laboratory did not compensate for the loss she felt when she had to leave her newborn child to a caregiver. "I was trying to do two jobs simultaneously and feeling that I couldn't do either one well."

"I began to question how—emotionally and physically and, yes, financially—I could leave the upbringing of my children to another person," says Yolande, a former magazine editor who spent half of her annual thirty-one-thousand-dollar paycheck on care for her two small children.

> I had no time or patience left at the end of the day for my husband. And I had no time for myself. I was trying to live the Supermom myth and it wasn't working. I felt awful.

Emily's children were teenagers and did not require her constant care. As a single parent with an hour-and-a-half commute stacked on top of a full day of teaching, however, she felt torn between obligations. "My difficulties with my children were taking an enormous toll on my energy," she says. "My son was hyperactive, with learning problems. My daughter was unhappy in junior high and taking out her frustrations at home." Emily saw clearly the connection between her daughter's angry feelings about school and her own ambivalence about a career that conflicted with her ability to be emotionally and physically available for her children.

It is not only sadness that many successful career women

experience, but also the sense that they are deeply isolated from other women. In an article entitled "All Alone: The New Loneliness of American Women," author Margery D. Rosen describes the painful separateness of Sheila Fahey, a mother of three children and a manager in a medical-supply company who misses the deep companionship she once had with other women. Sheila's hectic schedule makes it difficult for her to find the time to connect with friends in a meaningful way. She describes a typical day in her life:

> I get up at five-thirty, take a fast walk around the lake behind our house, wake the twins, who are now three, at six-thirty and drop them at preschool on the way to the office. Jack [Sheila's husband] takes care of our seven-year-old son. I get home between five and six, and the evening's a blur of dinner, homework, baths. By nine o'clock I'm catatonic. I can barely manage to get myself ready for bed, so of course I put off calling a friend. I just don't have time for women friends anymore. It's a very, very lonely feeling.[7]

The loneliness of the successful woman, as Rosen points out, is a product of many things: the frantic busyness of women who are doing too much, the divergence of our professional and personal lives, the loss of neighborhoods that once gave us a common focus. Most of all, women suffer loneliness because the career culture isolates us from other women. It substitutes a connection to the work organization for connections with other people. It segregates us by rank, isolating some at the top, some in the middle, some at the bottom, and severing communication among the ranks. It heightens competition among us, whatever our rank, to the point where we are afraid to share details of our intimate lives with our colleagues at work because we cannot be confident that those details will not somehow be used against us.

All of this pervasive discontent—the sadness, the loneliness, the conflict over competing obligations—eventually becomes so painfully disturbing, so deeply distressing, that the stage-one career leaver realizes that the rewards of her career are not worth their price. Her first step toward getting control of her life is to let go of her attachment to her career identity.

31

CUTTING LOOSE

Women who begin to feel a deep disillusionment with their work and a profound loss of personal self may come to believe that they cannot continue to work as they presently are. They begin to detach and disengage themselves from their work, first on an emotional level, then behaviorally.

Helen Ebaugh, in *Becoming an Ex,* observes that people who are considering a role exit often exhibit what she calls cues. Cues are signals, conscious or unconscious, that indicate that we are dissatisfied with our current role and are seeking other alternatives.[8] Cues are the "early warning signs of erosion in commitment," Ebaugh says.

For me, the first signal of an erosion in my commitment to my work was my decision to make an unprecedented three-week visit to a friend in Italy. This trip, which I took two years before I decided to leave my career, was the first one I had taken in fifteen years solely for personal recreation. When I returned (and without seeing any special significance in my actions), I found myself taking an hour or more for nonbusiness lunches, coming in at eight o'clock in the morning instead of six-thirty, and trying to reduce weekend work. I cut down on work-related socializing and refused appointments to boards and committees, saying that I was overextended. My secretary and closest associates were probably aware that I was taking more time for myself, although I do not think they guessed from these cues that I was disengaging myself from my career commitment. At that point, even I did not recognize the signals.

Some women find, however, that the cues of their disengagement are read and responded to by others. Kay, a district sales manager, gave one of her salesmen a card congratulating him for doing a good job. "He was surprised," she said. "He asked, 'Are you giving me this card because you're not going to be here?'" His question made Kay wonder if that was what had been on her mind.

A day-care worker read Laura's cue to her desperately confused state of mind:

> I wasn't sleeping more than three or four hours a night and not doing a good job at anything. The day-care provider I was using

commented that she'd never seen anyone struggle so much when I left my daughter each day. That was the final straw. A total stranger had seen through me.

A close friend of mine, Vikki, had the experience of having her cue read—and responded to in a way she did not expect. After several years of mounting unhappiness with her career as a university administrator, she began to disengage from her work. "I'm thinking about cutting loose" was the way she put it. Because the next year's budgeting process was beginning, she mentioned to her boss in an offhand, tentative way that she might not be there next year. He put a substantial salary increase into the budget for her. When she gave him her resignation letter some months later, he was deeply hurt and protested that he had "bent over backward to keep her happy." He had even, at her request, given her a raise. "To this day, I don't know," she says, shaking her head, "whether he thought I had asked for a raise or whether he thought that a raise might keep me on the job."

Sometimes, looking back, we interpret cues as a justification for a role exit. Many career leavers interpret their health problems as cues. Leah's doctor told her that she was suffering from what he called battle fatigue and suggested that she take time off from the job. Leah was so glad to hear his recommendation that she immediately told her supervisor that her doctor was requiring her to leave work.

Virginia did not need a doctor's advice. Her cancer was a cue: "Facing the real and very fearful prospect of death, I reevaluated my priorities. Suddenly, my career slipped down the list. It just wasn't important to me." Although her condition would have permitted her to continue in her career, the cancer reinforced her feeling that she needed to make major changes in the way she worked.

Considering relocation can serve as a cue that we are no longer totally committed to our present work. Trudi, a vice-president of marketing at a large corporation, had for some time been uncomfortable with the large city she lived in, which she found crowded, dirty, and crime ridden. She vacationed in a small California seaside town, where life seemed slower, healthier, and much more relaxed. She made friends there and began to consider it as an attractive place to live—maybe someday, she thought. Once the idea of relocating had occurred to her, however, it began to grow, and she found herself wondering whether that someday might come sooner than she had thought. A few months later she consulted a psychiatrist, specifically, she says, "to work through my reasons for wanting to move, to get out of the city." The psychiatric consultation itself was another cue—an indication of her growing emotional discomfort with her position and her unhappiness with life in the city. A few months later, Trudi put her house on the market, a sign to both herself and her friends that she might actually go through with her idea of getting away from the corporation and the city. Thinking back on it later, Trudi recognized these first steps as early indications of her desire to get out.

Denise, an art professor at a major eastern university, felt herself disconnected from her career and ambivalent about the directions her art seemed to be taking. She spent a sabbatical year on the Maine seashore, painting, working out new artistic techniques, seeing in a new way. "I realized that what I wanted was to be able to live the way I had learned to live while on my sabbatical," she said later. When she returned to the university, she bought two acres of seashore property, which symbolized her desire "to lead a different life in a different place." She also began to develop workshop activities and other income-producing projects that could make her artwork self-supporting (another cue). She was not ready to make a move, but she was giving clear signals that her academic career was no longer the sole focus of her energies.

At this stage in the process of career exit, many women begin to consider alternative ways of earning money and may even try their hand at doing something else, even if it is only a symbolic gesture. In my last few months at the university, I wrote (late at night and on Sundays) a novel for children. While I did not begin the novel with the idea that writing could provide an alternate income, by the time it was sold I had developed the vague idea that I might be able to write for a living. The sale of that book was an indication to me that there was a feasible alternative to the way I was working.

Trudi made similar tentative explorations. Continuing periodically to visit the seaside town she liked, she casually contacted the free-lance public relations professionals in the area. "I didn't have anything special in mind," she said. "In fact, I was still pretty solidly committed to my career. I just wanted to see what was going on around there. I was wondering if maybe I could work out of my home, in case I decided to make a change." At this point, ideas and indefinite notions for alternative work are not usually plans, considered in a logical and deliberate way. However, they do serve as cues that the woman is beginning to think of other ways to make a living, should she decide to exit from her career.

Often, particular events take on a highly symbolic significance and are interpreted as cues. "My alcoholic father entered a treatment center," Nichole said, "and along with other family members I joined him there for family week. During those five days, I realized that I was a workaholic." Nichole traces her subsequent disengagement from her career to that highly charged event. For her, the weekend that brought her to a new understanding of herself and her work was a signal from a higher power that it was time for a major change in her life.

Shirley, a successful writer and television producer, was struck by the fortuitous coincidence of two different events. It seemed to her a cue that the moment had come to make a change in her work life:

> I recognized the synchronicity of two circumstances in my life: the natural ending of projects I'd been working on and my pregnancy. While I hadn't planned on taking off work to have a baby, it just felt right not to seek further projects at that time.

Judith received a small inheritance; she saw it as a cue that the time was ripe to consider alternatives to her library career. Carla was offered a promotion from her technical job to a management position; she now recognizes her decision to turn the promotion down as the first important signal, to herself and others, of her lessened commitment to her career. Her employer certainly read her cue rightly; when she rejected the promotion, the company made it clear that she should look elsewhere for work.

For many female career leavers, disengagement begins very gradually, even before they are conscious of it. Its duration varies greatly. Some women spend only a few months on the job after they begin to question their commitment. Others spend years riding a terrible emotional seesaw, periodically feeling up about their work, then feeling down. During the down periods, they disengage and begin to imagine themselves doing something else; during the up periods, they recommit themselves to the old choice and find a new energy for the career. Sometimes, something happens in the career itself—an unexpected raise or promotion—that encourages recommitment.

Among the factors that determine how long stage one lasts are the degree of the woman's awareness of what is happening and whether she is alone in her doubts or is part of a group of women who are also beginning to doubt their commitments. If we are conscious of the reasons for our discontent, we are more likely to act on it, one way or another. Our awareness of what is going on is likely to be heightened if we talk with others who are experiencing the same thing—or if we read a book, like this one.

Generally speaking, the period of disillusionment, discontent, and disengagement is a period when we are more and more frustrated by our problems and less and less confident that our careers are the solution. It becomes difficult for us to imagine that we can continue working as we are indefinitely, although most see no alternative at this point.

GROWTH AT STAGE ONE

The psychological growth we experience during the first stage of the career-leaving process involves the gradual recognition that the life pattern we call our career has become—or rather, has been from the beginning—limiting and confining. We begin to sense the need to grow beyond the narrow circle of self that our work has defined.

This growth is not easy, for it involves the rejection of a model of success that is introduced to us at home and taught to us through our entire educational system. For the past two decades, girls have been urged early in their lives—as early as secondary school, if not before—to select a career. Even very young girls and those with economically handicapped backgrounds are encouraged to imagine themselves growing up to be professionals and are often given a special boost in that direction with science and math classes designed to overcome traditional gender barriers in these areas.

Recently, I saw a television news story in which an eleven-year-old black girl living in rural poverty announced that she wanted to be either a lawyer or a paleontologist. Her declaration brought her a box of books and an invitation to visit a California paleontologist. I am not opposed to children in poverty setting high goals for themselves. I believe it is important and necessary for young girls to want to rise above their own devalued status and the devalued status of their mothers. While the young girl's desire to pull herself out of low-status poverty commands our heartfelt admiration and support, however, we also have to recognize that it is characteristic of our society to define economic and social enhancement in terms of narrow concentration in a specialty profession—which in the long run keeps us from realizing the broader potentials of our human experience.

With its near-total focus on career, American education has become a feeder system for the career culture, in the same way that college football and basketball teams are part of the big-league farm system that supplies trained athletes to professional sports. If a young woman has not chosen a career by the end of secondary school, she will be urged to start work on a career-oriented major during her freshman year in college; she will, typically, resent general-education courses, the breadth requirement in the curriculum, as distracting and a waste of time. When she graduates, she will be encouraged to pursue her career education through additional professional training. She recognizes that to become successful, she has to be educationally prepared in a narrow career field. The career culture rewards specialization, not generalization.

Many management experts, however, criticize the tendency of business and industry to seek out entry-level specialists with a highly trained, single-focus perspective. This degree of specialization makes for individuals who lack flexibility and adaptability, have few new ideas, and are unable to take a broader view of problems and solutions. What we need is not people who are trained and paid to think in terms of their specialties, but people who are trained and paid to think globally, across disciplines, professions, and methodologies. Our collective future may depend on generalization, not specialization.

If the early narrowing of intention and energy is not healthy for our culture, it is most definitely not healthy for us as ind uals. Early specialization narrows our definitions of ourselves and motivates us to see ourselves primarily, even solely, in the contexts of a specialty and a career. When we adopt a professional identity, we are encouraged to think of it as our whole identity and we have little time or energy to explore and develop other aspects of our personalities. The career culture places little premium on the quality of roundedness, but we cannot be whole people without being rounded. What is more, we cannot be whole people without caring for other people. The career culture allows us little time to pursue our caring in any meaningful way.

Unfortunately, the narrowed focus on career-based specialization occurs when we are very young, when the glamour of the workplace is most alluring and before we have either the opportunity or the maturity to know—confidently, authentically, independently—who we are, apart from what we do for a living.

Sandra, an ex-lawyer, is a case in point. Sandra first decided that she wanted to enter the law when she was ten. She began working summers in her stepfather's law firm at thirteen. When I asked if her law career had required her to replace her personal identity with a professional identity, she answered thoughtfully:

> When I entered the work force I don't think I had my own personal identity, separate from the expectations of my parents, peer group, and society. So in the beginning, I didn't replace a personal identity, I just adopted a professional identity.

Sandra's professional identity was in the beginning the only secure identity she had—a fact that is true for most career women. Sandra knew her strengths, her skills, her potentials only in the context of her work and through other professionals' expectations of her performance.

After a time, however, Sandra began to outgrow her professional identity and to see it as false and confining. Serious ethical issues in her law firm and pressing questions of personal authenticity forced her to compare her beliefs and values to those of the professionals (almost exclusively male) around her. The comparison revealed that her professional identity no longer seemed to fit. A voice inside began to suggest to her, she told me, that her whole personality was larger than the self she knew at work— the dressed-for-success self she thought she had wanted to be:

At first it was just vague disorientation, mild dissatisfaction with the things that went on in the office. But the voice inside grew until I could no longer ignore it. I was not one of them. I didn't want to identify with people who elevated their own esteem at the expense of others and took no personal responsibility for themselves or their actions. It was almost as if I was learning who I was in reaction to who they were.

As we begin to learn who we are in relationship to others who are supposed to serve as our professional models, we often feel the dissatisfaction that is the first push toward new growth. If we listen honestly to that dissatisfaction and honor it, we may feel a need to enlarge our self-definition beyond its career focus, as Sandra did.

This new growth, this wish for personal enlargement, may be at the least uncomfortable and, at the worst, severely disorienting, threatening, and painful. After all, we have spent years, perhaps even decades, striving for career success. We have poured endless hours into training ourselves, adapting to the rules, learning our roles. It is painful beyond measure to suspect that something might be wrong with the game and our participation in it. It is even more painful to suspect that we are going to have to do something about the way we feel. Role exit can be a very frightening thing.

Under these difficult circumstances, it is no wonder that we wish to deny our feelings of disillusionment, discontent, and disengagement from our work roles. It is no wonder that the first stage of career exit is almost always marked by ambivalence, anxiety, and a denial of our feelings. Because we have been fully acculturated to see our career and our job as desirable, any questioning, any doubting is initially likely to result in denial.

This denial can take a variety of forms. Sometimes we minimize our feelings and search for a distraction: "Everybody gets down in the dumps once in a while. What I need is a new health club (or a new diet, a new wardrobe, a new psychiatrist, a new lover)."

Or we attribute the pain of a cramped soul to being burned out because of a heavy workload. We hope to feel better after a certain project is finished (or after vacation, or after the next promotion, or when another person is hired). We try to stick it out until things get better.

We take a class on positive thinking and paste a few affirmations on our bathroom mirror: "This is such a *great* job, a great opportunity. Every day, in every way, it's getting better and better. Every day, in every way, I'm getting closer to the top."

We tell ourselves that the job is basically okay and that we are out of step, that it is crazy to be feeling the way we are feeling and complaining about a few minor problems. We think nobody else feels the way we do.

We remind ourselves of the long, hard road to the top, imagine telling them to stuff it in five years, and then pour another drink (or cut another piece of cake or buy another piece of jewelry)—trying to forget our feelings.

We have to learn to recognize and acknowledge the pain we feel about our careers and our work. Paradoxical as it may sound, we need to welcome it. For the discomfort and pain we feel in our career is an essential part of the process of growth. If we continue to narrow our experience to choices we made when we were in our twenties, we are not likely to open ourselves to new growth. Disillusionment with career and the career culture is a necessary, if painful, prelude to a thoughtful examination of our lives. It is the first step in an important, personally transforming effort to construct a new and more satisfying reality: work that is essentially our own, work that fits the persons we have become, work that leaves us with ample room for future growth.

Before we can move toward that new reality, however, we must understand the reasons for making our career commitments in the first place. That is the work we have to do at stage two of the career-leaving process.

THE SECOND STAGE: REFLECTING ON THE SELF

*F*or many female career leavers, the outward signs of disengagement with their careers—ennui, lack of involvement, sense of disconnectedness—are deeply troubling, sometimes disorienting. This is especially true because successful women are used to being in control of the way things happen, to being in charge. After all, they successfully completed the female equivalent of the hero's journey. Against heavy odds, they created a successful career in a highly competitive male-dominated world. They can expect to reap even greater rewards—broader responsibilities, another promotion, more travel, an increase in pay. Instead, they find themselves frustrated, deeply unhappy, and profoundly troubled. "This wasn't the way I thought I'd feel," one woman told me. "When I got to the top, I was supposed to be happy. I actually wondered whether I was going crazy. I felt I was completely out of control."

The feeling of losing control leads many women to ask serious, probing questions about the motivations that have brought them to their emotional crossroad. Why? they ask. Why do I find it so necessary to be a career achiever? Why do I drive so hard to get ahead? What part of myself am I feeding by my efforts to achieve in the career culture? What part of myself am I sacrificing?

The search for answers to these questions can, and does, occur at any time during the career-leaving process. For many women, however, the task begins when the disillusionment and discontent reach a painful pitch they can no longer ignore. For others, it starts when they can no longer reconcile the dissonance between their career and their relationship commitments. Whenever the search for answers begins, it always grows out of a woman's need to know the truth, out of a refusal to be held any longer in the bonds of illusion.

The answers do not come easily. They are rooted in the roles women have historically played in our culture. We are the first generation of women to experience both the opportunity and the obligation to move out of the narrow confines of the home and into the career culture. We are driven by the possibility of achievement and by the sense that in some sense we owe it to the generations of women before us who were not permitted to enter the workplace and to the generations of women after us whose success depends, in part, on how successful we are.

In a more personal sense, the answers are rooted, deeply and disturbingly, in our birth families—in our fathers and mothers and their interaction. Our birth families are a powerful shaping force in our adult achievements. In stage two of the process of finding work of their own, many women begin to explore their psychological connections to their families and attempt to understand how the family shaped their career commitments. They see that to grow and develop as individuals, they must re-mother and re-father themselves. They must find out who they are, separate from the powerful figures that influenced them.

CAREER-ONLY WOMEN

Many women who have achieved success in their careers are *career-only* women—that is, early in their lives they made a conscious decision not to have children. Most often, women make this decision during the teen years or in the twenties, when they are feeling the first heady rush of career commitment and believe (with justification) that marriage and children will interfere with the amount of time and energy they can give to their work. "How could I have children?" one woman asked me. "For a lot of years, I put in twelve or fifteen hours on the job. If I'd had to rush home at four-thirty or five to take care of the kids, I would have been operating under a handicap. And it certainly wouldn't have been fair to the children."

Many career-only women have strongly negative feelings about the traditional family, based on their experiences in their own birth families. When these women compare their mothers and fathers in terms of power, they generally see their fathers as being powerful people and their mothers as being relatively powerless. They do not want to reproduce that situation in their own lives.

The phenomenon of the powerful father is one that Patricia McBroom observed when she studied a group of professional women in the finance industry for her book *The Third Sex: The New Professional Woman*. Of McBroom's forty-four subjects, thirteen said they were not interested in becoming mothers. This group, McBroom says, "came from patriarchal families in which their fathers held high power and their mothers did not." She did not find a single woman who was the daughter of a "low-powered mother" who had children of her own.

> The fear of deteriorating into a state of feminine powerlessness, if they pursue love and marriage to its ultimate conclusion, forms a solid barrier for these women, who are in many cases out of touch with feminine identity. . . . Typically, the women who did not want children and who came from patriarchal backgrounds were reacting against femininity as soft, giving, and weak. . . . The feminine images they grew up with at the most intimate level are ones of being dominated and even degraded. Their defense against falling into the same state is to walk a wide circle around maternity.[1]

When career-only women reach the stage where they begin to doubt their career commitment, the experience is often so profoundly unsettling that they seek help in therapy. In the process of trying to understand why their work has taken such a high priority in their lives, they have to acknowledge and understand their feelings about their fathers and mothers.

Daughters and Fathers

Vanessa is a tall, striking-looking woman in her forties. When I met her, she was about to enter a graduate program in fiction writing. She moved and spoke with a compelling sense of personal authority, and I was not surprised to learn that until three years previously she had held a high-level management position in a large southwestern city. When I asked her why she had resigned, her answer was simple and direct.

> I got frightened. I had the feeling that my creative self, the part of me that's feminine, was being buried under all the executive demands I had to deal with. I knew that I had to leave, or there wouldn't be anything left of me—whoever *I* am.

Vanessa's search for her true self was much more complex than her straightforward answer might suggest. Two years before she resigned, she began psychotherapy. She wanted to discover, she said, "why I was so attached to big pay checks and superficial forms of public recognition. I had the feeling that I was symbolically replaying an early family role. This feeling of being trapped in an old script was very frightening for me."

In therapy, Vanessa began to examine the roles her father and mother had played in her life. "In a public sense, my father was extremely powerful," Vanessa says.

> He owned his own business and was recognized as a community leader. He wasn't a particularly good husband or father because he was self-centered and emotionally distant. But he was very interested in seeing that my sisters and I were successful in the ways he was successful—through work and public recognition. I wasn't conscious of it, but I think a big piece of my career drive had to do with identifying with him and wanting to please him.

Compelled by this unconscious need to obtain her father's approval and to become the kind of person he wanted her to be, Vanessa sought a position that would give her the greatest authority, the highest level of public recognition. Her work in civic management certainly met those requirements.

Career-only women often report that, as young girls, they admired their fathers and found them to be more competent and more successful than their mothers. In most cases, the daughters admired their fathers more than they admired their mothers.

Kay's father was a physician. "I had a special position with him," she says, thinking back.

> I could go to him and he would take my side. He seemed excited about me, about the things I did—much more excited than my

mother. I identified with him in many ways. I wanted to be like him. He was vibrant. And he had a position people respected.

Carla believes that identifying with her father propelled her into her corporate career.

My father's life seemed glamorous. He was in a managerial position and worked with people all day. He made things happen. My mother's life seemed incredibly boring. I couldn't understand how she could stand to stay home day after day and do nothing. I thought I might marry, but I never wanted to have children. I was afraid they'd leave me stuck at home like my mother.

"I identified more fully with my father," Jill says. She loved watching him get ready for work and waiting for him at the train station at night.

Once I even tried to shave my face, to my mother's horror. The effect of all this was that I grew up thinking I would have a profession and be a part of the work force just like a man. I might marry, but I would never have any children.

Psychologists say that the intense dynamic that can be formed between daughter and father is often the motivating force that compels the adult woman to commit herself to a career. In one of the first studies of successful women, carried out in the early 1970s, Margaret Hennig and Anne Jardim found that women who achieved high corporate positions had extremely close relationships with their fathers and were involved in traditionally masculine activities with their fathers when they were very young: "From [the father-daughter relationship] they drew attention, approval, reward and confirmation. It was an added source of early learning, a very early means of expanding their experience, and through it they gained a role model with which they could begin to identify." Hennig and Jardim add without interpretive comment: "They also developed a very early preference for the company of men rather than of women."[2]

Not all career-only women, however, have a strong and capable father they can use as a model for their adult selves. "It wasn't my father I admired," Marlene says now, looking back.

He was always so pressured trying to make a dollar that he wasn't there, and when he was, he was always angry. We were on tiptoes not to do anything to set off a tantrum, or he would get explosive, or he'd have a migraine and we'd have to be quiet. But my grandfather saved me. He was very important to me, and I loved and knew him better than my dad. He was able to make his way in any situation. He could scramble. He was a survivor and yet he got along with everybody.

Marlene's positive model of masculine acceptance was her grandfather; her negative model was her raging father, from whom she wanted desperately to escape. (Interestingly, her first choice of vocation, at age eighteen, was to become a nun: that is, to reject the male world in favor of the all-female world of the convent, subservient to and respectful of the male hierarchy of the church.) Escape was impossible, however, and throughout her life she remained involved in an ongoing psychological dynamic that was, in part, a product of her intense feelings about her father.

Fear of his frequent rages formed my personality to a great extent, because I put a lot of energy into anticipating what would set him off, learning to read very carefully and avoiding it. That made me a good reader of people and manipulative, too, in both positive and negative ways.

Like her father, Marlene has found her own anger to be a problem in her adult life. When she was feeling stressed in her work as a senior vice-president at a large communications agency, she reacted with rage at home—to the point where she feared that her anger might destroy a relationship she deeply wanted to preserve.

Whether we consciously adopt a positive paternal model or try to escape a negative influence, our need to identify with the masculine is compelling. As Patricia McBroom suggests in *The Third Sex,* this need arises out of the powerless, passive situation of women in our contemporary culture. Early in her life, a young girl absorbs the culture's devaluation of women and equates her mother's femaleness with weakness and dependency. She sees that in order to make things happen in the world, she must adopt male standards of thinking, behaving, relating, competing. She must form an alliance with the father and become what some psychologists call the father's daughter, remaking herself to meet the requirements of the masculine world.

Some women adapt to the masculine domain through an emphasis on their appearance, assuming a conventional image of feminine beauty and seductive behavior in order to make men like them. They attempt to gain power by relating to men sexually, through marriage and other arrangements. Others adapt by emphasizing their achievement. Rather than making men like them, they have become like men. Being respected for achievement probably provides more and deeper satisfaction throughout the adult years than being admired for appearance. Fundamentally, the two are equal. "Both are facades," say psychologists Polly Young-Eisendrath and Florence Wiedemann in their book, *Female Authority*. They are false selves, "adapted to the dictates of the patriarchy in order to gain patriarchal power."[3]

Gaining approval and confirmation from the father can be an empowering achievement for a young girl who is faced with a double bind: Either she is true to her feminine self and powerless, or she is true to the masculine and powerful. Realistically speaking, in view of the reward system of the career culture, it is better to be masculine and powerful. Young-Eisendrath and Wiedemann agree: "Adapting to male dictates for validation is actually a healthy transition . . . to greater independence in a patriarchal society. Identifying oneself with the culturally superior form of authority (i.e., masculine) results in greater self-esteem and mastery, and in less risk of depression."[4]

Adaptation can also result, obviously and emphatically, in substantial rewards during the adult years. The career successes of the women described by Hennig and Jardim testify to the long-term gains that can be achieved by the creation of a male-identified facade, or career self.

A male-identified career self has its psychological dangers as well as its cultural advantages and rewards, as I found to be disturbingly true in my own life. As I began to understand the forces that led me to overcommit myself to my career, I realized that I am a father's daughter. While my own blue-collar father did not have the kind of public authority that Vanessa's father had, in our working-class home he was unquestionably more powerful than my mother, and I worshipped him. As a young child, I clamored to go fishing with him; as I grew older, I admired his intellect and shared his enthusiasm for literature. We were never close, for he was frequently remote, angry, and unpredictable, and he suffered from alcoholism. Because he was unreachable, however, I idealized him even more highly. I was often afraid of his erratic moods, and I feared his punishment.

It was, nonetheless, my father's approval (and later, that of my male teachers and professors) that I sought in my efforts to earn high grades, to complete college and graduate school, to become an intellectual. To please him I was still in school (albeit a vice-president) at the age of forty-five, still striving for more responsibility, more authority—because no achievement is ever enough to satisfy the compulsion to achieve that is the burden of the true father's daughter. Largely in his image and for his approval, I constructed my male-identified career self.

Therein lay the hazard. My drive to succeed had become a driving compulsion, necessary to maintain the career self. It was this self that I had to cast off with such pain and struggle when I abandoned my career and began to search for work that would reflect the whole person I truly was.

It is not just the personal father that we are talking about here, however, for in a much larger sense, my father, Vanessa's father, Marlene's grandfather—all our fathers—are merely representative symbols to their daughters of the power and authority available only in the patriarchal world: the world of the Fathers. For a woman, achieving power and success according to a masculine model means acceptance into the patriarchy—an acceptance, of course, which is always conditional on her behaving like a good daughter, adapting herself to male-dictated behaviors. A daughter of the father is a daughter of all the Fathers. From the alliance with the personal father she turns to other powerful men—colleagues, bosses, employers—and to powerful masculine institutions: the university, the church, the corporation, the government. An affiliation with these authorities provides her with credentials and ratifies her own authority, which she gains by developing a male-identified career self. In the process, she sacrifices her feminine soul, for identifying with the masculine, psychologists tell us, necessarily requires the rejection of the feminine—the rejection of the mother, of the Mothers.

Daughters and Mothers

We glimpsed Vanessa's father in the preceding section. Now we will look at Vanessa's mother. She was not a passive, stay-at-home housewife. She had strong intellectual and artistic interests and a part-time job as a teacher in a pottery studio. As a child, Vanessa saw her mother as a powerful figure, although she felt her to be emotionally reserved, judgmental, and controlling. "But I understand now," Vanessa says, "that a lot of what I thought was power was Mother's way of covering her anxiety about herself. She had a brilliant and powerful aunt who had become a scientist and a female cousin who was a lawyer. She was trying to live up to the models they set."

Vanessa's mother, herself a daughter of the Fathers, must have felt that her own career achievements were overshadowed by those of her husband and her sister, both of whom were making outstanding contributions in male-dominated fields. Her discomfort was apparent to Vanessa, even as a child. "She was very ambivalent about her role as a mother. I sensed early on that there was a tension between the time that mothering took and her desires to be successful." Her part-time work clearly came second to her husband's career, and Vanessa saw her mother as performing a kind of unsatisfying balancing act between family and work. Although Vanessa rarely heard her mother complain, her unconscious picked up the clear message that it is impossible to be both a mother/wife and a woman with an independent career. The judgmental, controlling behavior, Vanessa accurately perceives, grew out of her mother's underlying frustration and anger at not being able to live out her own artistic life in a full and gratifying way.

Jungian analyst Marion Woodman describes such mothers as "patriarchs"—out of touch with their own instinctual lives: "Disempowered as a woman [the patriarchal mother] runs her household as she runs herself—with shoulds, oughts and have-tos that add up to power. Life is not fed from the waters of love, but from willpower that demands perfection."[5]

Asked how her mother's emotional imbalance colored her own career choices, Vanessa answers without hesitation.

> I've been playing out a kind of struggle between my identification with my father and my identification with my mother. I felt a really

strong tension between public administration jobs, which I identified with my father, and art, which I identified with my mother.

Vanessa's outer self, her career self, was modeled on her father's public power and authority. Her true self, buried underneath the high-powered, competitive, ambitious persona, was much more aligned with the essential feminine. "I finally decided," she says, "after a great deal of painful soul searching, that my real gifts were reflective and contemplative and artistic." Asked about marriage and children, she hesitates.

> Well, I certainly planned to marry, but it was . . . I don't know, how can I put it? It was always in the future, not in the present. So I'm not sure how deeply grounded the plan was. I was much more consciously conflicted about children. In some sense, I wanted to live a traditional life. But in another sense, I was aware of how acutely uncomfortable my mother had been in her own mothering role.

Still feeling her mother's ambivalence, Vanessa continues to reject the idea of having children, although she is able now to incorporate her mother's feminine creativity in her life in a different way. She has recently completed her studies in fiction writing, is working on a collection of short stories, and teaching writing. She is consciously working at the task of re-fathering and re-mothering herself, cleansing herself of the old relationship to her father and discovering her own feminine nature.

Many other career-only women recognize themselves in Vanessa's conflict: between the outer career self, designed and constructed to please the Fathers, and the inner true self. Jeannie is one. Shortly after she began to doubt her commitment to her twenty-year career in the airline industry, she happened to attend a seminar on dysfunctional families. When she recognized her own situation in the presenter's description, she sought counseling in an attempt to answer such stage-two questions as Who am I, really? and What do I really want? In her search she began to explore the ways in which her choice of a career and her acceptance of difficult career conditions had been influenced by the dynamics of her dysfunctional birth family. She began to seek out ways of re-fathering and re-mothering herself and to create a healthy environment for her further growth.

Jeannie's career began at the age of eighteen when her father coaxed her to enroll in an airline school. "He encouraged me to get into the school because he loved flying, loved traveling," she says. His flying, hunting, and fishing hobbies took him away often during Jeannie's childhood. She traces her idealization of him to the fact that he was rarely there, either physically or emotionally. As a result, she adds, "I spent a lot of time trying to imagine his response to me. I spent a lot of effort trying to please him." He was not easy to please.

> No matter how well I thought I had done, he never praised me. He would always want to know why I hadn't thought of this or that, or he'd find a flaw and quickly point it out. Years later, I realized that my boss and my working environment were frighteningly similar to my father and the environment I grew up in. I was striving, striving, to prove myself worthy to a man who would never recognize me or my efforts.

With her father so often absent, Jeannie might have turned to her mother as a model for her own growth and development. That was impossible, however, for Jeannie remembers her mother as a woman totally lacking in personal power or authority. "I believe she got cancer," she says with infinite sadness, "because it was the only way out for her."

> I was raised in a small German community where the husband was the boss and the woman had no rights, so the women got very frustrated and turned into nagging people. My mother must have been frustrated, but she didn't nag. She just kept quiet, and she was sick all the time. When I was ten, she died. It was the only socially acceptable way out of a devastating situation.

Even though the daughter longed to be close to her mother, the mother's silent, passive withdrawal and her illness imposed an unbridgeable distance between them. "I never remember her hugging me or holding me or saying I love you," Jeannie says. Her family—the absent, autocratic father, and the passive mother who was self-abnegating to the point of self-annihilation—may be an extreme example of the patriarchal family, but it points up

51

with startling clarity why young women turn to the masculine world for satisfaction of their human need for power and personal authority. "I never wanted to be like my mother," Jeannie recalls without rancor. "Even though Dad wasn't around, he was the only strong one. He was the only one I could identify with."

Although Jeannie consciously turned away from her mother and the domestic world of the Mothers, her work in the airline industry ironically put her into a position not very different from that of her mother. In spite of the fact that she achieved a high-level management position, she still felt like an alien outsider with little real power to communicate and to get things done effectively. "In the male-dominated airlines, no woman manager ever really belongs to the corporate family," she told me.

> I was one of the first women ever in management in my airline. Those of us who made it were "tokens," and we were never totally accepted. We were discounted as not having the technical or professional acumen. My manager gave me raises grudgingly, and I always got less than the men.

Like her mother, Jeannie did not try very hard to be a member of the corporate family. She found she did not share its values or its commitment to twelve-hour days, and she withdrew, at least from its extracurricular functions.

> During the thirteen years I was in management I repeatedly saw unethical business practices, and I witnessed and experienced the consequences of working for men who strive for power and prestige. I could not, over the years, develop those [so-called] required traits. I preferred to go home in the evening to friends, exercise, classes at the university, than to stay at the office and work or attend functions at work just because that's what you do to get ahead.

Unlike her powerless mother, Jeannie was able to develop other resources and sources of strength and affirmation outside the corporation. Through her deep, probing stage-two self-questioning, she began to see the similarity between her birth family and her corporate family. Her new understanding put her well on the way to overcoming her unhealthy dependency on work that she no longer enjoyed.

Interestingly, however, Jeannie's first impulse was not to leave the corporation, but to fix it. Going to school at night, she had earned an undergraduate degree in psychology.

> My big dream was to get my master's and go back to the airline and do counseling, because we had so many alcoholics and drugs and divorces and all this stuff. I thought, if I can mix psychology and business, I can really help this company. But I finally said, this is bullshit, Jeannie, you've got to get out. You don't want to leave the airline, it's been your whole life and you've loved it. But it's sick, it's like a sick family, and if you don't get out, you're going to stay enmeshed.

When Jeannie eventually left the airline, she enrolled in a graduate program in psychology. Now, several years later, she is about to open her own counseling practice. She feels she has worked through the resentment and unhappiness about her mother's death and her father's abandonment, and she understands the dynamics that compelled her to work as she did. For her, re-fathering herself has meant discovering a new understanding of ways to relate to authority and to men; re-mothering herself has meant discovering dimensions of her own feminine self that have been hidden to her, concealed beneath her mother's passive dependence.

Not all mothers are as unresponsive and as closed to emotional contact as Jeannie's, of course. Many career-only women, however, feel that during their childhood they lacked another type of contact with their mothers: intellectual contact. As daughters, these women often believed their mothers to be intellectually less competent than their fathers.

MaryAlice, who grew up to become an executive in radio broadcasting with an annual salary of a hundred thousand dollars, remembers her mother as flaky and flighty. "Mother was fluent in Czech," she says, "but my father wouldn't allow her to speak it to us, because it was lower class, uneducated."

> As a child, I thought Mother was totally incompetent and I disassociated myself from her as fully as possible. She loved to dance, play poker, go to the horse races, go to Vegas. But I saw her fun-loving ways as superficial and silly, in comparison to my father's meticulous attention to getting things done right. For a long time I held the belief that women weren't as smart as men.

The daughter's perception of her mother's intellectual incompetence is sometimes casually pitying, sometimes bitter and deeply resentful. Jan, who grew up to become a physician, remembers that her father—a college graduate and a department head in state government—would not permit her mother to work outside the home. She also recalls that her mother, who had not graduated from high school, was convinced that she was not as smart as the rest of the family: "Mother had a difficult time living with three very intelligent people," Jan says.

About her father, she remarks, "I don't think he actually tried to make Mother feel dumb, but he certainly didn't try to make her feel intelligent." Like her father, Jan began to think she was quite a bit smarter than her mother and to find extreme ways of showing her intellectual superiority.

> I wouldn't let her touch me. I wouldn't speak to her unless I had to, except for basic information. I repudiated my mother's role. I said, I am not going to be a mommy or a housewife. At the age of four, I decided to become a doctor. But my mother's message to me was that little girls didn't grow up to be doctors.

With an unconscious irony that reveals how much Jan truly coveted her mother's approval of her wish to be accepted into the male world, she adds, "I hated her for not believing in me." Between the lines of Jan's story, we can sense the despairing wish of the mother to hold the little girl to herself, at the same time feeling herself helpless against a masculine world that could beckon with such seductive promises of power and confident intellectual authority.

Sometimes it is the mother herself—perhaps compelled by repressed anger, perhaps by the frustration of being excluded from power and wishing broader opportunities for her daughters—who forces a daughter to choose the father. Trudi was earning a hundred thousand dollars a year as a marketing vice-president in a cosmetics firm when she began to experience doubts about her career and entered therapy to try to resolve them. In therapy, she examined the dynamics of her birth family and explored her antagonism to her mother. "I was much closer to my father than to my mother," she recalls.

Dad wasn't home a lot—he was a workaholic—and when he was, he'd bring work home. I'd sit at his knee and he'd dictate letters to me, and that's how I learned to write letters. He was my mentor and taught me how to act and react in business.

Trudi's mother, however, resented the fact that father and daughter were so often closeted together. "She felt left out of my father's life. She harbored her resentment of him and his work for the rest of his days and continues to cling to it still," Trudi says. An event that occurred when Trudi was thirteen years old seemed to exemplify her mother's unspoken anger at Trudi's growing identification with the father—although it could just as easily have exemplified the mother's wish for a life of broader potential for her child. "She had been ill," Trudi remembers.

She was in bed, and I went in to cuddle with her. Something was said about Dad and having to make a choice between them, and she pushed me and said, 'Well, then, go to your father.' It was clear to me that I had to make a choice between them. It couldn't be her and him, it had to be him or her.

Following her mother's instruction, Trudi went to her father, and symbolically to the world of Fathers. "I felt terribly resentful and angry at her for forcing me to choose," Trudi says. "In the end, I became like my father, a workaholic with a successful career." To this day, in spite of her therapy, she sees herself as having rejected the feminine and feels herself much more aligned with the masculine.

I learned early on that I preferred working for and with men. I thought like them and reacted like them. My traits are so much closer to a man's traits. I just don't have patience with women.

According to the recollections of other career-only women, their mothers expressed their anger and frustration much more openly than Trudi's mother did, often through unpredictable outbursts of rage and violence. Even though they may have used every strategy they knew to hold their daughters, they literally drove them into the arms of the Fathers. Here again, we have the "mother as Patriarch," in Marion Woodman's terms. Within the family, this angry woman (sometimes a housewife, sometimes employed outside the home in a job below her ability) plays out the masculine role, using her daughters (and often her sons) to mirror herself and to fulfill her deeply frustrated need for power and personal authority.

Sandra's mother was a patriarchal mother. "Our family was dysfunctional in many of the same ways an alcoholic's family is," Sandra says, "yet no one drank."

> My mother's deep-rooted insecurities and lack of self-esteem were manifested in her obsessive-compulsive manipulation and control of everything and everyone she could reach. I was born to suit her needs. I tried to be like her (or like her fantasy of how she wanted to be as a little girl) in order to stay in her good graces. I loved her, but I was also enormously frightened of her unpredictable wrath.

For the first thirteen years of Sandra's life, her mother was a single parent, which created an especially strong bond between the two of them. "Not only did I identify with her," Sandra says, "but she was my identity. Or perhaps more accurately, I was hers."

As early as ten, Sandra expressed a desire to become a lawyer. Her mother, a legal secretary, approved of her choice. When Sandra was thirteen, her mother married a lawyer. "As Harry integrated into our family, he and I formed bonds of our own," Sandra says. "I admired his integrity and the respect he'd earned in the community. All these factors reinforced my decision to enter the law."

At first, her mother supported her decision, but when Sandra was ready for college, she did an about face and strongly opposed her daughter's decision. Seeking a way to separate herself from her mother, Sandra was more determined than ever to become a lawyer.

> I pursued the notion of law school, not only because it appeared to be a lofty goal but because it would also provide the perfect opportunity for me to openly and publicly defy my mother, as well as reject her views.

Sandra's mother clearly fits Woodman's description of the patriarchal woman who wants her daughter to fulfill the dreams that she could not fulfill. Sandra's desire to be a lawyer must have both pleased the mother (who had once unsuccessfully studied for the law) and at the same time invited comparisons. When the mother married a lawyer and was able to project her own career ambitions onto her husband instead of her daughter, it was no longer necessary for her to encourage Sandra to surpass her; it must even have seemed dangerous, awakening jealousy at the thought that her daughter might succeed where she had failed.

Sandra's decision to enter the law was shaped, like the decision of many other women, by the dynamics of her birth family, especially by the conflict between the powerful masculine and the less powerful feminine. In this instance, the choice was shaped by the mother's rage and frustration rather than by her passivity, but the outcome was the same: The daughter fled into the arms of the Fathers.

CAREER-FIRST WOMEN

The women I have just described, Vanessa, Jeannie, Trudi, and Sandra, represent career-only women. Early in their lives they rejected the traditional female role of bearing and raising children, chiefly out of fear that they might be forced into the role of the passive feminine. The daughter's image of her mother's wounded and devalued self shaped her response to opportunities in her own life.

Many career women, however, are what I call career-first women. They plan to establish themselves in a career during their twenties; then, when the career is firmly in place, they plan to establish a family. They expect to coordinate their career and family obligations in a way that will allow them to meet both simultaneously—and successfully. These are not women who plan to drop out of their careers in order to raise children. Instead, they wholeheartedly and confidently accept the superwoman model that became so popular in the 1980s at the urging of feminists who believed that a woman can reach her full potential only through a full-time professional career. Career-first women expect to integrate their work lives and their personal lives successfully. "I knew it wasn't going to be as easy as falling off a log," one woman said to me, "but the women's magazines kept running these articles about women who were handling both a career and kids. I figured if those women could do it, I could too."

Career-first women experience the same kinds of doubts that the career-only women do—workplace dissatisfaction and disillusionment, lack of respect for colleagues and superiors, discomfort with the level of competition, concern about questionable ethics, and conflict between the values of the workplace and their own personal values. These doubts are intensified, however, as women with children struggle to cope with the difficult physical and psychological challenge of carrying two careers at once. In fact, family obligations sometimes provide a welcome escape from a career and a work style about which these women are increasingly ambivalent. "If you want to know the truth," one told me, "I was relieved when I found out I was pregnant again."

> I felt I had to get out, and having another baby was a good way to explain it to people—although it wasn't the real reason. The real reason was that I was beginning to hate my career and the way it made me feel about myself.

When a career-first woman begins her stage-two investigations into herself in order to understand the source of her career doubts, she often looks no further than the family situation she is currently trying to manage. "I finally woke up to the fact that I wasn't Super Mom," Sonya said after she left her position as the manager of a hectic graphic arts business.

> It took a lot of tears and frustration for me to admit to myself and my husband that I just couldn't do it all. I couldn't climb the career ladder and at the same time be the kind of mother I wanted to be.

For the career-first woman, problems at home are likely to seem more troublesome than problems on the job. This perception has been heightened by an otherwise excellent book by Arlie Hochschild, *The Second Shift: Working Parents and the Revolution at Home.* Hochschild herself sees the workplace as a significant part of the problem and its redesign as a crucial step in moving toward gender equity: "I repeatedly heard career women in this study say, 'What I really need is a wife.' But maybe they don't need 'wives'; maybe they need careers basically redesigned to suit workers who also care for families. This redesign would be nothing short of a revolution."[6]

But the media and most readers of Hochschild's book focus on the other part of the problem: the strain between working wives and husbands that Hochschild says is a result of the "stalled revolution." When a career-first woman tries to answer the question "Why am I so unhappy with my career?" she often sees the most immediate and pressing side of the difficulty. She concludes that she is unhappy because she has insufficient help with the second shift at home. For that reason, if she undertakes therapy, she usually seeks marriage and family counseling with her husband in an effort to ease the second-shift strain and seek help for the troubled family. Family counseling is likely to be pragmatic, aimed at fixing the immediate problem, relieving the stress, and more equably distributing the work load between the two marriage partners. It usually does not address the root of the problem.

Another reason the career-first woman is more likely to skip the deep, internal probing of stage two is that she does not experience as many deep conflicts involving her relationship to her mother and father as do career-only women. While she may be desperately unhappy with the present situation, her unhappiness is not the angry disaffiliation from the feminine that so many career-only women experience.

Daughters as Mothers

The career-first women I interviewed were not as frequently compelled to probe their birth-family conflicts as were the career-only women I talked with—for the simple reason that there seemed to be fewer conflicts. In general, career-first women seem more realistic than career-only women about their fathers' work and the power their fathers wielded, both in the family and on the job. On the whole, they admire their fathers less and see them more realistically. They idealize the masculine less than do career-only women.

More importantly, however, these women admire their mothers as much as or more than they admire their fathers. In general, while career-only women identify with their fathers and often say emphatically that they never wanted to be like their mothers, career-first women say that they regard their mothers as good role models. "My mother was competent and authoritative," they report. "I'm more like her than I'm like my father."

Sarah, thirty-five years old, left a high-paying position as a vice-president of a large bank to mother her two young children and to establish an at-home business. Her father was a college math professor (she calls him the typical absentminded professor), and her mother ran a home-based catering service. Both were practicing Jews. Although there were obvious discrepancies between the kinds of power the two wielded, Sarah saw her mother as a person of strong personal authority, high energy level, and abundant emotional warmth.

> She always did a lot. We'd sit down to watch TV at night, and she'd be finishing up a catering job. Her energy is what, even in the present tense, I admire about her. And Dad was proud of her, although he didn't show it very well.

In spite of her mother's energy and creativity, the family structure was still patriarchal, outwardly, at least: The father was nominally the most powerful person in the family, and the mother acquiesced to his wishes. Even as a child, however, Sarah saw through the outward appearance of her father's authority and recognized her mother's real, practical power in the family:

> My mother planned around him but allowed him to control. He didn't really have authority over anything, except that things were centered around him. It was, 'we can't do this, we can't do that because your father wouldn't want to'—that kind of thing, even though he was probably oblivious to whether we did it or not. He was very, very bright, and I admired his intellect, but he wasn't very competent around the house. He couldn't hammer a nail in a wall. And he always rode a bike, he didn't drive a car. My mother was chauffeur, and where we went was dependent on her.

When I ask Sarah if there are ways in which she is like her mother, her response comes quickly and without hesitation:

> Yes, I'm high energy, and I'm well-organized. I can be controlling, the way she is. She has this thing about having all the family home for a meal or something. I can see that in myself, the heavy maternal stuff, and it's sometimes a negative thing. But there's a lot that's positive about it, like the idea of doing everything and being complete as a person. Having a family, having work to do, all that.

What Sarah responds to most positively in her mother's character is her ability to do two things at once—to have a family and to have work to do. Although her mother did not have a career in the contemporary sense of the word, Sarah saw her as being interestingly and meaningfully employed, in addition to taking pleasure from her family.

When Sarah left her career in banking to build a business-consulting practice at home, she recreated the same combination of family and at-home work her mother had created. Her new work fits her needs as a mother (and a mother-identified daughter) much more than did her former career, which felt to her, she says, like a disguise. She describes her behavior on the job as a kind of masquerade, in which she was dressed to fit the part. Interestingly, the suits she wore were sewn by her mother, who supported her daughter's wish to have a career.

> Being in the corporate world was like attending a costume ball. My identity was covered over by my business suit. Part of my identity, a strong part, is my motherhood. In the business environment, you're not supposed to show that.

Sarah's insight about her business suits illustrates another observation about the career self: that part of our personality that we develop specifically to meet the demands of the career culture. The career self, of course, is not the whole self, as Sarah is clearly able to see. She now jokes, as did many of the women I met, about the power suits hanging unworn in her closet. "There's nobody to wear them," she says. "That person doesn't live here any longer."

Lisa, the African-American woman introduced in chapter 2, also says that as a child she was closer to her mother than to her father. She speaks of her mother with love and affection.

> My mother spent time with me and my sisters. We went shopping, attended church, and visited relatives together. My father worked twelve-hour days, six days a week in his own business. He was either working or at home resting.

Lisa's mother combined her family responsibilities with work in what Arlene Rossen Cardozo calls a "sequencing" arrangement.[7] While the children were small she stayed home with them; as they grew older, she taught grade school full time and worked as a school librarian. Lisa initially planned to combine her career with child raising, but when she was actually confronted with her first pregnancy she realized that she wanted to leave her career.

> Identifying with my mom has had an effect on my work life. I, too, have decided to focus on my children's development in their younger years—to stay at home with them full time.

Sarah and Lisa come from family backgrounds (Jewish and African-American) in which the mother-center is traditionally strong and authoritative—what Pat McBroom in *The Third Sex* defines as "a tradition of maternal power."[8] Female authority can also be strong in other families. Emily's account is typical:

> I vividly remember my first visit to the library. My mom took me, just the two of us, as soon as I was old enough to have my own library card. I'll never forget it. I walked into the womb of the world that day.

Emily consciously chose to become a teacher because her grandfather, whom she idolized, was a county superintendent of schools. However, when she began to feel a conflict between her career as a teacher and the needs of her teenaged children, she resolved the conflict by taking a lower-paying job (she saw it as a job, not a new career) that would enable her to provide more mothering for her children. Her new work is in a library, where her mother first introduced her to the power of books.

Crystal, who left a position as executive director of a large employment-and-training program to develop a women's spiritual network and newsletter, remembers her mother as having the power and authority in the family:

> My father built and equipped small businesses, grocery stores, convenience stores. He was gentle and kind and humorous, but when it came to making the choices, it was my mom. She has a lot of power in herself, and warmth, and she's very loving. My grandmother had a great deal of power, too.

Crystal always expected that her life would include children. Now the mother of a teenage son, she sees herself as a blend of both parents:

> I'm a lot like my mother. I'm kind, I'm also charismatic, I'm self-possessed, like her. At the same time, I also have a lot of the risk taking that's my father, and my father was very inquisitive. I'm like that. He wanted to be extremely well-informed, and I'm like that. I kind of went back and forth between the two of them.

Among the women I studied, the mother-identified women were more likely to combine their careers with mothering by establishing their careers first, then their families. Unlike the father-identified career-only woman, the career-first woman sees the feminine not as powerless and passive, but as authoritative and capable of carrying out plans and desires. Armed with her mother's strength, the career-first woman believes that she can incorporate her mother-wish for children into a life pattern that also honors her father-wish for a career. While she insists on creating a career before she establishes a family (a practical choice, given the need for specialized training and the strong youth orientation of the career culture), she knows clearly that she wants to do both—equally well.

Therein lies the stage-two dilemma for career-first women. Many of them suffer both from a deepening disillusionment with their work in the masculine career culture and from a profound disappointment at not being able to give their children the kind of mothering they want and expect to give. Some suffer guilt and anxiety when they leave their children to someone else's custodial care, fearing that their children will suffer from the loss of a mother's attention. Others feel that the loss is theirs and resent the career (which they may already experience as being deeply unsatisfying) that takes them away during their children's growing-up years. Many no longer have confidence that the rewards (both material and psychological) they may gain from their careers will be more satisfying than the rewards they and their children will gain from being together. These mother-identified daughters are faced with the difficult question of whether they want to continue to devote their days to the Fathers or take on, full time, the career of being a mother.

Here is a sample of the deep emotional questioning that is centered around this very difficult dilemma:

> If I had returned to work after the birth of my son, I would have had to entrust his care to day-care centers or babysitters. I felt enormous guilt at the thought of placing him in such sterile, un-loving environments.

> After my first child was born, I stopped wanting to work late or socialize with colleagues. The only thing I could think of was getting home. My career took a backseat.

> I began to question how, emotionally, physically, and, yes, financially, I could leave the upbringing of my two children to another person. With the birth of my first child, I felt an unexpected, overwhelming, emotional bond. I couldn't bear to leave his care to others. It was a terrible time because I was so torn.

The introspection and self-examination that these questions demand take the stage-two career leaver deep into herself as she begins to examine her alternatives.

Daughters in the Workplace

In a book called *Family Ties, Corporate Bonds,* author Paula Bernstein quotes Dr. Mel Roman, professor of psychiatry at the Albert Einstein College of Medicine: "The family we grow up in, the family that teaches us more than we'll ever know, is our family of origin. And when we leave to make our own way in the world . . . we attempt to recreate that family in the same way."[9]

The corporate workplace as a recreation of the family setting is a concept that many women affirm intuitively. We begin shaping ourselves through our identification with our fathers, as one woman indicates:

> As a girl, I had more of a kinship with my father than my mother. My career has patterned several of his work traits: independent decision making, problem solving, focus on process rather than outcome, low tolerance for "errors" in others' work.

Often, our fathers become our mentors, teaching us what we need to know in order to succeed in the masculine work world. Alexandria, for instance, was her father's namesake, his favorite child, and, following his lead, an avid golfer and bowler. Her father encouraged her to be highly competitive in sports, and she sees that competitive spirit as giving her the edge in a successful career in which her annual salary topped sixty-five thousand dollars before she left the corporation.

Of course, many women do not have a close, supportive relationship with their fathers. In this case, a woman may try to develop such a relationship with the significant males who are responsible for the upward progress of her career. Her mentor becomes her father. We often see our fathers in our supervisors, in our employers, and in the institutions we work for; moreover, we often develop the behavior of the so-called good daughter in an attempt to meet their needs and requirements.

Recently, psychologists have begun to focus on the ways in which corporations encourage us to replay the roles that we initially learned in our families of origin. This is a particularly relevant issue when the birth family is dysfunctional (due to alcohol or substance addiction or to a process addiction, such as workaholism). Anne Wilson Schaef and Diane Fassel explore this problem in their book *The Addictive Organization* and remark that "many of the behaviors considered 'normal' for individuals in organizations are actually a repertoire of behaviors of an active addict or a nonrecovering co-dependent." They continue: "Many of the organizational processes deemed 'acceptable' in companies are just more of the same addictive behavior masquerading as corporate structure and function."[10]

Schaef and Fassel cite a client's recollection of her work-aholic father. Her words could have come from many of the women I interviewed:

> Everything revolved around my father's work. If we got too play-ful or made noise we would be quieted because Daddy was either working or sleeping. When work went poorly, he was moody, an-gry, and destructive. When it went well, he was jolly. We were con-stantly watching him to see what kind of day he had had so that we could act accordingly. . . . Work was the overriding excuse for everything; family celebrations, plans, and vacations all bowed to the demands of work.[11]

This daughter is describing a father who is addicted to work and a dysfunctional family that has become co-dependent on his addiction. Sharon Wegscheider-Cruse defines co-dependence as a caretaking disease, an "addiction to another person or persons and their problems, or to a relationship and their problems."[12] If the daughter does not seek treatment for her disease, she is likely to exhibit its symptoms and become a workaholic herself.

As Schaef and Fassel point out in *When Society Becomes an Addict*, co-dependent behavior is highly valued in the career cul-ture because caretakers are willing to do almost anything for ap-proval, and their caretaking often "progresses to the point of workaholism."[13] Most corporations rely on this kind of behavior. "The problem is," one woman told me, "that you get such fantas-tic brownie points for being a workaholic and never having a life away from the desk." Obviously, the corporation derives many benefits from its employees' workaholism; the most obvious of these are increased productivity (to a point), long-term commit-ment, and enhanced allegiance to the company. Although many corporations have launched therapy programs for alcoholic em-ployees, there are none to my knowledge that have instituted such programs for their employee workaholics.

Many women, once they define their birth families as dys-functional, attach that definition to the workplace. Jeannie left a high-level management position with an airline after she real-ized, at age forty, that her boss and working environment were frighteningly similar to her father and her childhood environment. With her new insight, she was able to define the man she worked for as what some psychologists call a rageaholic:

> He was emotionally unbalanced. This man would throw temper tantrums and scream and walk out of the room. He never supported us, never patted us on the back, never paid us a compliment. We were all, male and female, co-dependent. He was the father figure, and we wanted more than anything in the world to get some iota of approval from him.

When Jeannie started therapy and began to probe her relationship with her father, her efforts to please him, and her deep anger at what she felt to be his abandonment of her, she began to free herself from her unhealthy relationships on the job.

> As I worked through that anger, I realized that it was just in my mind that what I accomplished would impress him. He had pushed me into the airline career. But if I wanted to do something else, or if I wanted to quit one day, it didn't have anything to do with him anymore. It was my decision.

It was only when Jeannie could re-father herself by separating herself from her father and by no longer using her career to obtain his approval that she could also separate herself from the situation at work. By separating herself, she was affirming herself as a strong, healthy, and independent woman:

> I left [my career] because I became aware that even though I refused to play their games (I never slept with anyone or brown-nosed), I was still a part of the system and the sickness. I was still trying to prove myself to my father, too, as long as I stayed there. When I got to the point where I could choose to leave, that was healthy.

Christine, a graduate of a well-known divinity school who left her position as an ordained minister in a prestigious church, also sees her separation from a paternalistic bureaucracy as an affirming statement of her feminine individuality. As her discontent and disillusionment grew, she began to perceive ways in which the church acted as a dysfunctional family. She saw that her choice of a career in pastoral ministry was a natural choice, given the dysfunctionality of her family background: "I was masculine-identified and a raving co-dependent," she described herself to me in a letter. "And God was simply a larger version of my father, my professors, and the church Fathers."

Even though Christine tried to play the role of the obedient daughter, she was never able to mold herself to its requirements. She eventually interpreted this fact as an early, positive sign of spiritual and psychological health hidden under a career-self mantle of compromise and accommodation:

> I definitely felt like I didn't belong to the corporate family. (And don't think that the church is any different from corporate America: It's big business, without the profit!) My language was different from church language; my priorities and my sense of the relative importance of things were different; my whole world view and vision for living was different. Ultimately, I don't think my authentic self wanted to belong, because it knew that if I did, it would mean death—the death of Me. There was a large internal barrier to my belonging, which I'd [now] call health—growing psychological and spiritual health. Thank God!

Through her searching self-examination, Christine found a new way to understand her growing disaffiliation from the work she had chosen as the center of her spiritual and material life. As she began to reinterpret her discontent and disillusionment in terms of the dysfunctional model, she came to a clearer understanding about the direction her path would take. She was moving toward a more integral, more whole, more authentic vision of her work and her life. Her task involved re-fathering herself by yielding up the supernatural authority she had given to the masculine principle.

STAGE-TWO GROWTH

Psychologists tell us that challenge is one of the first prerequisites for adult growth and development. Growth comes about when we are confronted by situations, however painful, that upset our equilibrium and demand change. Without challenge, we are likely to cling to the familiar life structures—our career roles, our relationships, our social responsibilities—that fix us in the present, anchor us in the past, and obligate our futures. As we become increasingly committed to these roles, relationships, and responsibilities, we become less flexible and open to change. After a time, we find it very difficult, if not impossible, to break away from these rigid adult roles. Even though they feel uncomfortable and confining, even though we suspect that they are inappropriate to our current needs, we may deny our feelings and suspicions and continue to act as if the roles meet every need perfectly. Many women are imprisoned at mid-life and beyond within life structures that were created in the mother-father patterns of their birth family. They can wake themselves to the realities of the present only through challenge.

We do not change and grow, however, just because something new challenges us to change. For personality development to occur, two significant things must happen in our lives. First, we must be willing to allow ourselves to be genuinely confronted by challenge: to experience it, to feel it. Many of us avoid confrontation, and when the challenge comes, we turn our backs on it. We prefer the stability and security of our established life structures—however uncomfortable and confining they may be.

Second, we must be willing to undertake serious, conscious self-reflection, for unless we engage in deliberate self-examination, the behavioral changes we make will not lead to growth. Among the women I studied, it was this act of self-reflection that characterized stage two of the process of career exit. When a career leaver feels disillusioned about her career and unsure about her future direction, she turns within herself to discover why she invested so much of herself in her work life. She begins—sometimes with the help of an analyst, sometimes with friends and support groups, sometimes alone—to explore the deep inner reaches of the self, asking always, Why? Her search takes her deep into her past, to her earliest experiences of women's and men's roles. When she can see that the choices she makes in her work environment are largely conditioned by the male-female dynamics of her family, she can begin to understand her own motivations more clearly and less judgmentally. She is more free to make knowledgeable decisions. When she is able to re-father and re-mother herself by separating herself from the old models and creating new ones, she is well on the way toward healthy feminine growth.

Although not all career leavers consult a therapist or undertake an intensive self-study before they decide to abandon their careers, most engage in some form of serious self-examination.[14] They may join a formal or informal group, such as a feminist consciousness-raising group or a twelve-step group, an addiction-recovery program based on the model of Alcoholics Anonymous. They may discuss their feelings and present options with friends, coworkers, spouse, or partner. They may read self-help books, attend classes, or go to workshops.

These self-investigations are passionate, purposive, and above all, painful, for no one can dismantle a life structure that has been created and maintained at great personal cost without experiencing deep anguish. Phyllis spoke of the pain after she left a twelve-year career as a social worker:

> The hardest part of the process was digging down into stuff I had buried years ago. Once I got started, it all came welling up—old fears, old bitterness, old anger toward my father and mother, toward the whole family situation. I had no idea how much of that ancient history I was living out every day on the job. It was like an old script I just kept rehearsing numbly, sort of mumbling through my part in a fog. The pain of seeing the truth—it's impossible to describe. When people ask, I tell them: Don't start the process if you're not willing to suffer the anguish of the old wounds all over again—and maybe worse, because you've denied it for so long.

The pain of old wounds, once allowed to be felt, is severe, sometimes almost debilitating. In most of us, there are buried resentments, unexpressed anger, unacknowledged anguish. Many of us suffer stoically, silently, because there is no safe outlet for our pain. We veil our hurt in addictions to alcohol and drugs, in compulsive eating and compulsive working, in physical illness, in depression, in unsatisfying relationships. We armor our vulnerability in intellectualism, in career success, and in pride of overachievement. Those of us who achieve career success often shroud our anguish in that very success. Seeing our achievements as symptoms of our deepest and oldest losses rather than as signs of our great and powerful gains is in itself a painful act.

The commitment to deep self-examination and the search for answers can take place at any time during the career-leaving process. Some women begin to explore their feelings as soon as they are aware of them. Others delay until they are so emotionally exhausted by their conflict that they have no other choice. Looking deeply into ourselves is a difficult process—so challenging that many people would rather live as long as possible in their present misery than undertake it.

In one sense, of course, it does not make a great deal of difference when we begin to examine our feelings as long as we do it. The sooner we see through our inherited patterns of behavior and awaken to our own needs and wishes, however, the sooner we can choose new ways of feeling and behaving. Our self-analysis can and should be continuous. We must continually search our feelings, question our behaviors, examine our motives, and ask why. The answers are always only temporary answers. They provide us with a tentative, guiding knowledge that opens us to new knowing. If we are truly committed to self-discovery, what we find within us always leads us to search out more, so that we allow ourselves to be confronted by another and even more penetrating series of why's.

The problem for many of us, however, is the denial of our urgent need to look inward. Denial is a habit of long standing: From girlhood on, we have denied our feelings of inferiority, our fears of failure. Such denial of the need for self-examination is not only a personal habit, it is also a social habit. The truth can set us free, and no contemporary society I know of comfortably incorporates genuinely free people, particularly free women— women who no longer need to act and think and feel either like traditional women or like men.

Whether our denial comes from personal habit or social shaping, it can be costly. Some women deny their career conflicts and delay any serious self-investigation until after they have experienced a work-related emotional breakdown or a career crisis that requires them to make a change in their work situation. At this point, they are faced with the frightening fact of change, not just the prospect of change; they may have no control over the situation. The emotional immediacy of it is terrifying, sometimes paralyzing. The consequences of denial here are severe, for a woman who has not faced her own inner conflicts and identified her own needs and wants has only two choices. She can either delay her efforts to find work of her own until she has explored her work issues and has understood why she worked as she did; or she can take the path of least resistance and find another job in the same career field, sentencing herself to a repetition of the very same pattern in another few years. Many women, confronted with the pressing need to find some kind of paying work, will take the best thing that comes along, trapping themselves within a no-exit cycle of conflict and denial of conflict.

A few of the women who shared their stories with me are victims of denial. They are still hiding behind the facade of the career self and delaying their encounters with the deep self. Although they have made some changes in their work situation and say that they intend to make more, it is clear from their behavior that they are still working in the same fearful, compulsive way—still burdened with psychological structures from the past. They are not able to make a complete role exit.

One such woman, Carrie, held a high-level corporate management position. She took several months off to recuperate from a stress-caused illness and flirted with the idea of leaving her career. "I know it would be the best thing to do," she told me. "I'm a wreck, physically and mentally. My job is killing me." Six months later, she was back at work. "They needed me," she said defensively. "And I had to pay the bills. Anyway, the stuff I was getting into in therapy was kind of . . .well, I didn't like it. So I decided I'd get back into the swing of things and stop all that soul-searching." Carrie's latest way to cope with her continuing symptoms of physical and psychological illness is by maintaining a daily program of stress control and exercise in the executive health club that her corporation has recently established.

Jodie showed her denial in a different way. When she introduced herself to me, she said she was leaving her career, *again*. During the past ten years, Jodie has left three different jobs, in three different career fields. "When I first start a job, I like it," she said. "But then I find out what it's really like and I have to get out. But I know I'll find something that's right for me, sooner or later. It's just a matter of looking."

Most of us are acquainted with women like Jodie, women who frequently switch jobs and careers to find something better but never find true satisfaction or personal fulfillment in their work. In a sense, it does not matter where they work or what they are doing, for they are only living out the old patterns in each new situation. The lesson we can learn from failed career leavers like Carrie and Jodie is clear: if we do not consciously and deeply search ourselves and our souls, if we do not open ourselves to the pain of self-knowledge, no amount of career leaving or career changing will lead to growth.

If we are able to relax the rigidity of our confining roles and are willing to open ourselves to challenge, however, we will be able to see new possibilities. What we need are new spectacles, a new vision, a new way of finding our way through the world. It is this new vision that comes to us as we enter stage three of the career-leaving process.

| 4 |

THE THIRD STAGE:
WEIGHING OPTIONS

$\mathcal{T}$he emotionally painful exploration of one's personal history can be the prelude to a period of hope that includes weighing options and sorting through new possibilities. Most career leavers experience this stage of growth as a fairly rational time, and they begin to think of other ways of working.

Although the first two stages of career leaving often include some awareness of possibilities for new work, these insights are usually blurred and unfocused. The stage-one career leaver is too preoccupied with the anguished uncertainties of her present to give much thought to an even more uncertain future. To the stress of simply coping with everyday problems are added pervasive feelings of disillusionment and discontent, often combined with a sense of failure for not being good enough or tough enough to work wholeheartedly. For a woman with a family, the strain of trying to juggle the needs of her children and spouse with the demands of her career is an added psychological burden. In the early stages, most career leavers do not feel centered enough to take on the serious work of discovering more suitable work. Nadine, a former public-school administrator, told me:

> All I could do was stew about it, I mean really obsess about everything that was wrong with me and my career. I was so tangled up in my feelings that I couldn't think—let alone think clearly—about options. I wasn't sure who I was. How could I figure out who I wanted to be?

In the early stages of career leaving, a woman may give herself seemingly good reasons for not considering alternative work. These reasons do not usually address the issues of what the woman wants to do or even the problems posed by her present career; rather, they refer to the rewards that the career brings.

The woman might have a financial obligation that her high salary enables her to meet comfortably. She may have a special need for the low-cost health insurance that her employer provides. She may be influenced by the promise of future benefits, such as a retirement plan, stock options, or other incentives to stay with a company.[1] She may be responding to the special needs and expectations of someone else—a spouse, a parent, or dependent children.

Nadine's biggest problem was that she could give herself a dozen so-called practical reasons for not making a radical change in her work.

> Whether I was happy or not didn't seem to be the deciding factor at that time. My daughter had a chronic illness. If I left the insurance program we had at work, I would end up with no coverage for her. Sometimes I felt that the insurance was more important even than my salary. I knew I could always earn money doing something. But I didn't know if I could ever get insurance for Alexandra. Emotionally, I felt stuck.

Nadine's dependency on her company's benefits was a major factor in her denial of her need to change the way she worked.

The rational consideration of alternative ways of working is not a part of stage two, either. If the career leaver undertakes serious self-reflection at this point in the role exit, her inner explorations sap her energy and occupy her attention. During this stage of the process she usually shelves any plans for a career change that she might be tempted to make. This is especially true if she is in therapy; therapists usually encourage clients to postpone life-changing decisions until they have resolved the underlying problems that initially brought them to therapy.

Career leavers who engage in intensive self-study usually find that their inner work enables them to answer many of the highly emotional questions that troubled them during stage one. Often, a woman's deep self-reflection enables her to stop blaming herself. She sees that the problem is not with the way she is working but with the working environment itself. She cannot function comfortably in it, not because she is sick but because she is, or is becoming, basically healthy. Freedom from self-blame gives her greater clarity and a sense of confidence. She feels capable of making rational choices.

75

Stage-two self-exploration also helps a career leaver to free herself from the bondage of unconscious emotional patterning, especially where her work is concerned. This new freedom gives her greater distance on her situation and enables her to see herself and her career more objectively. She becomes capable of dealing rationally with the major task of changing her work life.

Compared to the emotional and psychological challenges of stage one and stage two, the work of stage three is much more rational. At this point in the process of role exit, we attempt to determine, more or less deliberately, what is at stake. We try to calculate the loss of our current career against what we might gain by doing something else. We ask what-if questions about the future. The process is not entirely a logical one, of course, for nonrational and emotional elements are necessarily threaded through it, as are the synchronicities and coincidences that in some mysterious fashion often seem to contribute to our choices. Still, the activities involved at this stage in the process include such complex logical tasks as analyzing the present situation; exploring skills, interests, and experience; seeking out and evaluating possible alternatives; and assessing the losses and gains involved in making a major change at mid-life.

ANALYZING THE SITUATION

"I wasn't in a very logical frame of mind," Dee told me when we discussed the way she felt before she made the decision to leave her career in real estate.

> I really felt trapped. There were all these good reasons for staying put—kids in college, a mortgage, car payments, the money I was giving Mom every month to help her out. I couldn't just up and leave a job that brought in seventy thousand dollars a year without having something to fall back on. I was pretty confused about what I wanted, but I knew I had to try to figure out some options. The trouble was, I was so depressed at the thought of having to go to work every day that I couldn't seem to summon any logic. It was a vicious circle. The harder it was to go to work, the more depressed I got. The more depressed I got, the harder it was to think of some rational alternative to my career.

Feeling that she was being swallowed up by her depression, Dee found a therapist. For several months, she worked through her confused feelings—focusing especially on her relationship with her idealized father, who had made a great deal of money as a commercial-property developer. After a time, Dee felt able to step back and take a more objective view of the situation. "I made a list of the things I didn't like about my work," she said. "It was hard to be rational about something I *felt* so much about, but I tried."

> I put down having to cut ethical corners in order to make deals, not being square with people, having to work weekends and always be on call—a lot of stuff like that. Then I made a list of the things I enjoyed, like being in charge of my own time, not being supervised, helping people get what they want. The two lists really helped when it came to figuring out my options.

Analyzing the present situation is not an entirely rational process for most people. For Dee, it was clouded by her despair. For Martha, it was blurred by anger and frustration.

At the time when Martha first began to feel a need to make a change in her work life, she had been a critical-care nurse for more than ten years and a working mother for four. Several times, she had been offered promotions to management positions at the hospital but had always refused. She enjoyed caring for patients, and she enjoyed the challenge of critical care. Then the hospital invited staff nurses to undertake new training in an area other than their specialty so that the hospital could more flexibly respond to changing health-care needs. After giving the matter a great deal of thought, Martha asked for training in the newborn nursery. Her reasons for making the change were very clear.

> I wanted to deal with young healthy people. I wanted to help women and children. Also, I had been interested in midwifery since nursing school, and now I was a mother. Mothering was important to me, and the well-being of babies. I decided that I wanted to work with infants and mothers, so I asked for training in the nursery.

When Martha's request was rejected because her supervisors felt she was needed in critical care, she became angry and frustrated. Her unhappiness with her critical-care responsibilities intensified. A few months later, a full-time position in the nursery came open, and Martha applied. After a great deal of negotiating, Martha was told she could have it but was then refused again. At that emotional moment, the first thoughts of leaving her career occurred to her.

> I thought, God, maybe I should just quit. Maybe this isn't worth it. It was really awful to be told I had the job and then suddenly find out I wasn't going to get it. They were stringing me along to suit their needs, not mine.

Finally, after a great many more emotional ups and downs, Martha got the nursery job and the training she wanted—only to find her assignments continually shuffled around by the hospital:

> I was officially still on orientation in the nursery, but they began floating me back to Intensive Care. I became this movable cog that they could put in the nursery and yank out of the nursery whenever it suited them. I was very frustrated, very disillusioned that they would treat me like this. If this was the way it was going to be, I thought I should just quit.

What began with reasoned logic (Martha's rational decision to work with infants) was quickly colored by her emotional frustration at not being able to implement her choice. She investigated the option of taking a job at a hospital farther away but discarded it because the job would have meant a longer commute; she did not want to cut down her at-home time with her children. Putting together her increasing desire to be more of a mom to her own children and her wish to work with babies and mothers with her hope to make a difference when there is a chance to make a difference, Martha came up with a logical alternative: She would leave nursing and set up her own at-home infant day-care facility. She would also prepare herself and her family to meet the requirements for providing a foster home for babies affected by cocaine and AIDS.

Martha was able to carry through with her plans. Recently,

she wrote to me that in addition to caring for her family, she finds time to school her children at home, volunteer at a local hospice, and serve as a contributing editor for a nursing journal. The combination of activities that make up her new career fully meets her need to be not only socially responsible in the work she does, but also responsible to her family and herself.

Exploring Skills, Interests, and Experience

Martha was able to analyze her situation and make a choice within a few months because she was confident of her skills, interests, and experience—and because her new work grew out of the work she wanted to leave. For many women, however, the process requires several years of sorting through experiences and testing out various skills in order to find different work, unrelated to the careers they are leaving behind.

Carla fell into her first career when a college counselor suggested computer programming. She agreed because the burgeoning computer industry promised ready employment at what she considered good money. Within a few years, Carla was a systems analyst earning thirty-four thousand dollars annually, but feeling that her work persona was not her authentic self and that her reasons for entering the computer field were not adequate or sound. "I don't even think they were my reasons," she told.me. "They were the counselor's reasons. I couldn't think of anything better, so I just went along."

Carla decided to make three radical choices. She rejected her company's offer of a management position, moved from full- to part-time work, and began to fulfill her childhood dream of studying art. She also enrolled in some sociology courses—including a women's studies course. Going back to school enabled her to explore her interest and skill in art as a career, and her studies of women's issues helped her to understand that her alienation from her career was not exclusively her personal problem. Her new, more objective feminist awareness helped to pull her out of the depression she had suffered ever since she first began her career:

> I realized that a lot of what I was feeling was not unique to me but was culturally based, and that a lot of women feel the same way. I

started to see that work—not just the work I'd been doing, but work in most corporations, maybe all—was completely male-dominated. I began to see what that meant in terms of the effect it had on my work life. I had always tried to be one of the boys, and when they didn't accept me, I blamed myself for not being good enough. But now I know I wasn't accepted for reasons that had nothing at all to do with my work. I know it's okay to be a woman.

Carla's college work gave her the confidence to imagine new alternatives for herself: "Computers weren't the only thing I was good at; there were other things I could do." By the time she earned her bachelor's degree in fine arts, she had decided that she could not support herself doing the kind of art she wanted to do. She also decided that she did not want to continue part-time programming work indefinitely—just to support her experiments in art. Her other consuming interest over the past five years had been her own personal therapy, which she had undertaken in order to deal with her depression. Her experience of therapy had been positive, and she felt she knew a great deal about how the psyche functions. As she sat down to assess her interests and experience with the rational goal of choosing work of her own, she found herself putting psychotherapy at the top of her list, even above art. At the age of thirty-eight, nearly ten years after she left her full-time career as a systems programmer, Carla returned to school to work on a master's degree in clinical psychology. She is only a year away from becoming a psychotherapist with her own private practice.

During this part of the process, many women attend seminars, enroll in workshops, or read books like Richard Bolles's outstanding self-help manual *What Color Is Your Parachute* and Marsha Sinetar's inspiring book, *Do What You Love, the Money Will Follow*. Kay, the district manager we met earlier, was one of these.

Kay became ill with a low-grade viral infection and chronic fatigue. She was also suffering from serious depression. Her physical and emotional symptoms were caused, she was sure, by the stress created by her frantic, highly competitive sales position in the communications software industry and by the compulsive drivenness that had pushed her to an annual salary of one hundred twenty-five thousand dollars. Her physical and emotional condition deteriorated so seriously that she began to consider leaving her career. She could not bear the thought of taking another job in the same competitive, stress-charged field. She did not have the strength, however, to consider training for a new career. She felt, she says, abysmally stuck, emotionally confused, and deeply depressed. She knew she had to do something, but she had no idea what that something was.

Then Kay happened on a book called *Inventurers*, by Richard Lieder and Janet Hagberg. It was a life-examination kind of book, she says, that helped her see that she could rebuild her work life with resources she already had. She would not have to go back to school to learn new skills or to gain new credentials. If she approached the task creatively, she could translate her already-substantial abilities into something she truly wanted to do.

Kay could perhaps have gotten this message from a variety of sources, but the book was a fortunate find. Encouraged by her reading, she sat down with a pencil and paper and figured out what it would cost to buy herself a year's leave of absence that would give her time to recuperate from her stress-caused illnesses and to explore some new possibilities. She discovered that, if she was careful, her savings and her equity in her house would give her enough money to live on for eighteen months.

Kay asked for a leave of absence. She spent the next year and a half reading, traveling, setting criteria for the kind of work she wanted to do, and creatively exploring various options. She knew that she did not want to work in the same driven and compulsive way she had worked in the past. She decided that she would like to work for a small firm rather than a large corporation, that she wanted to work in a cooperative, rather than a competitive environment, and that she preferred to work with women. Over the next few months, she developed some very clear guidelines for herself about what she wanted to do—and what she did not want to do.

In Kay's search for work of her own, she arranged interviews with several executive search firms. To her surprise, she found herself enjoying the search process itself, so much so that when the female president of a small executive search firm offered her a position, she accepted. "My work combines my interest in building relationships with people with my need to achieve," she says. Kay remains flexible where the future is concerned however, and is not sure that her own search for rewarding work is over.

> I hope that in some way something I am doing today will open doors to continuing growth for me. I am very interested in helping girls and women to be full partners in our society. I want to use my skills and experiences to benefit others, and I'm still figuring out how to do that. Maybe I'll always be figuring it out.

The key to success in Kay's and Carla's stories lies in their willingness not to force themselves to come to a premature conclusion in their search for work of their own. Instead, they permitted their needs and wishes to mature and ripen as they became alert to changing possibilities and to new applications of their substantial skills and abilities. They remained open to new roles and to new ways of seeing themselves. They solved the problem of how to live in the interim by using their ingenuity and by tapping their resources: Carla traded her programming skills for part-time work; Kay traded her savings and real estate equity for time to heal herself, physically and emotionally.

The experience of these two women teaches us an important truth about work: Our ideas about the best work for us will change as we grow and mature. Our best work expresses our interests and abilities, and these expand and develop in a widening spiral throughout our lives as we become stronger and more confident in what we do. It expresses what we know, what we are capable of, what we believe in. That knowledge, those capabilities, and those beliefs change as we change.

Because the best work arises from our deepest center, it also expresses our conception of ourselves as developing, living beings, dynamically responding from the depths of our human selves to the changing world of people and ideas around us. In a sense, our best work has very little to do with outcomes—that is, with the service we perform or the product we create or sell. It has, instead, to do with process: the process of growing, of maturing, of letting our spirits enlarge.

Seen from this angle, our best work is never done. To fix ourselves to a single career too early in our lives or to grasp a new career too soon during the process of career leaving can be a self-limiting mistake.

SEEKING OUT AND EVALUATING ALTERNATIVES

Some career leavers do not plan. They respond to alternatives that present themselves synchronistically and demand an immediate response. Take Emily, for example.

Emily, a single parent, was a highly successful secondary-school teacher of English—popular with students and recognized statewide for her abilities. In spite of her success and confidence in the classroom, she says that she felt miserable teaching in a school where the morale was low and the working conditions wretched. She hated her hour-and-a-half commute and constantly worried about her two preteenage children, who were left alone in the morning and evening. When the new principal of her school "high-handedly" removed several novels from the library with no staff consultation, Emily felt her patience snap. Without a plan or a strategy, almost without thinking, she took her work life into her own hands:

> On the way home, on impulse, I stopped at the university employment center and saw a notice for a library job. I knew I could do it because I had worked in the English department library in college. I applied and was offered the job. I had to make a decision to quit teaching cold turkey—didn't even have time to figure out if I'd be able to make ends meet. But my car was paid for; I had no debts other than the low mortgage on my two-bedroom duplex; I wouldn't be paying for day-care; and my commuting costs would go down.

Emily sacrificed nearly ten thousand dollars in gross annual income (the net loss was less) to take a position that offered few prospects of professional advancement. She gained, however, the satisfaction of having brought her work life into balance with her family obligations and her own personal needs. Although she made the decision quickly and without seeking other alternatives, she was comfortable with it. Five years later, still working in the library, she is beginning to explore other possibilities for creative work and to see this time as a period of preparation for whatever work she may do in the future. As Emily thinks back over the past five years, it is the balance and harmony she has achieved in her new life that brings her the greatest satisfaction. She can see her calm spirit manifested in everything around her:

I can see my inner peace and self-determination in the quilts I've made, in the flowers blooming in my garden, in the fresh meals I cook with farmers'-market produce. But most of all, I can see it in my children's lives. Their happiness and growth is what tells me that my decision to step out of the professional career path—quickly made as it was—was the right decision.

Other women who decide to make a role exit spend far more time and effort seeking out and evaluting work alternatives. Dee left the real estate firm and sold her house. Like Kay, she used the money to buy a year for planning.

For the first few months I just recovered from all the bad stuff I'd been letting myself in for. Then I got serious about finding work. I talked to a lot of people about sales, which is what I knew, but when I evaluated the positions, there was always something that made me say, This isn't for me. Then a friend asked me to help her start a newsletter, and I realized that one of my big skills was putting a publication together—the way I did when I put out the home-finder booklet for my real estate firm. So I began thinking about desktop publishing. At the same time I volunteered at a local women's group to help with their publications. It was good experience, because I got to use their equipment and figure out what I needed. I also got some free training, and I made some first-rate connections with other businesswomen that I wouldn't otherwise have made. Later, their support made the difference between succeeding and failing.

Dee continued to study the field of desktop publishing for eight months, talking to publishers, equipment vendors, and possible clients. At the same time, she developed a business plan. Then she bought her equipment and put out the word on her new business.

Dee's investigative work during her planning year plus the experience and connections she gained as a volunteer enabled her to design her new work with confidence in both the financial soundness of the new enterprise and herself as an entrepreneur. "But it's not a career," she says emphatically. "I'm not giving myself to any job, ever again. I enjoy the work, but I'm not wedded to it. Other things in my life—my family, my own growth—are far more important."

Other women find it possible to evaluate their alternatives while they are pursuing further education or training. In the process, they engage in what Helen Ebaugh calls role rehearsal—the opportunity to learn about and identify with the values and norms of a role before it is actually assumed.[2]

Gail's experience is a good example of role rehearsal. In her late twenties, she left her successful career as a college administrator in order to study for the priesthood. When the bishop rejected her bid to become a postulant, she was bitterly disappointed and felt she had nowhere to turn. After a few months of what she calls just being, she applied and was admitted to the social work program at the local university—her "second-choice calling." Several semesters later, she began an internship at a church retirement community, where she says she felt a sense of mission:

> I felt that the retirement community was a place that needed my help, needed some things changed, and that I could make a significant difference there. I hadn't felt that in my work for a long time.

Still without a firm idea of what she wanted to do, Gail continued to work experimentally, following the direction her explorations seemed to lead. She volunteered to raise funds for a battered women's center in order to see how it felt to be a fundraiser. She sought out a second internship as a legislative aide for health and human service issues with a state representative in order to test out her skills in governmental policy making. She is now about to receive her master's degree in social work. As she thinks about her future work, which she is designing for herself out of the several alternatives she has already evaluated, she is still guided by the positive results of her various role rehearsals.

Gail's experience is typical of that of many women who try out and evaluate several alternatives before they find work of their own. Judith, who became disillusioned with her thirteen-year career in library management, returned to the university to pursue a master's degree in business administration thinking that she would like a private-sector business career. After a year, she realized that although she enjoyed her studies in management and marketing, she did not want an MBA degree. More

85

significantly, she was beginning to perceive that the poor management practices she saw in the library were also present in business. They were, she said, built into the system. Evaluating her experience in business school, she commented:

> It is important that we find alternatives to the academic educations we sometimes think we need and don't. Workshops, retreats, and classes led by women for women can help ease us through transition periods. We need both practical and more intuitive kinds of education. We can learn from each other as well as we can from school.

Judith began to seek alternatives that would give her a practical and intuitive education. She considered several jobs in business, but she could not bring herself to take seriously the idea of working in a corporate structure. She felt it would be, as she said, "the library all over again, only worse." She managed a restaurant for a year while she considered going into the restaurant business, debated whether to start a service business of her own, and then happened to find a position as assistant manager at a feminist bookstore. "I knew it was for me," she said, "from the moment I walked in the door." Soon she was managing the bookstore.

> I tripled sales in the three years I was there. But more important, I felt that I was helping women find themselves. To help a woman locate just the right book or tape to make her know that she is not alone, that other women have had the same experience—that's important. That's what made it all worthwhile for me.

With the bookstore job, Judith had become what she was seeking: She was manifesting in her work her life's conviction that we can learn from each other. Three years after she began working at the feminist bookstore, she felt she had enough experience and know-how to make a long-term commitment. Confident in her management skills and her knowledge about books, she moved to another city and opened her own feminist bookstore, working with money she had saved and with a small inheritance. Recently she wrote to me that her new bookstore is more than just a store:

It is central to the women's community and is a meeting place of ideas. I love it. It puts me in the middle of women's culture *and* I'm even paying myself now. It's not easy to leave patriarchal jobs, but if you 'do what you love, the money will follow'—eventually.

With a healthy sense of tongue-in-cheek humor, Judith adds: "Maybe in five years I'll even be making a decent middle-class salary."

Judith's wry comment offers us another important insight. Judith could have chosen to feel frustrated and angry because her new work paid less than her old library career or the other business alternatives she had considered and rejected. Instead, Judith chooses to reject financial reward as her criterion for successful work. The other rewards of her work—personal growth, the opportunity to help other women grow—mean far more to her than the money.

When we stop to think about work as an end in itself and begin to think of it as a means toward our personal growth, we realize that our search for work that expresses our deepest selves may not yield its richest results overnight. One woman, after several years of anxious searching for at-home work that would produce income while it permitted her to be a full-time mother, finally came to the conclusion that she was managing her efforts to find the right kind of work in the same tense, uneasy way she had managed her career. She wrote to me:

> I think that much of my anxiety and discontent has come from trying to jump the gun on career concerns too soon. I'm learning to let go of my need to control and plan everything. If I just start doing something I like, maybe it will lead me into other things that I haven't thought of.

And that observation, I believe, opens the way to another valuable truth. If we learn to trust ourselves—to trust our skills, our experience, our interests, to trust the process of becoming who we truly are—we will be far more open to possibilities for creative work.

Evaluating Losses, Estimating Gains

As we consider whether or how to leave our careers, the first major loss we think of is the loss of salary and benefits. Women career leavers also face other, less tangible losses, however. When we leave our careers, we lose our social identity and the reputation and status that we gained on the job. Our long-term investment of time and energy in a particular career path seems to have vanished and our working relationships and friendships have disappeared with it. In stage three, the career leaver weighs these losses against what she hopes to gain by finding or creating work that expresses a greater part of herself.

Crystal had a comfortable career managing a women's employment and training program—an area in which she had worked for nearly fourteen years. It was work she enjoyed. "I liked counseling low-income women, helping empower them through economic equity," she told me. "I felt there was meaning and purpose to my work, and helping other women was deeply satisfying."

Rewarding as it was, however, Crystal's work did not satisfy all her needs. In her free time, she began to explore a growing interest in women's spirituality. When she could not find many women in her area who shared her interest, she took a new counseling job in a larger city where she found a large number of women of a like mind. Together, they started a women's spirituality group that soon held more meaning and significance for Crystal than did her counseling career. As the group grew larger, members began networking locally and nationally; they developed publications and an educational program. When these activities grew so extensive that volunteers alone could not handle them, Crystal decided to leave her career and undertake full-time leadership of the program. At that point, the risks seemed large indeed, particularly the loss of financial security:

> I found myself going through some pretty intense processing, trying to decide whether or not I really wanted to give up my traditional career. I was going to a job that I had created and loved, but there was no retirement plan, no security, maybe no future. It was very iffy, very tentative. At any moment, the sources of income could run out, and there was my son to support.

For a long time, Crystal went back and forth on the question, trying to decide whether she should leave her career and risk her financial security. She made her decision when she understood where, in herself, the hesitation was coming from:

> I finally identified my mother's voice in me, saying: This is a risk, this is not the kind of job that good people get—you know, good people get good jobs.

Crystal decided that she was ready to stop listening to her inner mother's cautions and to confront the potential risks. She resigned from her job and left her career. The women's spirituality program she leads is now the largest such activity in the United States, and her first book has found an eager audience. The financial risk is still there, of course, but it no longer figures in her thinking about what she does. "I get paid a living wage," she says, "but I don't work for money. I work for joy. *All* my work is my true work."

Loss of income is a major risk for almost all career leavers. In some cases, the liability is lessened by the realization that the woman can return to her former career, either full- or part-time. "If worse came to worst," Judith put it wryly, "I could always go back to being a librarian." In other cases, the financial risk may be cushioned by some form of available capital: Some women withdraw retirement funds; others sell houses or other property; some receive substantial severance pay; a few receive inheritances. Some are able to cash in on skills that allow them to replace some portion of the lost income.

Some women, however—those whose new work is full-time mothering—know that they cannot replace the lost income because their new work is unpaid. Often, these are women whose salaries made up a substantial portion of their families' incomes. For them, the financial risk of career-leaving is one that is shared and felt deeply by the entire family.

Sonya left her career as manager of a service business and an annual salary of forty thousand dollars to work as the full-time mother of her children—an unpaid job. It was not a decision that came easily. "The financial aspect will be a major obstacle for us to overcome," she wrote to me shortly after her husband, Doug, reluctantly agreed that she should return home to care for their two children:

We are feeding one more mouth [Sonya had given birth to their second baby], and we have forty thousand dollars a year less to do it with. If, in a year's time, we are eating peanut butter for dinner and burning candles for light, we'll consider my return to work part-time in a night-shift position.

But weighing the lost income against the gains she expected to see in her own life and in her children's life, Sonya added: "Somebody has got to start thinking of our futures. Sooner or later the money isn't going to be as important as family and friendships."

Now, two years later, the loss of Sonya's income has created a serious split between wife and husband. Over time, it has become clear that while Doug assented to Sonya's wish, he never fully supported his wife's career-leaving decision. He deeply resents the responsibility of carrying the full income burden for the family. He points out that he married a career woman, not a full-time mother, and that he always expected Sonya to carry what he calls her fair share of the family's financial responsibilities. Because she chooses not to do paid work, Doug sees her labor at home as a liability, not an asset.

The couple's financial situation has gone from bad to worse. Desperate to relieve themselves of high mortgage payments (they had bought a large home in a rural subdivision the year before Sonya decided to leave), they put their house up for sale. It did not sell. Forced to give up that plan, they concentrated instead on reducing everyday expenses—food, clothing, entertaining, transportation. Sonya accepts this new way of life and even finds it rewarding because she feels that they formerly spent too much, too mindlessly. "It's important for me to save, even in small ways," she says. "It's almost like a philosophy of life."

Doug, however, rebels at the drastic cost cutting. "He accuses me of living in lala-land when it comes to money," Sonya says with a sigh, "and maybe I do. I don't need a lot of stuff to keep me happy. The big difference is that my values have changed, and his haven't."

I don't mind driving a dumpy car and saving on clothes and haircuts and entertainment. For me, that's just part of what I have to give up in order to be at home with the children. But Doug minds.

He works hard, and I'm sad to see him doing without little things he enjoys—a new pair of running shoes, even a six-pack of beer or a pizza.

Feeling her husband's despair and resentment over their worsening financial situation, Sonya began to take in day-care children and started a small home-based craft business that brings in some cash during the holiday season. They expect to be able to manage in the short term with her small earnings and their tax refund, but the long–long-term outlook remains problematic. Sonya plans to look for part-time evening work in the field she left. An outsider might say that she has failed in what she wanted to do, but Sonya refuses to judge herself against the standards of the career culture. "It's amazing what you can do when you have to," she says, weighing the loss of her income against what she feels her children have gained.

> We've survived, with major adjustments to our lifestyle. Those adjustments have been painful, but I feel I have grown by making them. And even if I have to go back to work part-time, I know it's been worth it, being at home with the children for these two years. I'll never again work the way I used to, sixty hours a week, all-out effort, just for a high salary. I don't have those values anymore. I only want enough money, not lots and lots.

Sonya's comment about enough money is important for us to remember. As Marsha Sinetar observes in *Do What You Love, the Money Will Follow:* "Each person has the ability to produce something that someone else wants, and in so doing to produce at least enough wealth and reward to support himself [sic] and his family."[3] Our problem, of course, is to define our needs in a way that matches our ability to meet those needs—to define what is enough. As we have seen, the central problem that Sonya and Doug face is their inability to agree on what is enough.

In general, women who place a high value on financial reward are not likely to leave their careers for what is, at best, an uncertain financial future. Career leavers are people who believe—more or less firmly—that their high salaries are not sufficient compensation for what they are giving up or what they can potentially gain. Here is a sampling of comments about money from career leavers I interviewed:

> I was making over a hundred thousand a year, but the money didn't mean anything to me. I was never home to enjoy the house and the lifestyle the salary was buying. I could afford all the expensive salon treatments I wanted, but I didn't even have time to get my hair cut!

> I spent three hours daily commuting, and I ended up with less than half my paycheck after I'd paid for child care. I got to the point where I was asking myself, what are you working for? If it was just for money, it wasn't worth it.

> After a lot of soul-searching, I decided that I had to change the way I was working, even though it meant a big cut in pay and benefits. I didn't want to stay trapped in the vicious cycle of working at an unpleasant, meaningless job in order to support an expensive lifestyle that got costlier every year.

Most career leavers expect that the lost income will be balanced out by gains in personal freedom and in time—time to be creative, time for the self, time for family and loved ones.

Less tangible but no less important losses are also involved in exiting from our careers. When a woman gives up a highly visible job and elects to do something that the culture judges to be less important or less valuable, she surrenders not only her high salary and excellent benefits, but also the social prestige of being at the top, and the strong sense of identity that she had developed with her career. The loss of status and social identity can be a higher price to pay for abandoning a career than the loss of income, although only a few women see this risk and weigh it. For most, the significance of the loss of status is not actually understood until they experience it, until, stripped of their career trappings, they have to face themselves and others. We will explore this loss at length in examining stage four and stage five of the career-leaving process. Now, I would like to look at the kind of growth that occurs during the process of weighing alternatives.

STAGE-THREE GROWTH

The rational process of analyzing the situation; exploring skills, interests, and experiences; seeking out and evaluating alternatives; and estimating losses and gains is complex and demanding. Most middle-class mid-life adults have developed a philosophy of life and a secure place in the world that buttresses them against change—even when that change represents potential personal growth. Career leavers, however, feel that the time has come in their lives when they have to make a significant shift in the way they work, even if this means sacrificing much of what they have gained—salary, status, acceptance, personal and professional identity. They may even reason that it is not a sacrifice to give up financial dependence on a career that makes them unhappy or physically ill.

The psychological growth of stage three emerges out of the task of serious, responsible life planning. Many women never focus in any thoughtful, in-depth way on what they want to do, as opposed to what they are expected to do or what is simply available to do—not until they begin to consider leaving their careers. Many never seriously examine their work skills, their work styles, or their work preferences until they think of making major changes. Many, moreover, never give any substantial thought to the future directions their lives can take—that is, to their own personal potential in a future that stretches out beyond the next few months—until they must make a serious commitment to a new future. For most, the idea that they can direct, rather than be directed by, their work lives is a startling and new idea.

Many female careerists choose their first career before they enter college, in their freshman or sophomore year of college, or when they begin professional study. At that time, in their teens and twenties, they often feel the need to make a career choice that will please a parent, a teacher, or mentor—or, if they are negatively reacting to a powerful authority figure, a choice that will displease that person. A career that is chosen under these circumstances is someone else's career. It is not the choice of a freely electing adult with enough experience to test another person's suggestion against her own wishes. At age eighteen or twenty-two, even at twenty-six, how many of us (women and men) know our own wishes? "I didn't have any firm ideas about myself, other than the ideas my mother and father gave me," Paula, a former government official, told me. "How could I? I was too young to have a self of my own! So it was natural for me to choose something that would please my father and show my mother how capable I was."

Women who are not guided by another person in their choice of careers may be guided by happenstance, in the sense that they seize the best opportunity out of several—none of which seem absolutely right. "I took the first job that came along after I got my MBA," Patricia says. "I never intended to stick with it, but fifteen years later, there I was. I didn't like it any better after fifteen years than I did that first day."

"I happened into my career," Andrea reports. She had a doctorate in English and Medieval Studies, but there were no teaching jobs available. She took a job as an associate editor of library reference materials, which ultimately led to a lucrative position as an executive editor for technical books. This was not the kind of work she wanted or was trained to do, but it seemed to be all she could get at the time.

Whether they chose their work too early or chose among too few options, many career leavers feel that at the beginning of their careers they did not actively explore what they wanted to do. They did not assess their strengths and their skills; indeed, most feel that at that point they had few skills. They did not fully investigate their options. For them, the stage-three process of personal life planning—of rationally examining their potentials, assessing their personal and professional strengths and weaknesses, and seeking out alternative kinds of work—proves to be a growth-inspiring activity, putting them in touch with inner resources of which they often are not aware.

This stage-three growth is apparent in the lives of most women who are successful in redesigning their work lives. When they begin the process of role exit, they are comfortably established in a mid-life career pattern that rewards them in ways that only a small percentage of women in our culture are rewarded. Stage-one growth occurs when they are willing to acknowledge that their successful careers are uncomfortable and limiting and, in some cases, physically or psychologically debilitating. Stage-two growth occurs when they are willing to undertake serious, sustained self-reflection, to get at the roots of the unhappiness they feel. Stage-three growth occurs when they are able to become rational about the emotional situation in which they find themselves; when they can see themselves in the context and process of choice making and can ask thoughtful what-if questions about their choices; and when they can—often for the first time in their lives—see themselves as risk-taking people. When I asked Dee what she had learned in the process of leaving her career in real estate, she gave a response that is typical of stage-three career leavers: "I learned how to take my life off automatic pilot and fly it for myself."

The process of making conscious, responsible choices at a time in our lives when we are able to see and evaluate the consequences of our choices is enormously growth enhancing. For most women, the achievement of stage-three growth is the prerequisite for successful career exit. Not all women are able to complete the important planning work of stage three before they leave their careers, however. For some, the rational evaluation of possible alternative work is interrupted—often in an almost cataclysmic way. In chapter 5, we will hear their stories.

THE FOURTH STAGE:
THE CAREER CRISIS

*M*any women evolve into their new work roles gradually, coming to the decision to make significant changes in their work lives over a period of months or years.[1] These women find their first careers unsatisfactory or limiting in some significant ways, look deeply into themselves to seek out the causes of their discontent, and begin to sort through possible kinds of new work; often, they develop that new work as a sideline while they continue in their careers. When the new work becomes fairly well established, they are able to move into it without great disruption in their lives.

Crystal moved gradually into a new, self-created work environment. The process of leaving her former career in counseling for a leadership role in the women's spirituality movement took twelve years. Because she made the change gradually, the transition to her new work was smooth and, for the most part, enjoyable: "I just kept moving toward what I wanted, without any major disruption," she says. "I grew into my new work. It was a comfortable way to change."

Some of us do not have the opportunity to develop an alternative work life while supporting ourselves by remaining in our careers. Instead, the orderly process of exiting from our careers—moving through the disillusionment and emotional turmoil of stage one, the self-examination of stage two, and the rational life planning of stage three—is abruptly terminated by some sort of career crisis. We are precipitated out of our career by an event, usually unforeseen. These events can occur either in the workplace or in our private life—or, sometimes disastrously, in both areas at once.

In *Becoming an Ex*, Helen Ebaugh describes these cataclysmic events as turning points.[2] She defines them as "occurrences that crystallize one's ambivalence toward a current role and place the choice to exit [from the current role] in bold relief." Sometimes an event is clearly recognizable as significant: a "bolt from the blue that changed my life," as one woman put it. The event may appear to be relatively insignificant in itself, but later, when we look at it in the context of the career-leaving process, it seems highly charged with meaning.

A series of events—some significant, others seemingly insignificant at the time—pushed Cassie to leave her position as a senior manager in a large West Coast accounting firm and to set up her own tax-accounting business at home. When she was a college freshman, Cassie wanted to major in music. She rejected the idea because she felt she could not "make a living at it." Instead, she followed the advice of her father (a lawyer) and majored in accounting. She stayed in her first job for five years, then accepted a position in a relatively small accounting firm with a relaxed, pleasant working environment. Within fifteen years of becoming a certified public accountant, Cassie was earning sixty-two thousand dollars a year and supervising six to ten junior accountants in addition to handling a heavy client load. Although there were a number of things she did not like about the work, she was basically content with the choice she had made.

Two events then happened that significantly affected her work life. Cassie became pregnant, and her small company was acquired by a much larger national accounting firm. During the acquisition, the original owner failed to vest his existing staff— that is, to establish their benefits from the date they were initially employed by the company, rather than from the date of the acquisition. Cassie discovered this disquieting fact when she learned that she would receive only two weeks' paid maternity leave instead of the nine weeks' leave she had earned. Angrily, she told her boss how she felt:

> I said to him, I will be very disappointed in you and the firm if you don't find a way to give me the credit that I'm due for having been here nine years. At that point, I was thinking that I might as well leave. I was very angry that he didn't care enough about me and the others, after all the unpaid hours we had worked, after all the blood we had shed for his firm, to get us vested.

After months of dickering, Cassie received the benefits she had accrued. Her son was born and she went back to work after her maternity leave as she had planned. "Part of me wanted to stay home," she said, "but part of me felt that I needed to be on the job. It was loyalty, I guess. I felt like I owed the firm something."

When Cassie returned to work, however, she found that she could no longer make a neat separation between her personal life and her professional life. Because she wanted to be home with her son, she was no longer willing to commit eleven or twelve hours a day to the job. She began to do some serious soul-searching, examining her commitment to her career in accounting management and asking herself whether she wanted to spend the next few years feeling torn between two loyalties.

The situation at work was rapidly deteriorating. Under the new ownership, administrative paperwork had mushroomed, support staff had been cut, tension was high, and morale was low. The original owner of the firm (now an employee of the new company) began sending oblique signals about more change to come. "I don't know whether I'm going to be here a year from now," he would say, and indirectly suggest that the managers (including Cassie) start looking for work elsewhere. "It was never direct," Cassie said later. "He would never just come out and say, This is what's happening and here's what you should do. He would just hint that something was going on behind the scenes."

Cassie began to explore other possibilities. She set herself the task of making what she describes as a cost-benefit analysis of the pros and cons of resigning her high-paying management position. "I analyzed it just like any situation I would analyze for a client," she told me. "I figured out what percentage of my current salary the family absolutely had to have and how many clients I would have to carry in order to make that amount. I also calculated the cost of doing business at home and weighed that against the cost of child care and the other costs—lunches, clothes, transportation, things like that—of working at the firm."

Cassie was still thinking through her options when the company abruptly made a decision to cut administrative staff. "I've got to let a manager go," the former owner told her. "If you want to stay, I'll fire Gloria [the other manager]. Let me know your decision tomorrow."

Cassie was furious at being asked to make such an important decision on such short notice and angry at being forced into what her boss called a "you or her" situation. The next day, she gave six weeks' notice. During that time, she established the client contacts that would enable her to open a home office where she could be with her son, choose her hours, dress as she pleased, and work in a comfortable and relaxed environment. At the end of the six weeks, she moved into her new work life: a self-employed, self-reliant professional, working on her own terms. The entire process, from her discovery of the loss of benefits to the career crisis itself, had spanned fourteen months.

Marilyn's career crisis was much more emotional and tumultuous than was Cassie's. She experienced what Helen Ebaugh calls the last-straw type of turning point: a gradual buildup of feelings and events that culminates in an explosive situation.[3] The events contributing to Marilyn's role exit, like those in Cassie's, were both personal and professional.

Marilyn had happened into her career as a programmer analyst for a large state agency. Intelligent, cooperative, and a hard worker, she advanced quickly; within six years she was making fifty-two thousand dollars a year as a project leader in software development for the agency's computer system.

Then a series of disturbing events began to occur. Marilyn's supervisor asked her to misreport her team's progress on a new software system to the agency's supervisory board. Marilyn felt that his request was unethical ("He was asking me to lie to cover his mistakes!" she says). She uneasily did as he asked, not only once but several times. During this difficult period at work, she experienced several exhausting personal crises: a close friend became ill with cancer; two other friends died; and a long-term relationship came to an emotionally traumatic end. "I felt like I was coming apart," she said. "Between having to lie to keep my job and all these other things happening in my life—I just couldn't hold on anymore."

Marilyn took disability leave and began a serious in-depth study of herself. She entered therapy to work on her relationship problems; at the same time, she began to attend a support group for adult children of alcoholic parents. As she acknowledged the impact of her parents' alcoholism on her life, she saw that she had given in to her boss's unethical demands in the same way she had given in to her parents. "A lot of times I had to lie to cover up bad things my parents did when they were drunk," she said. "By lying to cover up my boss's mistakes, I was doing exactly the same thing. I was caretaking for him just the way I had taken care of my parents." When she began, as she says, to get well, she felt that she had to leave her work situation. The job compromised her emerging sense of herself as a strong and responsible person:

> I began to see the dishonesty and I was distressed by the manipulation and the deceit—*his* manipulation, *my* deceit. If I were to stay in recovery, I couldn't continue in my previous roles at work.

Marilyn went back to work at the agency after her disability leave when her stage-two self-exploration was already well advanced and she was beginning her stage-three exploration of alternatives. She did not, however, return to her former job. Instead, she asked to be transferred to the training division so she could learn new skills. "I wanted experience with people, rather than machines," she said later.

> I wanted to teach people how to use the new software system I'd helped to design. I wanted to help them learn how to handle on-the-job problems. I thought that in this way, I could change some attitudes and help people. I was even optimistic about changing the system.

Things did not turn out as Marilyn hoped. Three months after she began her new work, she encountered what she felt was another deeply dishonest practice. The workshop she had developed was supposed to create an environment of trust, where employees felt safe in learning to deal with difficult managers and colleagues. After the workshop series was under way, however, the agency head demanded information about participants' attitudes and performance. Marilyn felt angry at being asked to betray a trust. What is more, she felt that her earlier perceptions about the agency were being reconfirmed.

> His asking me to do that was the last straw, the clincher. I could see that the whole operation was dysfunctional. And I no longer had any illusions that I could make a change in it.

By the time the actual career crisis occurred—when she recognized the last straw—Marilyn had prepared herself to meet it. She had moved through the disillusionment of stage one and into the self-exploration of stage two. She had grown skilled in using a model of addiction recovery to explain and deal with things that she perceived to be out of balance both in the workplace and in her personal life. Although she had not carried out a full-scale examination of alternatives or a complete survey of her strengths, experience, and abilities, she was in the process of doing stage-three work—as is indicated by her request for a transfer so she could try out something new.

At the same time, Marilyn was exploring a different kind of skill and interest: She had started to write a book about her traumatic experience of coming to terms with the alcoholism in her family. On the surface, at least, the book was a stage-three experiment to see if she had the skills and commitment to be a writer. When she quit her job, she told people that she was leaving because she needed the time to do research on the book. Reflecting on the still-incomplete project several years later, however, she was able to see that its real significance in her life lay in allowing her to continue the self-study that she had already begun through her therapy and group work:

> To tell the truth, the writing was almost like a smokescreen. Of course, I didn't feel that way at the time. I convinced myself that the most important thing I had to do was to write, and that it was maybe going to develop into a new career for me. But now I think it wasn't so much the book itself I needed to do. The book was an excuse to take the time to do the research and the reading and the learning. I had to try to understand things in a new way.

When Marilyn left her career, she had twenty-five thousand dollars in retirement money and seventy-five thousand dollars of equity in her house. She cashed in on both. The money bought her nearly three years of free time—time to do the reading and the learning she wanted to do and to do meaningful volunteer work. She spent fifty hours a month working for an AIDS support group and for other community projects. Recently, having decided that she is not cut out to be a writer, she has returned to work as a programmer at thirty-five thousand dollars a year.

"Taking the time off from a 'real' job was the best possible choice I could have made," she told me in a letter.

> From my time away from work I gained serenity and a realistic acceptance of my abilities. I have that inner sense of being okay, in balance. I know I won't burn myself out again in the real world. I'll never again let a career take control of my life.

Rachel's experience demonstrates very clearly the complex interplay between the two careers that many women pursue simultaneously: a profession in the career culture and the profession of mothering. The career crisis occurs when a woman decides that she can no longer carry both careers.

Rachel decided in seventh grade that she wanted to be a scientist. She began her career as a microbiologist in a Seattle clinical laboratory, where she conducted research, published her findings in scientific journals, and performed routine technical analyses. She enjoyed her work and was soon promoted to a management position. As she later wrote, however: "The administrative work seemed monotonous, and I couldn't help wondering if this was all there was to life." She was disillusioned, she told me, with the hierarchical structure within which medical technologists worked:

> In the hospital setting, technologists are unseen and unheard. We feel high[ly] pressured, underpaid, and underappreciated. The [private] laboratories are run like totalitarian governments. We sometimes have dress codes, are required to repress any dissatisfactions or risk being labeled "unloyal" to the company, and are often threatened with punishment for infractions of rules or policies.

In addition to working as a clinical technologist, Rachel was also a mother. Her first child, born a decade after she began her career, had been accidentally conceived—"probably due to subconscious desire," she wrote later. She welcomed the pregnancy, not just because she wanted a child, but also because it gave her an opportunity to escape temporarily from an unpleasant work environment:

I think that having a baby provided me a way out of my career position, a good excuse to get out of the situation I had created for myself.

After the birth of her daughter, Rachel began to feel a dissonance between her family and her profession. The second daughter was born three years later, and Rachel's dissonance heightened. The balance between career and mothering felt increasingly shaky:

As my children began needing more than just caretaking, I began to feel pressured, uncomfortable, and split. I no longer felt I was doing my best at either job.

At the same time that she was experiencing difficulty balancing her two-career life, the situation was worsening in the lab. Rachel no longer felt happy or comfortable with the work that had once been so rewarding.

Changes in the health-care system affected the professionalism in the lab. Those of us who were highly trained and experienced were being replaced by minimally trained technicians who could be bought for lower salaries. In my last position at a private clinical laboratory, profit was clearly more important than good patient care.

The career crisis came for Rachel when she confirmed that she was pregnant for the third time. Her youngest was five, her oldest eight. She was working a four-day week that gave her a long weekend with the children, but her ten-hour day was extended by a three-hour commute. "Being pregnant and having a baby once again offered some respite from job aggravations and a way to postpone career decisions," she says candidly. She decided to quit her job.

Now, several years into what she calls her retirement, Rachel works as a full-time mother, an active La Leche League volunteer, and a free-lance writer specializing in parenting topics. It is not, however, an entirely happy situation. She has found that the conditions that distressed her in the lab—low status and lack of recognition—are also true for women who choose to be full-time mothers. It is a fact about which she is vocally unhappy:

> The job of raising children is considered absolutely unimportant in our society. Likewise, day-care [which Rachel offers to supplement the family income] is spurned as a profession even as the outcry for more day-care heightens. Volunteer work, also, is not afforded the recognition it deserves because the importance of everything we do seems to relate to the presence or size of our paycheck.

Rachel's situation is complicated, for it is an example of what Kathleen Gerson, in *Hard Choices: How Women Decide about Work, Career, and Motherhood,* describes as blocked mobility.[4] Throughout the latter part of her professional career, Rachel suffered from the sense that her advancement was blocked by forces over which she had no control. As her enthusiasm for her career waned, she turned toward motherhood—only to find there, too, a kind of blocked mobility. Like all mothers in our culture, she was denied the recognition she deserved.

Rachel's story also exemplifies what Helen Ebaugh calls the fourth type of turning point—the excuse. The excuse, Ebaugh writes, involves some event or authority figure that makes it clear "that a [role] exit is necessary for the well-being of the individual . . . regardless of the individual's supposed degree of role commitment."[5] As Rachel's two-career life evolved, she found that her negative feelings about her work radically decreased her commitment to her professional career and increased her commitment to mothering. Her third pregnancy provided her with a good excuse to leave the work world. Unfortunately, Rachel took her feelings home with her. She sees herself as a mother in almost exactly the same terms in which she saw herself as a career professional: low status, underpaid, underappreciated.

Pregnancy is not the only excuse that is used for career leaving. Among women who experience a career crisis, health problems are often given as a reason for their role exit.[6] Of the women I studied, two were diagnosed as having cancer and others as suffering from various stress-related illnesses. One woman's doctor flatly told her to leave her work, and others were counseled that reducing their commitment at work was necessary to recovering their health. Sometimes, career leavers feel an obligation to continue with their careers; the medical advice they receive, however, provides a rationale and a socially acceptable justification for leaving. The illness often makes it easier to reach a decision to leave, because it offers proof that it is not their fault that they are no longer able to continue in their careers.

Other women reach what Ebaugh calls an either/or point of exit from their career roles. Nicole's experience was typical of this:

> In November my alcoholic father entered a treatment center and along with other family members I joined him there for Family Week. During those five days I realized that nothing in my own life was working and I needed to make major changes. So I quit my job as director of public relations in an advertising firm, sold my house and sports car, and moved. I quit drinking and drugging and focused my entire life on recovery.

Nicole felt that she had no choice: If she did not leave her career, she was doomed to continue her uncontrollable compulsions.

Amy's either/or turning point is similar. She was confronted at work with the offer of relocation and promotion—the fifth transfer to a new location in ten years. As a district manager of a Fortune 500 company, she earned an annual salary of seventy thousand dollars. Her negative feelings about her work now crystallized as she analyzed the impact that her constant moves had on her relational life.

> I was traveling sixty to seventy percent of the time and struggling with meaningful primary relationships. I realized that I wasn't around enough to create healthy relationships. So I refused the transfer and was offered six months' pay to leave the company, plus pension and stock benefits.

Amy had a clear choice: She could continue to do what she was doing and accept the transfer, or she could trade her stressful, unbalanced professional life for what she hoped would be more balance between work, self, and relationships. She opted for greater balance. "I was far too heavily into work," she says. She took two months for what she calls basic recovery, including stage-one and stage-two work. Having taken a massage work-shop, she found herself interested in bodywork, the use of mas-sage, exercise, and nutritional therapies to facilitate physical and mental health. "My next step was massage school," she says, "for a license and more healing of self and my body-mind-spirit con-nection." A year later, she became a licensed, self-employed pro-fessional in the growing field of bodywork and physical therapy, remarried, and began a family.

For women who have already prepared themselves by do-ing intensive stage-two and stage-three work, the career crisis, while abrupt, is not so difficult that they cannot manage it. Some, however, are not prepared for it. It occurs after they have entered stage one (they were becoming disillusioned with their careers) but before they have done much self-exploration or weighed many alternatives. The crisis is usually far more difficult for these women, because they find themselves without sufficient psycho-logical or financial resources on which to fall back.

Forty-eight-year-old Eleanore was devastated when she was let go by the bank corporation where she had worked for twenty years.

> It felt like an earthquake. I was totally rattled. Losing my job was hard enough, even though I'd been thinking for a while that what I was doing wasn't really right for me. I didn't have enough control over what I did at the [savings and loan corporation], and I had to do some things I didn't feel were right. But losing the job came at a very bad time—when I didn't have much to fall back on except for my retirement money. I hated to spend that just to buy groceries.

In the beginning, Eleanore was simply stunned by the enormity of what had happened to her. Then depression set in, and for the next few weeks she lost all energy to meet the crisis. "I just sort of muddled through," she said. "The days were a blur. I slept a lot, and when I wasn't sleeping I was watching old sitcoms on TV. It was a very low time. The worst in my life."

When she finally sat down to figure out her finances, Elea-nore found that her unemployment insurance would pay the basic bills until she found another job. She eliminated unneces-sary expenses, mustered what mental resources she could pull together, and began to think about looking for another job in the banking industry. What happened next surprised her.

> I dragged out my old résumé and started to update it. But working on it made me think back on a lot of my work experiences, and I realized that I really didn't want to go back to finance. It wasn't something I was interested in or cared about, even in the beginning. I was competent and people respected me, but I'd been working out of habit and routine, not because I gave a damn about what I was doing. I didn't really like doing what I was doing, either. There were a great many questionable loans, poor practices, unethical stuff. The industry deserves its bad reputation.

For Eleanore, it was progress of a sort to figure out what she did not want to do. But she still had not come up with work that challenged her—until her sister called and asked her to become a working partner in her new catering business. It meant investing part of her retirement funds and moving halfway across the country, but Eleanore was ready to take a risk. Now, three years into a successful business partnership in a working situation over which she has control, Eleanore can look back philosophically on what was a very difficult time:

> I felt terribly hurt and betrayed at first—worthless, depressed, like I was a miserable failure. Losing my job was a real crisis in my life. But now that I look back, I see that it was necessary. While getting fired wouldn't be my first choice of a way to make the break, it turned out to be the cosmic kick in the pants I needed to get me out of a deadend career and make me confront the question of what I wanted to do with the rest of my life. Maybe, at some level I don't understand, I asked for it.

Nearly all of the women I interviewed whose career was terminated through a firing or a layoff said in some way "maybe I asked for it"—not in the sense of setting themselves up as victims, but in the sense of hoping that somebody else would do what they could not do for themselves. These women are voicing the truth that when change becomes necessary in our lives, we have a choice. We can take the direct action that will resolve the situation and let us move forward, or we can block ourselves from that direct action. When we block, events have a way of doing for us what we cannot or will not do for ourselves: We may be the recipients of what Eleanore called a cosmic kick in the pants. The terrible, gut-wrenching experience of being fired or laid off can turn out to be a genuinely liberating event, for it may force us to begin the necessary work of stage two and stage three.

In other cases, a happier event initiates the career crisis. Andrea was working as a technical editor when, she told me, her husband inherited a modest amount of money that enabled the two of them to leave their work and start a publishing business of their own. "Perhaps I could eventually have quit," Andrea said. "But getting the inheritance made it happen sooner and a little more comfortably."

Judith was still working at the feminist bookstore when she unexpectedly received an inheritance of several thousand dollars of extra income a year. The money enabled her to leave and start her own bookstore. More important, it was a psychological lift, a "kind of insurance," Judith said, that gave her the courage to make a somewhat risky investment.

What Dee called her gift from the gods came in a slightly different way. She had left her real estate career and was casting about for alternatives when she received an unexpected settlement of an automobile insurance claim several years old. She used the money to buy the equipment that would get her one-woman desktop publishing company under way. "I saw it as a signal that I was on the right track," she said.

Mary Kay, whose story is told by Deborah Arron in *Running from the Law*, was involved in an accident that resulted directly in career leaving. For some time, she had been deeply unhappy in her work as a prosecuting attorney. After much soul-searching, she left that position to teach in a law school. Even that career change, however, brought no satisfaction, for she felt that what she had found wrong with the law was also wrong with teaching law. "Students are taught to advocate any position, to separate moral issues from legal issues," she told Arron. "Your humanity and sense of right and wrong get whittled away."

Mary Kay's career as a law-school professor came to an end after she was injured in an automobile accident. Before the injury, Mary Kay had been an avid backcountry hiker. Afterward, she could no longer carry a backpack, so she began to experiment with llamas as pack animals. The accident, and her newly discovered love for llamas, led to a new career:

> When I realized that there were a lot of other people out there like me—people who love to hike but can't carry a pack—I convinced my best friend, another lawyer, to start a pack animal hiking service with me.

It was not easy for Mary Kay to leave the security of the legal profession for a precarious life in the backcountry.

> I feel like I had to be driven to get where I am today. Otherwise, I don't think I ever would have bought the idea of quitting law to move to the mountains. I'm glad I got here, but there's no question that I did it out of my own desperation.[7]

Whether our career exit is precipitated by a change in the work environment, by an accident, or by a personal change, it gives us an opportunity to experience a new kind of growth: the growth that occurs when we allow an existing life structure to be torn down and another to emerge to take its place.

STAGE-FOUR GROWTH

Growth usually occurs only when we face a crisis: a decisive turning point, a clear fork in the road, when we must decide whether to stay on the same path or to choose a new direction. The choice that a woman confronts—to stay in her career or to leave it—has life-changing consequences not only for herself but also for her family and her loved ones. The decision she makes now to redirect her work life will affect her for the rest of her life.

In stage four of the career-leaving process, growth occurs when we confront a career crisis and make a deliberate choice. As we have seen, some women make choices about the direction of their work life over a period of time, gradually and incrementally redirecting their path, so that when the time comes to leave the old career, the course of the new is already established. For these women, growth occurs as they make each small choice—a growth that is often not recognizable at the time the choice is made but that emerges in retrospect. "I'm not the same person I was at twenty-five," Crystal told me from the vantage point of forty-one and her position as director of the women's spirituality network.

> I wasn't aware of it when it was happening, but now I can see that I made some really significant choices—like moving to a different city to find other women who shared my interest in women's spirituality. Every choice made a change in me. Every choice was important.

For other women, the choice of whether to stay with a career or take a new direction intrudes more abruptly into their lives, sometimes with a frightening emotional jolt. The diagnosis of a serious illness, the discovery of a pregnancy, a firing or layoff—these events require the individual to make a choice, whether or not she has done the necessary work to ready herself for change. In fact, the degree of the emotional impact depends a great deal upon her readiness. If the event triggering her choice comes out of the blue, it can create a great deal of uncertainty and trauma. If it is expected and prepared for, even to a minor extent, the emotional impact is easier to handle.

The nature of growth during stage four has two components. The first is the act of choice itself. Our present generation of women has been presented with choices that no other women have faced; in that sense, we are pioneers. Early in our lives, we choose to pursue a career, marry, bear children—or to combine two or all three. Some of these choices are open-ended, some have time limitations. Theoretically, we can choose to marry any time we find an acceptable partner. We can choose to begin a career even in late adulthood, as many women have done. We cannot, however, choose to give birth after we are about forty-five.

The choices made early in our lives do not always seem right in later years. Many women who initially chose only to pursue success in the career culture find themselves saddened by their childlessness and feel empty. Feeling that they cannot create and maintain a marriage relationship and a career, they willingly give up the rewards of the career culture—the genuine worth of which they have begun to question—for a less intense work environment that permits them to devote more time and energy to a relationship. Or, if they wish to have children, they often choose to trade their careers in the public world for the relative obscurity, lower status, and intangible rewards of the domestic world.

Other women choose early in life to combine three activities—career, marriage, and mothering—without asking themselves how they are going to manage all three. Some of these women find, as Rachel did, that they simply do not have the time, energy, and physical endurance to meet the demands of the choice they have made. They feel they must leave the workplace or choose to endure what Arlie Hochschild has termed a two-shift job, a work life that consists of a thirteen-month year of work on the job and at home, all the time avoiding or suppressing the frightening conflict over their two-career commitment.[8]

These are the women who choose to leave their careers and return home. Many of them say that although their departure from the workplace is temporary, allowing them to meet their child-rearing obligations, their departure from the career culture and the rejection of its work style is permanent. "I'll never again work in that blind, driven way" was a comment I heard during a number of interviews with women who traded careers for mothering. Or: "I had a career once—I don't want another. I don't care what kind of work I'm doing as long as it's work that means something to me and isn't stressful. I'd trade status any day for less stress."

The choice, temporary or permanent, between being in the public world or the world of the home is not, however, the only choice career leavers make. Some choose to conduct their business at home rather than in the marketplace. Others decide to do, on a free-lance, self-employed basis what they are presently doing for a salary. Others elect to stay in the workplace but seek a less stressful work environment—full- or part-time—in which they feel they will not have to compete, manipulate, carry out unethical practices, or curry favor with the boss. Still others choose to return to formal education and to train themselves for new work, often in fields that will allow them to be self-employed.[9]

ABANDONING THE CAREER SELF:
AN INVITATION TO GROWTH

The growth involved in making choices of this magnitude is substantial. Most often, a career leaver has a financially secure situation in which her future is easily assured, if not in the position she holds, then somewhere else in the same field. She chooses to abandon what she knows to be a secure work future for the insecurity, uncertainty, and challenge of a new kind of work; usually this work is less financially rewarding. Most importantly, when she leaves a successful career, she chooses to abandon an old self—one that can no longer satisfy all of the needs of her emerging personality—and to construct a new one.

That brings us to the second component of the growth involved in stage four. The act of leaving our careers involves abandoning our career selves, the masks we have put on to meet the demands of the career culture. Carl Jung describes the persona, which can be considered the same thing as the career self, in more encompassing terms:

> Fundamentally the persona is nothing real: it is a compromise between the individual and society as to what a [person] should appear to be. He [or she] takes a name, earns a title, represents an office, he [or she] is this or that. In a certain sense all this is real, yet in relation to the essential individuality of the person concerned it is only a secondary reality, a product of compromise, in making which others often have a greater share than he [or she]. The persona is a semblance, a two-dimensional reality.[10]

For many successful women, the career self is far more than a secondary reality. Just as the power suit becomes the primary career costume for many, the dressed-for-success career self can become our primary life reality. In the workplace, this self is absolutely crucial. Not only does it represent the compromises we have made to effectively meet the career culture's expectations of our performance, but it also functions to shield and defend our vulnerable feminine personality with its learned insecurities and inherited feelings of valuelessness. Without the protection of our powerful and successful career selves, we can fall prey to the many negative lessons our culture teaches us about women's worth.

Because the career culture is a male-dominated culture, the successful career self is by necessity masculine-adapted. This adaptation can become extremely problematic in terms of a woman's overall psychic health and wholeness, leading her, as psychologist Jane Wheelwright suggests, to be "stuck for life in an inner patriarchal system of her own." In a male-dominated society, our masculine-adapted career self can overexaggerate its despotic rule, as Wheelwright puts it, to the point where it totally suppresses our feminine personality. [11]

Now, there is nothing necessarily and inherently evil in developing a masculine-identified career self. When a woman adapts her behavior to create personal achievements that gain men's approval or respect, she is rewarded by a high level of self-esteem and a strong sense of competence and mastery. What is more, if a woman wishes to achieve independence and authority in our patriarchal culture, she will find it necessary to identify with men at some point in her life and to some degree. [12] If the career self is kept in balance with the feminine ego, if the authentic feminine personality is allowed room to grow and develop, a woman's masculine-adapted career self can serve her quite effectively in the workplace.

The career culture is extraordinarily seductive, however. It feeds a woman's masculine-adapted career self a steady diet of rewards—money, recognition, status—to the point where the career self becomes inflated: larger than life, more confident, more vivid, more powerful than any other aspect of the personality. When the career self rules the personality, other aspects of the woman's self are not permitted to manifest themselves. That is where the difficulty lies, for as psychologist June Singer says: "The stronger and more rigid the persona and the more we identify with it, the more we must deny other aspects of our personality." [13] In her outer life, the woman becomes her career self, identifying so closely with it that she does not quite know where it—the president, the manager, the doctor, the lawyer—ends and the real, authentic self begins. In her inner life, the denied aspects remain unexpressed and buried in the unconscious, where they can create anger, frustration, discomfort, disease, and a terrible sense of wasting away.

During the career crisis, stage-four career leavers are presented with a choice. They can choose to maintain the rigid, limited, limiting career self, or they can begin the task of replacing it with a more elastic self-concept that retains personal power and authority and shares it among all the aspects of self. This task is formidable, for deposing the career self from its position of power is like signing the death warrant for an old friend—one who has served the woman well and faithfully as she made her way in the world. The task is made even more difficult by the fact that it is the masculine-adapted career self, not the whole, authentic feminine personality, which is rewarded in the career culture. Once this part of myself is gone, the career leaver quite rightly asks herself, how will I function? Will I be respected for what I really am? Or, more desperately, Who *am* I, really?

Dissolving our identification with our persona—in this case, releasing our attachment to the career self—is not an easy task. It is easiest for women, like Crystal, who are able to go about it over a period of time, gradually fashioning elements of the new self even while they live through the agency of the old. It is most frighteningly disruptive for those who find themselves suddenly without a job and faced with the choice of retaining the old career and the old career self or making rapid and dramatic changes in the structure of the personality.

Whether the change is gradual or abrupt, however, it remains a challenge, and its aftermath can be chaotic. In many instances, the self seems wounded, disabled, unable to function without the protection of the career persona. Life systems appear to collapse, burdens previously borne lightly now seem unbearable, tasks once accomplished quickly and well now seem impossible. The life seems to be totally out of control, and there is nothing we can do to redeem it. This is the moment during role exit that Helen Ebaugh calls the vacuum. One of the women in my study called it the black hole.

We have come to stage five of the career-leaving process.

THE FIFTH STAGE:
THE BLACK HOLE

*D*uring different stages of the career-leaving process, career leavers experience a wide range of emotions, both painful and positive: disillusionment, frustration, anxiety, fear, and anger, but also euphoria, a sense of personal liberation from the binding constraints of attitudes and expectations, and the hope of a promising future. The single emotional experience that almost all career leavers share at some point during the process, however, is an intense feeling of alienation: the sense of not belonging, the feeling of being disconnected, out on a limb, isolated, disaffiliated, estranged.

I NEVER BELONGED

Because women have been only recently and marginally accepted into the career culture, it is not surprising that we experience some degree of alienation, even under optimum circumstances. Female careerists often report such perceptions as not belonging to the old boys' club that operated in the office, being left out of lunches and after-work happy hours, or feeling out of place, out of sync with male values. One woman who worked for ten years in a predominately male office put it this way:

> It was as if I was on one side of a fence and they were on another. It felt pretty lonely, even though I knew them pretty well and we all considered ourselves friends. Lots of times I'd have one view, and everybody else would have a different view. I often had to go out on a limb to defend my ideas. Sometimes I felt that they ganged up on me.

Several women I talked with observed that their organizations tried to make everybody (including the women) feel like one big happy family. Generally, they said, these efforts were phony. "The old boys played family-style softball on the weekends but hardball all week," one woman told me. "All that baloney about teamwork," she said, "was a ploy to cover up the really brutal cutthroat stuff that was going on." Another woman said: "There was one other woman at my level. The two of us agreed that the stuff we kept hearing about the corporate family was a lot of corporate BS." She added with a giggle: "If they were a family, we were the black sheep!"

Many career leavers cite their feeling of never having belonged as a significant reason for deciding to leave. The experiences of the women I studied suggest that alienation is a strong indicator that a woman will leave her career. The more intense and conscious a woman's sense of alienation, the more likely she is to leave her position to search for a work environment where she can feel affiliated with her coworkers and in sync with the values and purposes of the work organization. If she feels that the work style and values she is deliberately rejecting pervade the entire industry and not just her workplace, she is likely to leave her career and look for entirely different work.

I HAVE TO PUT FIRST THINGS FIRST

Many women feel the most intense alienation while they are doing the stage-two inner work of self-exploration and self-discovery prior to exploring alternative ways of working. They often describe their sense of estrangement not in terms of a disaffiliation from the workplace but in terms of the intense self-engagement of personal therapy.

"I became more interested in my therapy than in my work," one woman said. "Working on myself was the important thing." Another, still in the process of leaving her career, comments: "I'm feeling that the career doesn't matter any longer. I matter. I have to put first things first."

Many career leavers are involved with some form of group therapy, ranging from discussions with close friends to formal participation in twelve-step programs, encounter-style groups, or feminist consciousness-raising groups. The strong emotional bonds that are formed within these groups often take the place of bonds with coworkers, and the values of the group can replace the normative values of the workplace. When this occurs, the career leaver is likely to feel increasingly isolated and alienated from her career, but increasingly affiliated outside her career. One former executive observed:

> Looking back, I realize that my focus on my career narrowed my viewpoint on the world very dangerously—and that my company had to have it that way. They made sure that we all toed the corporate line, mouthed corporate values, had corporate friends. When I began to really listen to the women in my support group, I was amazed at their views about the workplace. It gave me a very different perspective on my career—and a rather frightening one, at that. But after a while, I had to admit that they were right in their criticisms.

This change in perspective may be most striking when the group openly condemns the values of the workplace, as do some separatist feminist groups and many twelve-step groups. For instance, several career leavers used the phrase "corporate recovery" to describe their process, suggesting that the corporation was an addictive substance from which they were freeing themselves. This radically alienated view can be traced in part to the best-selling work of Anne Wilson Schaef and Diane Fassel, whose books *The Addictive Organization* and *When Society Becomes an Addict* were read by many of the women I interviewed. Both these books have profoundly influenced the thinking of many career leavers, giving them a strong vocabulary and a set of definitions against which to evaluate their interactions with their work environments. John Bradshaw's *Bradshaw on: Family* was also mentioned as influential. A number of women reported having watched Bradshaw's popular television series, which enabled them to see that they were living out the values of their patriarchal families rather than living out their own values. Another significant, often-cited book was futurist Riane Eisler's *The Chalice and the Blade*, which challenges the traditional concept of humans as a naturally competitive, warlike species. The book offers a model of personal and communal power that Eisler calls "actualization" power, as opposed to the "domination" power of Western society. Eisler's description of a cooperative partnership society created in female readers strong feelings of estrangement from the dominance-driven workplace and a hope that they might be able to find or create a work community oriented toward teamwork and shared values.

JUST LIKE DYING

The women who are abruptly jolted out of their careers by some form of career crisis may feel the sharpest sense of alienation during stage five. In many cases, the feeling of isolation and aloneness is overlaid by sadness and grief: the deep grief we feel when someone close to us has died. In fact, career leavers often told me that leaving their careers was just like dying.

Their grief is also mixed with uncertainty and fear and dozens of difficult questions: Now that I can no longer identify myself with my career, who am I? What am I going to live on? Where am I going to live? What am I going to do? Without a career to give meaning to my life, what meaning can I find?

Unless the stage-five career leaver has successfully completed the evaluative and exploratory tasks of stage three and is able to step immediately into her new work, she usually undergoes one or more identity crises—all arising from the fact that she has lost her visible, well-paying position, her status in the career culture, and the concept of self-worth that was conferred upon her by her profession.

In addition to losing the outer trappings of her career-culture success, the career leaver has probably lost many of her friends as well, at least those who were her professional colleagues. Her new downward mobility makes their own situations seem frighteningly tenuous. Many avoid her, as one woman put it, like an "office Typhoid Mary." Although a few friends may be envious and say that they wish they could make a change in their work lives, for the most part friends and colleagues are critical of the woman's decision to leave—or, if fired, not to seek reemployment in the field. Often, too, friends find that the career leaver has changed, is no longer her old self, and is disinterested in activities she formerly enjoyed. The common bond they once enjoyed—a bond formed primarily in the workplace, around workplace issues—no longer joins them together.

Some women can choose the time and the conditions under which they leave their careers. They have some control over the leaving process, although they may later feel out of control. Other career leavers are thrust into the experience without much advance warning and without any control over the situation. For them, the alienation and despair of stage five—the black hole—is devastating.

Out of Work, Out of Community, Out of Luck

When Diane's career crisis occurred she was forty-three years old. Although she was involved in a long-term live-in relationship, she was a career-only woman: Early in her life, she rejected marriage and children in favor of career. She had been employed for fifteen years by a midsize publishing company, where her degree from a Seven Sisters' college and her professional experience earned her only a typist's job when she was first employed. From this entry position, she worked her way up to what she later would call the "female-pioneer" executive level.

A vocal feminist, Diane was openly critical of the firm's employment policies and played an active role in prodding the local publishing industry to comply with its civil rights obligations to female employees. Her outspokenness was tolerated by her employers and her frequent promotions and pay increases were testimony not only to the esteem in which she was held but also the job security she thought she could expect. Famous within the company as the only secretary who had ever risen into management and then to editor, Diane played an increasingly visible role in the corporation. When the firm was acquired by a Fortune 500 company, she was promoted, given another raise, and asked to relocate to New York.

"The move was very difficult personally," she says now, reflecting. "I had to bulldoze my private life in order to make it." Even though the relocation was personally costly, she felt it was worth it. The opportunities for advancement in the larger company were much greater, and she felt that her promotion was a sign that she had made it at last.

119

I was filled with an energy and self-esteem that came from knowing I had pioneered a woman's senior editorial career path in a house that was singularly resistant to women. I was fueled by having established my own worth in a man's world and having paved the way for others.

Diane's feminist pride and sense of self-worth, so thoroughly rooted in her acceptance by men in a man's world, was about to be put to the test. She was fired by the respected male mentor who had promoted her for over a decade. It was Monday. He gave her until Friday to get out.

> The firing was violent and brutal and hard to accept. But the worst of it was the way people acted. I felt as if I'd had a miscarriage on the floor of the reception area in my office and everybody was stepping around it. Nobody would talk to me or even acknowledge what had happened.

Diane was stunned. For all her long-term dissatisfaction with the firm's personnel policies, she had thought her job was secure, especially after her promotion and relocation. She had always been confident that if and when she decided to leave for a higher-level job somewhere in the industry, she would be able to dictate her own terms.

The abruptness of the firing caught Diane totally unprepared, and her isolation sapped her energy and made her feel like a nonperson. Her first response was to look for a new job in the same field, but because of industrywide cutbacks, she found nothing. Her professional difficulties tragically compounded an already-difficult personal situation:

> The term on my illegal sublet was due to expire in two weeks, which meant I had to find another place to live with no salary coming in. If I'd had my own apartment, I might have hunkered down and waited it out. But I found myself out of work, out of community, out of luck, out of a home, and out of money.

Through the dark cloud of her growing despair, Diane realized that there was no advantage to her in finding another job in New York City. "I would simply learn a new set of management tapes and the same thing would happen again, sooner or later," she said. "So I decided that New York was a major deadend. I'd be better off back in Boston, where I at least had a house."

As part of her negotiated severance, she was able to force the company to pay her relocation expenses back to Boston. After that minor triumph, however, things got worse instead of better. Her house was rented out, so she, her lover, and her pets were forced to move in with a friend. She felt utterly humiliated.

> I had left for New York on Cloud Nine—the Big Time, the Big Apple, look out! But when I came home, I crawled. I was deeply shamed. Not only did everybody else have jobs and money, but I didn't even have a place to live!

Over the next few months, Diane discovered that nothing in her life was as permanent as she had thought.

> My partner and I withdrew emotionally and physically from our life together. My old dog and cat died. I was totally depressed and completely isolated. I was as stuck as a person can get, professionally and personally.

Trapped in her desperate isolation, Diane was given temporary reprieve when a biologist friend sent a prepaid, openended plane ticket and an invitation to join her at a research site in a remote jungle area. She packed her bags, paid her bills for two months, and, she says, "vaporized." She spent a year traveling, across Africa, through Europe and China. The journey had a liberating and healing effect, because it freed her from the necessity of measuring herself or being measured by the standards of the career culture from which she had been forcibly ejected. It was a freedom—and paradoxically, an isolation—that she responded to immediately.

> When I got off the plane in Africa, I was able to live in the present. I wasn't being judged by anyone. Nobody had the slightest interest in what I had done or who I was. The values I had held didn't have any relevance any longer. They weren't good, they weren't bad—it was like high heels and pantyhose in the jungle. They just didn't fit.

When Diane finally returned home, she found herself, she says, violently out of sync with the culture and completely cut off from everything that she had known. Her partner was gone. Her house was filled with "ghosts, outdated Rolodex entries, lost domestic dreams, and a booming silence." She spiraled down into what seemed like a bottomless depression. The next year was a blur of sadness as she grieved the death of her corporate persona and began the painful work of developing a new relationship with a self that she barely knew existed.

> I crawled to therapy, developed new support systems, confronted my feelings, tried to find balance, learned meditation and yoga, published some writing, detached from most emotionally disruptive people and from my own sense of shame, grieved and grieved and grieved, and made no plans for any time past this afternoon. I learned acceptance, kicking and screaming all the way.

After several months of therapy, Diane read a newspaper notice about a research project at a nearby college. The project offered counseling and support for women over forty who had lost their jobs. Her participation in the group led her to see that her experience was neither unique nor her fault. This realization freed her from her burden of anguished guilt and enabled her to accept the fact that her tragic downfall was due more to corporate bad management than to her own inadequacies. "The group was my first lifeline out of my isolation," she said. Further, being a member of an over-forty group forced her to come to terms with what she now saw as her own ageism and the daunting truth that she was no longer a perennially young Yuppie.

By now, the stage-five agonies of black despair and alienation were fading, lightened by the group and her new colleagues and friends at the college women's center. Small free-lance jobs and what she thought of as dire economies—cutting out every unnecessary expenditure—had enabled her to get by financially, and she had staunchly resisted the temptation of taking a job that would drag her back into dependence on a corporate system she no longer trusted. Instead, she began to think about launching her own business as a publishing consultant and a literary agent specializing in women's writings. Then she was offered a part-time job with a nonprofit feminist periodical, where the workplace style was consciously cooperative and mutually empowering. Although Diane was glad to have a steady salary and a position on which she could rely, she was not fully able to appreciate the dimensions of her new situation:

> I saw the job as a stopgap. The terms were ludicrous, measured against corporate standards and my publishing experience. It was only later that I realized I had no context to evaluate the full possibilities of the opportunity I had accepted. I knew just enough by then to try the job on for size and go where it led.

Although Diane's corporate experience had given her no basis for understanding her true work potential, the anxious trauma of the past two years had gifted her with flexibility and a willingness to experiment. She took the job, and then began to shape it to fit her needs. After a year, she was able to see it as an important asset to her central work as an agent and consultant to women writers:

> The position [with the feminist periodical] keeps me visible in the publishing industry whether I have clients' work for submission or not. The publication's values match my own feminist politics. The work environment is free of stress, which took months of getting used to, and the management style is enabling.

Now, five years into her new work life, Diane is pleased with the new self that arose like a phoenix out of the despair, anguish, and alienation of what she called the black hole. The way she describes herself and her work style reflects her heightened, confident self-esteem and her new ability to trust her own substantial resources. More importantly, it reflects her new sense of herself as a flexible, resilient person-in-progress, growing and developing by seeking out new challenges.

> Today I make choices about work based on what fits my values best as well as on what challenges me in an affirming way and on what opportunities are actually available. Since I no longer live on a corporate salary, I have far fewer performance anxieties and temper my ambition to suit a low-key work life. I am in the process of integrating work and private selves and of redefining success

and achievement. The result is a new way of being in the work world and of managing my life as a whole.

As a consequence of revisioning her work life in a new way, Diane changed many of her feminist attitudes. She is no longer driven by the ambition to climb to the top rung of the corporate ladder. Her career-leaving experience has enabled her to completely redefine her earlier feminist understanding of success:

> To shape my career I spent much energy on denying feminine values in order to do well in the masculine work world. Now, I hold myself apart from the masculine values I served for nearly two decades, though I move in and out of that system as my work demands. I now view it as fraudulent.

What Diane sees as fraudulent is a belief that is widely held in the career culture: The only way to go is up, and the only way to work is competitively. She now works by the powerfully transformative values of colleagueship, cooperation, and mutual empowerment.

THE BACK-HOME-AGAIN BLUES

Our second stage-five story differs from our first in several important respects. When Tracy found herself out of work, it was not because she had been fired. She resigned by her choice—a thoughtful, much-discussed decision that had been half a year in the making. When she left her career as marketing manager, and her annual salary of fifty-two thousand dollars, Tracy was not out of a home. Instead, she went home again—to her lovely house in the suburbs and to a job as the full-time mother of ten-month-old twin daughters. Tracy's career leaving was warmly supported by her husband, whose recent promotion and raise meant that his income would adequately support the family, and by Tracy's mother, who lived in a nearby community.

Even though the conditions seemed optimal, Tracy found that leaving her career was not as easy as turning in the keys to the office and collecting her final paycheck. Stage-five feelings of alienation, despair, and isolation caught up with her, too, as they did with Diane. She named her feelings the back-home-again blues, and she admitted later that they nearly swamped her and sent her running back to the corporate office.

Tracy identified strongly with her father, a bank president. When she was a small girl, she admired his outgoing, charismatic way with people. Tracy's mother, in contrast, was shy and introverted and subordinated herself to her husband in ways that even a very young girl could recognize.

> I understood before I went to school that my father was the absolute boss in our family. Mom had graduated from college, but I never saw her read a book or get interested in anything besides her children and playing the organ at church. She gave in to Dad on everything, but especially where money was concerned. He gave her what she needed for groceries and household things and clothes. Mom wasn't in on the family finances.

Like her mother, Tracy had an artistic bent. She thought of majoring in art in college and becoming a teacher. Her father, however, strongly encouraged her to get what he thought would be a more rewarding degree in marketing; since he was paying her tuition and living expenses, she followed his suggestion. Her degree and a good word from her dad gained her an entry-level position in a large corporation at a salary that enabled her to declare her financial independence. "Getting that job liberated me," she said. "I had my own money. I had grown up."

A career-first woman, Tracy imagined that she would marry and have children at some point in her life. She had not given any special thought to either event, however, and her attitude toward children was decidedly casual: "I thought that if I had kids, I'd fit them in around the career." Her sharply competitive style and her willingness to work long hours gave her a career advantage. She had earned two promotions and a salary of more than thirty thousand dollars a year when she met Richard, a rising star in an investment firm and, as Tracy says, a real whiz with money—a trait that she valued highly as a symbol of personal autonomy and authority. The two were married the next year, when Tracy was twenty-nine. When two years later she became pregnant, she was delighted. For one thing, the birth would give her a chance to take some time off from the office.

The stress level had gotten unbelievably high, and I was feeling burned out and pretty disillusioned by then with the way the company was managed. I'd been running at top speed for ten years, and the job was getting awfully cutthroat. I'd been thinking about looking for a different job, but I knew it would be just more of the same. So when I got pregnant, I began to think it would be nice to stay home for a change and be a mom. It would mean a big loss of income—I was making thirty-eight thousand dollars a year at that point—but we could manage for a few months without my salary, especially when we considered the cost of child care. When we found out I was carrying twins, that decided us.

Staying home for a change was nice, Tracy discovered, and when it was time to return to work after her daughters were born, she was not quite ready. One of the twins needed minor surgery, which gave Tracy an excuse to stay out another three weeks; then she had trouble finding a day-care provider she felt she could trust. When the twins were four months old, Tracy realized that she didn't want to go back.

Getting out of the rat race gave me a different view of it. I just didn't want to go back and start fighting all those old battles again. It wasn't that I'd lost my nerve—it was more like I'd lost my taste for war. And there were the babies. I never expected this to be true of me, but all of a sudden I wanted to raise my daughters. The career didn't matter any longer—the children were far more important.

Richard agreed with Tracy that it would be better if she stayed home with the twins. His salary would cover expenses, and they had accumulated a hefty savings account. Tracy returned to work for several months but says, it was "just because I felt guilty at taking the maternity leave, even though I'd earned it." Then she came home—to stay.

Tracy's homecoming was not as idyllic as she had expected, however. After the first several weeks, she began to feel unaccountably depressed. "It was like I wasn't sure who I was anymore," she said. "I felt sad all the time, like somebody had died."

I know it sounds absolutely crazy, because I'd been home with the twins after they were born and things had been fine. But I had a career then. I had a title waiting for me when I went back to the office. And I was making good money, too. Now I wasn't making a nickel. It was very depressing.

For Tracy, the money proved to be the central issue; it was a symbol of her ability to take care of herself, of her personal independence from her father, from her husband, from all male authority.

> I guess I just didn't understand what the money meant to me. Mom never earned a penny and she was always under Dad's thumb, to the point where she didn't have any say in her own life. When I was young I vowed that I'd be my own woman, and now here I was, just like her. Richard and I had a joint checking account and he never questioned me about what I spent. But now that I wasn't putting money in the bank I felt I had to ask him before I took it out. It was humiliating, demeaning. I felt bankrupt and totally dependent.

Tracy's self-esteem, which had been inflated by her stimulating career and by her excellent earnings, fell to a serious low; she suffered from a sense that her life was no longer under her control. In her depression, other feelings grew to gigantic proportions. She missed her friendships with her former colleagues and felt hurt and rejected when they failed to make time for her. She was also deeply wounded by others' attitudes about her decision to stay home with the children and toward stay-at-home mothers in general:

> It never failed. I'd go to a party and somebody—usually a woman with an important title and a big paycheck—would ask, And what do you do? I'd say I'm an at-home mother, and the eyebrows would go up and she'd edge away, as if I had the plague. Sometimes I'd be in a room with a bunch of people and feel totally alone, isolated. I might as well have dropped in from another planet. It was obvious that these people, especially the women, didn't value mothers or mothering. It was a low-level job you hired other people to do while you did important things in the big wide wonderful world out there.

To complicate matters, Tracy's mother, recently widowed, began to drop in for several hours a day. The birth of the twins had drawn them closer, but her mother's emotional situation further depressed Tracy, for now she could identify with it.

> Since Dad died, her life had become a total vacuum. I had to ask myself, would I be that way someday? Was it true that women who chose to mother their children couldn't be a real part of the real world? I felt alone, isolated in my home, just the way my mother had been. I kept remembering that old saying, You can't go home again. It was a horrifying, black thought. I had no place to go.

Tracy's family expected that her depression would lift after a few months, but it steadily worsened. She lost interest in herself, in the house—even, most frighteningly, in her children. She had no friends and saw no one except for her mother. She seriously considered going back to work, but that seemed like giving up on her determination to raise her daughters herself. Even though she knew it would not be difficult to reenter her career field, she says she felt dismayed at the thought of "getting eaten alive by the rat race." Her inner state of mind was mirrored in her outer life by a series of illnesses and by an automobile accident in which her inattention might have injured her and her children.

The accident, which occurred during the lowest point of her isolation and depression, forced Tracy to seek help. She found a feminist therapist who encouraged her to join a women's support group. "I wasn't very excited about it," she says. "In my experience, women weren't as interesting as men. I thought an all-woman group would be pretty boring."

Tracy's group therapy, however, enabled her to trace the root of her difficulty to her own devaluation of her non–wage-earning mother—a devaluation that had been fostered by her father's treatment of her mother and by the society's treatment of all mothers. She saw that her personal sense of isolation was an expression of the way our society has typically treated mothers and children, secluding them in the domestic world, away from the heart of the community.

With the group, Tracy read and discussed Adrienne Rich's *Of Woman Born: Motherhood as Experience and Institution,* a book that enabled Tracy to see her personal situation in a broader cultural and historic perspective. She particularly resonated to Rich's statement about the isolation of women at home: "For

128

mothers, the privatization of the home has meant not only an increase in powerlessness, but a desperate loneliness."[1] As she dealt with the issue of women's powerlessness, represented by her and her mother's financial dependency on their husbands, she seemed to be dragged deeper into the black hole:

> I realized that I had succeeded in my career because I'd been tough the way a man is tough and because I'd been willing to give up almost everything in my life for my work. In return I got a nice paycheck. But that really made me sad when I started thinking about it. I mean, if the only way to be recognized is a man's way, what's the use? I had brought two daughters into the world, but they were going to have to practically turn into men before anybody would grant that they were worth something!

Tracy's mood began to change as she dealt more deeply and constructively with the issue of personal worth—not as it is measured by the financial standards of the career culture, but by the individual woman's ideas of what really matters.

> The big change came when I realized how totally I'd bought into the bottom-line values of the corporate culture. In business, if a product doesn't show a profit, it isn't worth bothering with. But I knew that was wrong when it came to children. You can't measure mothering by the bottom line. What price do we put on our commitment to our children and our grandchildren—to all the children? When I realized that, I stopped worrying about what other people thought I was worth and just became grateful that I could afford the luxury of being a full-time mother.

Once Tracy had done the stage-two work of sorting out the personal and cultural issues that had affected her so traumatically, she was able to recognize that she really wanted to work in the public world—although not in the way she had worked before—rather than stay at home all day. This recognition led her to ask the rational questions of stage three, such as What do I do now?

Her first obligation, Tracy felt, was to her children, so she refused to take full-time paid employment. She had begun to believe that what she now saw as her special privilege—her education, her upper middle class lifestyle, a supportive husband who could provide financially for the family—gave her an equally special obligation to the children of women who could not afford to be full-time mothers. With that obligation in mind, she joined a community-action project seeking to fund improved day-care for children from low-income families and, using the skills she had honed in the career culture, helped to sell the project to local businesses and civic organizations. Recently, she was elected to the city council and is looking ahead to an even greater involvement in municipal politics. She is confident of her own personal worth and her worth as a mother and a supporter of other mothers—not as it is measured by the career culture but as she herself measures it.

> I value the lessons I learned in the marketplace, but I'll never again put a bottom line on my own work. When the twins are in middle school, I may look for a time-share job—a job, not a career—so we can save for their college. But for now, it's enough to watch my daughters grow and to join other women in helping mothers and their children. Maybe, through what we're doing, people will see what mothers—and the day-care providers who are surrogate mothers for so many children—are truly worth.

The black hole that Tracy stepped into when she left her career required her to face her own misconceptions about the value of women's unpaid work as mothers. Her creative encounter with the darkness within enabled her to transform her depression and her sense of alienation into a productive contribution to her community. Tracy's new work—as mother, community activist, and supporter of women and children—has energized and changed not only herself, but also her community. She has truly found work of her own.

Stage-Five Growth

When we look at Diane's and Tracy's experiences as they moved from a secure, well-buttressed psychological position to a place of insecurity and darkness, and finally to a new, more vibrant, and more-encompassing encounter with the world, it is impossible not to think in terms of psychological growth, self-realization, and self-actualization. Carl Jung's term for this process was individuation: the work of realizing our full selfhood, our unique individuality. It is a necessary activity, he said, to complete our task of being fully human. It is work that every individual, if she wants to consciously live out her fullest potential, must undertake.

That does not mean that we are all equally capable of accepting this challenging assignment, or that the process of becoming ourselves is a comfortable one. It is, on the contrary, a task that most of us avoid as long as possible and undertake only if we are forced to do so by the events and circumstances of our lives. It is difficult and painful work, charged with moral conflicts and agonizing decisions. This is particularly true because the first and most crucial task of individuation requires us to question the values of our culture and begin to establish our own principles of rightness and goodness, of truth and beauty, of success and failure. In *The Development of Personality*, Jung writes:

> The achievement of personality means nothing less than the optimum development of the whole individual human being. . . . [But] the development of personality from the germ-state to full consciousness is at once a charisma and a curse, because its first fruit is the conscious and unavoidable separation of the single individual from the undifferentiated and unconscious herd. This means isolation, and there is no more comforting word for it.[2]

In the psychological sense, then, becoming ourselves, realizing and integrating all the possibilities inherent in us, stands totally opposed to unthinking conformity with other people's values and wishes. It stands opposed to unthinking adoption of other people's definitions of success and failure. If we want to become our true selves, we must examine and reject the conventional attitudes and definitions on which most people prefer to base their lives.

Examining our conventional attitudes is very difficult to do, however, for we live within our culture as fish swim in the sea, as oblivious to its most fundamental rules for existence as fish are oblivious to water. It is only when we are somehow cast out of our culture that we are able to gain the distance and perspective that makes it possible for us to see it objectively and to question it.

Diane was cast out when she was forcibly evicted from what

131

she thought was a secure place in the higher echelons of her publishing career, a place she had obtained only through great personal sacrifice. Her travel to Africa and China gave her a broader view of human cultures; when she returned to the United States and found herself still without a job, without her former status, and without a partner, she was completely set apart from the society in which she had grown to adulthood.

Tracy was cast out when she elected to leave her place in the career culture for what she thought was the safety of home—a place where she eventually felt as alien and homeless as Diane felt when she lost her sublet because she could not pay the rent. Tracy was further cast out when she experienced for herself the way the career culture marginalizes mothers and motherhood— a marginalization that goes back at least to the beginning of the Industrial Age, when men's work was moved to the factories and rewarded with a paycheck, leaving mothers isolated at home in unpaid work or confined to the lowest-paying jobs in factories and offices, their children unmothered.

It may seem ironic that we should describe Diane and Tracy's act of career leaving as a rejection of society's standard for acceptable behavior, given the fact that both these women embarked on their careers by challenging society's expectations of what women do with their lives—at least as those expectations were expressed in the era in which they grew up. Neither of their mothers had careers, yet both Diane and Tracy were among the first females to be promoted in their companies. Neither of their mothers were independent, yet both Diane and Tracy led their own lives and made their own ways in a very difficult world.

The man's world to which these women were admitted, however, works only by men's rules. There, the standard of acceptable behavior for successful people, men or women, requires that the individual focus on career to the virtual exclusion of every other human activity. When Diane and Tracy reject this standard of behavior, they are rejecting one of the most fundamental assumptions of the career culture. At the same time, they are opening themselves to a range of possibilities for their lives other than an exclusionary concentration upon career—opening themselves, in psychological terms, to all their inherent inner potentialities.

It is in that sense that the black hole of stage five—the despair, isolation, and alienation that we fall into when we reject the rule of the dominant culture—becomes the fertile under-world that can eventually support a lushly vibrant, productive new life that may include paid work but is not dominated by it. The essential growth of stage five takes place in the cold, com-fortless dark, where we must be alone to work out what matters to us and to build a solid foundation for our own personal mean-ing in a life that once was jury-rigged upon meanings supplied by authoritative others. In doing this inner work, we are, as Diane put it, "violently out of sync" with the culture, for nothing in this society encourages us to work out our values for our-selves; rather, we are schooled to accept our family's and our so-ciety's dominant values—patriarchal values.

When we first separate ourselves from the prefabricated values of the culture, working out our own values is by necessity a very private and lonely affair. It must be private and lonely, for if we attach ourselves to another person or to a group too soon or too unthinkingly, we are likely to transfer the task to them and fail to do our own work: We will have adopted their values rather than seeking out our own. But at some point along the way, we make a decision. Either we will continue in isolation or we will join other fellow travelers (for women, these are usually other women) who can support and affirm our efforts to find out who we are and what we are about. Diane's and Tracy's stories illus-trate both the isolation that is a necessary part of stage five and the affiliation that enables us to accept the fact that we are women who need other women to help us grow.

For American women working in the last decade of the twentieth century, the task of defining our work values provides both an extraordinarily unique opportunity and an extraor-dinarily difficult challenge. It is unique in the sense that we are the first generation of women to be confronted with this task, and difficult in the sense that every step we take is a step deeper into uncharted territory. Our foremothers, with the exception of the few who had the education or the inclination to create their own paths, lived out the values of their male-dominated society, playing roles acceptable to their fathers and husbands and male children. In the last two decades, even though women have been admitted to men's workplaces, we have, like our foremothers, also lived out the values of the male-dominated society, playing roles acceptable to our organizations and our male employers (who in many cases function much like our fathers). If we wish to take our own direction, to realize our own individual personhood, we must examine these values and, where it is necessary, reject them. This examination and rejection are necessary first steps toward becoming our essential selves.

This task is sometimes almost incomprehensibly difficult, however, as nearly every female career leaver testifies. For when we say to the career culture, I no longer want to work by your rules but by my own, we may be sentencing ourselves to a life of no work at all. No paid work, at any rate, and relatively few women have the luxury, as Tracy recognizes, of a life without paid work. When we say, I will no longer judge myself by your standard of success but my own, we risk being seen as dropouts, copouts, failures. And when we say, I will no longer live by the rules of the career culture, we may find ourselves alone in a very lonely place, without friends and allies, for in this decade in America, the career culture is the dominant culture. If we forfeit our tickets to success, we may at the same time be sentencing ourselves to a life on the cultural margin. For some, this marginal life with all of its pioneering challenges may be far preferable to continual performances in the center ring of the vast American circus; for others, it may represent an intolerably lonely exile into strange and forbidding territory. The possibilities that we see in the world beyond the corporation may encourage us to leave or may keep us from making our exits.

If we choose to leave the career culture, we are confronted with an equally challenging task: to construct a new kind of work, based on values that we as women find livable and workable. What kind of work will it be? Judging from the lives of the career leavers I studied, it will be work that is creative and energizing; work that supports rather than violates our values; work that does not occupy all our time but permits us to pursue other interests and challenges; work that endorses our commitment to community and allows us to make a contribution to the lives of others; work that provides us an acceptable standard of living— acceptable by our terms, not those of the consumer society. Whatever work we choose, it will be work of our own.

In chapter 7, we will look at the lives of women who found new work.

THE SIXTH STAGE:
WORK OF HER OWN

In Do What You Love, the Money Will Follow, Marsha Sinetar quotes St. Francis of Assisi: "It is no use walking anywhere to preach unless our walking is our preaching."[1] It is no use talking about the right kind of work—what the Buddhists call right livelihood—without doing it.

In our technologized society, which is oriented toward careers that consume us and consumer goods that entice us to pledge years of future work against their purchase, the right kind of work is frighteningly elusive. Many working environments are toxic (both physically and spiritually); many working relationships are hostile, exploitative, or emotionally abusive; many goods and services are morally and ethically questionable. As employers, corporations are impersonal; small businesses, unreliable; and all businesses, at the mercy of a volatile economy in which furloughs and firings are an everyday affair. Even bullish economists predict that the last decade of the twentieth century will be a decade in which American businesses and government will be required to discipline themselves to the difficult task of scaling down after the unprecedented, ungoverned growth of the previous two decades. Even those not committed to conservation have begun to agree that we must reduce our reliance on scarce natural resources—including soil, water, and clean air, which we once imagined to be without limit. Even the most optimistic of futurologists agree that the decades beyond the turn of the century are likely to be far leaner than this one, as third-world nations cope with burgeoning population growth and increasing demands for higher standards of living on a planet that daily grows smaller and smaller.

In the context of such challenging economic, ecological, and social constraints, the issue of right livelihood becomes more central than ever before. Although it remains a personal issue, one that each of us must individually confront, it has become an issue of much larger dimensions—a social and political issue. For we are beginning to understand that wrong livelihoods—the clearing of the rain forests, for example, or the building of unsafe nuclear power plants—threaten not just our individual well-being and peace of mind, but also the health of all peoples and species, the health of the planet for unnumbered generations into the future. We know now, whether or not we choose to act on our knowledge, that for our livelihoods to be right, they must also be responsible, just, and moral. To be whole and healthy, we must work with our hearts, not just our hands and our heads. We must work for others, not just for ourselves, for in the shrinking world of the future there will be little room for the elbows-out, every-man-for-himself individualism that has characterized the American culture since the first settlers confiscated Native American lands.

Right livelihood, then, is work that we choose to do because we want to do it—not because it is currently fashionable, or pays a great deal of money, or because Father approves, or because it was the best available. Right livelihood is chosen thoughtfully, mindfully, with a full understanding of our needs, the needs of those we care for, the needs of the earth. Right livelihood is work that challenges us to grow as wholehearted persons at the same time that it challenges us to develop an ever-widening range of skills and knowledge. Right livelihood is work that pays enough, by standards of responsible consumption. And right livelihood is work through which we affirm that we are caring, compassionate citizens of our communities, our nations, and our planet.

WHERE THE HEART BECKONS

The women I studied who created new work for themselves agreed on the basic principle of their choice: They chose to do what the heart called them to do. For some, this has meant choosing to give up their positions in the career culture in order to become full-time at-home mothers. Although the decision often requires a total reordering of the woman's personal priorities as well as a substantial reduction in the family's total income, almost every woman, over the long term, feels her decision was right. The stories they tell about their experiences reveal a high level of satisfaction with their choices, although they also reveal a realistic understanding about the challenges of the new work.

Marsha, who majored in math and received her master's degree in business administration, was the vice-president of a data-processing firm when she left her career. When I first heard from her, she had been at home for two years with two teenage stepchildren and a four-year-old son. She had already discovered that mothering was a job for which her academic degrees and her executive experience had not prepared her:

I have had to totally reorder my priorities. Because my identity had been so totally tied up in my job, I had to try to develop a new one. I had to learn to live each day at a totally different pace, learn this new job almost from scratch, and confront all my prejudices and ideas about how children should be and how life at home should be. I went from a very self-assured woman to a woman with many doubts about her effectiveness. My life has changed radically. I wouldn't have it any other way.

Nearly three years later, Marsha is still being challenged by her new work. Her comments are a realistic appraisal of what her new work is worth:

Being a mother-at-home is the lowest-paid, most difficult, and most rewarding job I've ever done. I also babysit for another little boy six hours a week, so my personal income went from seventy thousand dollars a year three years ago to twenty-four dollars a week today. My days are full and extremely busy—my day-to-day problems are much tougher now than when I had a staff of thirty-five. But I'm convinced that it's very important for me to be home. A lot of healing has been going on in the family since I quit my job.

Other at-home mothers echo Marsha's evaluation of their new work and describe themselves in ways that reveal the rich variety of the things they do—not only for themselves and for their families, but also for their communities. June was a regional staff supervisor for a multinational corporation when she left her work to mother her two small children. At first, it was difficult:

The initial period of euphoria gave way to a period marked by loneliness (everybody works!), personal confusion (my identity was wrapped up in my job, the job is gone, who am I?), and boredom. There was also a big financial adjustment because our family income was cut in half.

June sought new friendships. "I found people who liked me without the fancy wrapping paper," she says. She made it a personal goal to develop herself in ways that the demands of her career had prohibited. Nearly three years after leaving her career, there is a tone of wonder in her words as she considers the woman she has become:

I have watched myself with amazement go through a one-hundred-and-eighty-degree change from the person I used to be. One of the gifts I have received as the result of staying home is a clear perspective on my life—where it's been and where it's going. I'm an active member of Al-Anon and of a local women's club through which I do community volunteer work. My two-year-old vegetable garden gave way to my children's swing set, but I'm proud of my flower gardens. And I'm ice-skating again, something I haven't done in years! Prior to leaving my career, I was too caught up in the hustle and bustle to see where I fit into the picture. I used to be too busy keeping up to know that what I really needed was to slow down. Now I know I have choices about what I do.

June's experience in community volunteer work, which she began after she returned home, was instrumental in helping her see her choices more clearly. As her children grow older and she thinks about returning to work, she finds herself at an important fork in the road: "I'm trying to decide whether I want to return to my original path, which brought me financial success," she says, "or to pursue social work. That's where my heart beckons me to go."

Now that their careers are no longer the focus of their lives, career leavers are free to follow the path of the heart. Sylvia, a former molecular biologist, left her career in the 1970s. She presently lives in a cabin in the country and writes and illustrates books about awakening to the spiritual life (three have been published; a fourth is on the way). Besides writing, her work includes travel for readings, interviews, and workshops—mostly for women. When she wrote to me about what she does, about the place she works and the people she works with, I sensed that Sylvia meets the challenges of her life from a deeply fulfilled place in her heart:

> I love my work—writing and publishing—both alone and with other women. I also love my contact with the earth and the native plants and animals which live here too. I'm excited about the on-going discoveries in my life—the immense power of our thoughts and beliefs, the changes taking place beneath the surface of our outer world.

The spiritual life is an important focus for other career leavers, as well. Rena left her position as a senior investment officer to be an at-home mother, but her faith is a mainstay of her life; her outside work is focused on her church, where she serves on the executive committee and leads a weekly Bible study group.

Nancy was a teacher and music instructor. She left her work to become pregnant and to give herself time for personal work and the study of Native American spiritual traditions. Now, she is at work on the creation of ritual art and music. She composes, performs, and records her compositions, writes for several periodicals, teaches workshops, and mothers her two small children.

Crystal continues to lead the largest women's spirituality network in the country. She writes about the Divine Feminine, teaches, and lectures.

Ruth, a former lawyer, works as the coordinator of a spiritual retreat center in a remote mountain area of the Southwest, a position that has enabled her to grow spiritually and in her ability to live in community.

Suzanne, a former teacher, is mothering her three-year-old daughter, considering the possibility of having another child, and attending divinity school part-time. In five years, she expects to be a full-time minister and thinks that her new work may give her husband the freedom to leave his career—a goal they both cherish.

Molly left her mid-level management position in a large weight-loss business to care for her aged parents and to establish an elder hostel that provides day-care supervision for the elderly.

Her goal is to own and manage several hostels which will provide older people with the loving care that their families are unable to give.

The heart can beckon us also to become newly, energetically creative, on our own behalf and in the service of others. Lenore held a six-figure job in marketing that required her to maintain a feverish schedule, "working endlessly from five in the morning, when I would wake up to get writing done before the phone rang, meetings had to be attended, or planes caught, until late at night." When she quit, she sold her house and used some of the money to finance her work as a writer: books, plays, television and film scripts. Then she became interested in finding work that would, she said, "in some way prove helpful to people." Now, she is finishing a workbook for weight control, along with a diary and newsletter that she expects to market through the workshops she is planning. Leaving her all-consuming career has freed her to combine her creative talent with her desire to work with people in a healing environment.

At the age of forty, Janet left her career teaching college-level English to mother her four-year-old child. Her deep interest in the needs of mothers her own age led her to cofound a community network for older mothers; "late-blooming parents," she calls them. The network led to a successful national newsletter that enables her to do what she loves and does best: writing, networking with mothers to help them support each other in their parenting goals and personal needs, and working out of her home:

> I love having a home-based business. My husband also works from our home as a consultant. We are truly an 'electronic cottage.' Even though I am busier than when I worked in my career, my energies are freer and I appreciate the quality of my life more. And because I work at home, I am free to put home and family needs first whenever that's necessary.

With her child now in school, Janet is also teaching university-level classes on managing at-home businesses and has become interested in alternative health care. She sees her new work as evolving to follow her changing interests but continually focused by her concern for making a contribution to others.

The desire to help other mothers is also creating new work for Rosemary. Rosemary was an upper-level manager of a computer manufacturing corporation and earned a hundred thousand dollars a year when she decided that she could no longer cope constructively with the conflict between mothering her four small children and pursuing her career. At home with the children, though, Rosemary found that she needed to be doing something more. Working with her mother and her former child-care provider, she opened an at-home business: what she calls a nanny placement bureau that trains, places, and supervises highly qualified child-care workers. It is work that gives her, she says, the "ultimate in flex time." Here, her experience as a mother is a plus, not a continual distraction from what she is doing. She sees her work as contributing to the health and well-being of other families besides her own:

> I would like my children, particularly my daughters, to understand that while you can't have it all—a high-powered executive job, yuppie lifestyle, perfect marriage, and a large family—you can have a happy, large family and a business interest. I'm operating on the principle that my business will expand to absorb more hours and produce more income as my family requires less time and energy.

Michelle left her career as a research agronomist when she realized that it could not fulfill her wish to make a significant contribution to the fight against hunger. Now the mother of two home-schooled children, she shares responsibilities in a parent-cooperative nursery school and teaches classes in prenatal and postpartum exercise. She is also developing a support network for mothers who face postpartum adjustment and depression, and she is a local distributor for what is called a baby sling, a product designed to enhance mother-child bonding. She is planning to become a La Leche League leader, is hoping to move into the local and statewide organizational structure, and is exploring the possibility of becoming a midwife. Through Michelle's various jobs, she has shifted her focus from idealistically wanting to feed the world to doing what she realistically can do to help mothers and children in her own community. Recently she sent me this note:

I was asked last week when I'd be going back to agronomy, and I didn't feel the slightest twinge when I said, never. This is my new work. It's taken five years to leave behind all the second thoughts and have the confidence I have now. I love the interaction with the women in my classes. I really feel like I'm having a positive impact on them at a very important time in their lives!

Helping and supporting other women is a prominent theme in the work lives of the career leavers I studied. Jeannie, a computer programmer/analyst, left her career because the values of the for-profit corporate world conflicted with her values as a women's rights and peace activist. For the past four years, she has served as the coordinator of a project called Shared Housing for One-Parent Families. In addition to helping low-income families locate homes, she also does peer support counseling and advocacy and referral work on women's issues. "I've never regretted leaving the corporate world," she told me. "Even though it has meant a much lower salary, no benefits, and no job security, I've been rewarded with the knowledge that I'm working for something I believe in." Recently, she has decided to train to teach English to non-native speakers. "I used to think there was something wrong with me for changing fields every few years," she says. "I now think that it is a healthy growth process. Change is good. It makes life more interesting and has developed my mind and my spirit."

Jeannie is right when she observes that change and variety in our work lives encourages us toward growth—far more growth, in many more dimensions, than the lifelong single-track career encouraged by the career culture. Personally, I have found that the most precious thing about my freedom from the self-limiting constraints of my former career is the ability to follow my growing interests and to blend together a satisfying and rewarding mixture of different kinds of work that changes as I change. I still manage with my career self's competence, but instead of others' work it is my own various activities I coordinate. I still teach, but now I teach in many different settings and in different and changing topic areas for a wide variety of students. I write, giving myself permission to follow my own curiosity into whatever offbeat topic interests me, in both nonfiction and fiction. I enjoy different activities according to the season: In the winter I quilt and make wreaths; in the spring and summer my husband and I raise whatever combination of vegetables, flowers, chickens, ducks, geese, and peacocks we can fit onto our small acreage and into our busy schedule. This rich and varied— and balanced—combination of activities gives my work a playful quality. Underlying all that I do is the sense that my writing and teaching make a contribution to the lives of others. Duane Elgin's term contributory livelihood appeals to me as a description of the kind of work that engages us the most deeply and returns to us the greatest reward.

> My sense is that if we give less than our wholehearted participa-
> tion to our work, then our sense of connectedness to life itself will
> be commensurately diminished. Work that is not strongly contrib-
> utory may yield the income to feed our endless search for grati-
> fication, but such work seldom provides us with a sense of gen-
> uine contribution and satisfaction. Therefore, work that is largely
> self-serving will generate by its very nature a sense of alienation
> and unsatisfactoriness. However, when our work is life-serving,
> then our energy and creativity can flow cleanly and directly
> through us and into the world without impediment or inter-
> ruption.[2]

I think all of the women I studied would agree with the observation that it is life-serving work, not self-serving work, that
fulfills them most completely. Life-serving work is the special
calling, the special privilege of those who free themselves from
the constraints of the career culture and follow the beckoning of
their own hearts.

ENOUGH MONEY?

The answer to that question depends almost entirely upon how much money you have in mind, and *that* depends, of course, on the standard of living you need or want to support.

All of the women I studied reported decreases in earned income (income not gained from the sale of property or from investments) when they left their careers. The most substantial
losses (in percentage of household income lost) occurred for
those career leavers who came home to the unpaid work of

mothering. The loss of the mother's salary is a burden borne by the entire family. Those who bear it most easily are those who have prepared themselves for the loss by accumulating savings and by reducing their expenditures (particularly mortgage and car payments) to a level that a one-income family can afford. Those who are worn out most quickly by the burden are those who have no savings or who fail to alter their style of living to match the lower level of incoming resources.

However, only 18 percent of the women I studied moved to nonpaying work, such as mothering or elder care. Most career leavers have to do work of some kind in order to make a living: They must ask themselves whether doing what they love will pay enough to keep a roof over their heads, food on the table, and leave something for personal enrichment. About half (52 percent) of the total group was able to answer an enthusiastic yes—doing what they loved meant earning enough.

For about 15 percent, the less-enthusiastic answer was *yes . . . but*. Yes, there was enough money, but it was not nearly as much as they were used to or needed or wanted and it did not come in at a constant, predictable rate. Yes, there was enough money, but the benefits were much lower or nonexistent. (Health and life insurance are not affordable on a low income, and self-employed people must make their own contributions to Social Security.) Yes, there was enough money for current operating expenses but not enough to make payments on accrued debts.

For the remainder (another 15 percent), the answer was a dissatisfied *no*: I tried doing what I love but I could not make enough money. So I have to do more of what I do not love in order to get by—or go back to doing a great deal of that in order to have the lifestyle I want. In one case, the woman decided that she did not love her new work at all and went back to the old, which she loves even less but cannot find a way to leave.

The women who now do what they love and earn enough generally have excellent skills and a strong sense of their own competence. Most of them have been able to translate the skills they were employing on behalf of a company or corporation into work they now do for themselves.

This group includes women like Andrea, who left her position as a book editor to open a small home-based publishing firm with her husband. They combine publishing, travel for research, and their own writing in a rich mixture of satisfying kinds of work.

The group also includes women like Abbie, who resigned from a vice-presidency in an entertainment corporation and now has her own company. She offers a smoking-cessation program to large corporate clients and to individuals. "I outgrew my career," she said.

It took a while to find what I wanted to do, and I felt like a lost soul. During the interim I made new friends, grew a lot, lost a lot—forty pounds, to be exact—and quit smoking after thirty-three years! But now I am off the ground and find myself busy between teaching, doing presentations, marketing and selling. My plan is to become certified in stress management so I can offer more than one program—sort of a mini-wellness center. I love what I'm doing. I think I make a good contribution to people's lives.

The group also includes Elizabeth, who, at the age of forty-two, was working as a public relations director for a large firm. Feeling that she wanted more time for her own artistic work, she reduced her work commitment to thirty hours a week for a year and then took a year's leave of absence. During that period she began to build a clientele for her unique sculptures: delicate porcelain figures that are miniature three-dimensional portraits of her clients: typically brides, debutantes, and mothers with young children. She also purchased a computer graphics system that would allow her to design brochures, ads, newsletters, books, games, and computerized slide presentations. "The secret is to be flexible and diverse in the services you offer," she says about her eclectic business. In the first year of operation, she grossed enough to pay off her equipment. Now, three years later, she says that doors are opening up everywhere: Out-of-state galleries offer to exhibit her work; she has been featured in magazines and on television; and she has received fellowships for continuing art study. "I feel I am on a threshold," she says.

Other women find that with careful financial management, they can do what they love on a part-time basis. Lisa's story is told by Deborah Arron in *Running from the Law*. Lisa left her legal career in the high-pressure field of oil and gas shelters to start a family. Now, she works three days a week with a search firm that specializes in finding positions for ex-lawyers. She is able to combine her mothering with her new work, in which she finds herself working as "handholder, psychologist, career counselor, matchmaker, and mother to attorneys, all rolled into one."[3]

Then there is Anne, who left a full-time position as a college development officer for the part-time directorship of a private foundation. Sarah, a former bank officer, now heads up a community loan fund, working part-time, out of her home. Nancy left her career as a nursing-home administrator and now taps her strong personal interest and skills in sports to serve as half-time athletic director at a private school.

Rita came to her career as a computer systems analyst in her thirties, after her two daughters were raised. By the time she was fifty-three, she was making eighty-five thousand dollars a year as a project manager, most of which she spent to maintain a high standard of urban living. She enjoyed her work in software development, but as she grew older she became ardently feminist and more deeply resentful of what she called the "petty-tyrant politics and macho games" that permeated the environment in which she worked. Suffering from stress, burnout, and a variety of psychosomatic illnesses, Rita decided to leave the city. She quit her job, bought a seventy-year-old house on thirty-three acres of land, expanded her interest in dog breeding, took up gardening, and began to write. When she saw how fast her savings were shrinking, however, she realized (at the age of fifty-six) that she must go back to work—although she had no intention of climbing back on the career ladder. She sought short-term work as a computer consultant, traveling all over the northern hemisphere. When I last heard from her, she was working in an Alaskan city on a six-month contract that would pay enough to enable her to live several years without working. Her temporary assignments make her less involved in the inevitable politics of the local situation. These nine-to-five, five-day-a-week jobs also give her an opportunity to read, sightsee, and do research on a writing project:

> I went to Kenai last weekend and visited an old Russian Orthodox church. Next week, I'm going fishing for halibut and king sal-

mon—haven't been ocean fishing for forty-two years. What a kick! Later, I'm going to Russia and will take a three-day trip on the Trans-Siberia Railway.

Rita is also thinking about going home, where she expects to become more involved with judging dog shows and writing:

> My ranch is just about restored, the dogs and the garden are doing great, and my retirement fund should be adequate by the end of this year. Then it will be write, write, write and judge, judge, judge, with a little travel thrown in for spice. I finally did it. And I've done it my way. I felt so alone the whole time, but here I am with all my independence and proud to be living my childhood dreams.

Not Enough Money

Among the career leavers I met are two smaller groups: those who say that the money has followed from their doing what they love but not quite enough money, and those who say that the money has not followed. Both groups include women who find themselves doing more of what they do not love in order to maintain their lifestyle.

After eighteen years as a computer-banking specialist, Julia tired of the rat race and decided to downshift her eighty-thousand-dollar-a-year job. She reduced her hours and worked out of her home via her computer. That strategy, however, did not take her far enough out of the career culture, so she and her husband of eighteen years (who was in the process of leaving his teaching career) bought a second home in a West Coast seashore resort and relocated there, with the intention of developing family real-estate and bed-and-breakfast businesses. To add to their excitement, Julia unexpectedly became pregnant. Then the recession hit, the real-estate market crashed, and tourism plummeted. The family was forced to give up doing what they loved and go back to full-time jobs. To support the mortgages they cannot get rid of, Julia now works in a resort-area bank and her husband teaches in San Francisco, taking their three-year-old with him to be cared for during the week by relatives. Julia is frustrated by their work-enforced separation but also sees the bright side:

> For the first time in our twenty-year marriage, I now view my husband as the primary caregiver and nurturer. In this light I have found him to be patient and endearing. He is doing a great job taking care of our son and seems to derive a great deal of pride that he can do it. And the week-long separation gives me an opportunity to care for no one else but myself. I enjoy the flexibility and calm it has enabled me to have. It has made me realize that being by myself is okay.

Kerry's story has a similar theme of frustrated hopes but a much different tone, for Kerry can find no bright side. For seventeen years, she owned a veterinary practice in a small Southern town. She was exhausted by the long hours, frustrated by people's attitude toward animals, and felt she was, as she said, "running on empty." Her life was complicated by the fact that she was the single parent of an eleven-year-old daughter who demanded a great deal of attention. Finally, at the age of forty, she sold her practice. The monthly proceeds from the sale (she took a personal note from the buyer) would provide basic support, which she planned to supplement from her savings and from a home-based business—exactly what, she was not sure.

Things did not go according to Kerry's plan, however. Her daughter ran away. The vet who bought her practice defaulted on the note. She reports that she was never able to "emotionally connect with" something she wanted to do—or when she did (she genuinely enjoys doing crafts), it did not pay enough to support her. Now turning fifty, she recently described her situation as "panicky semi-destitution":

> I'm still attempting to find a market for my crafts with no success, including a try at my own shop. But winter arrived, my savings were essentially depleted, and the economy still hasn't picked up in this area. I'm actively looking for a job to pay bills and to pay for the continuing education hours I need to maintain my vet's license, as I could still make a living at it, if worse came to worst. I'd prefer to do creative work, but I *do* have to eat.

GOING BACK

Of the eighty career leavers I studied, only two decided to return to their original jobs and their original work styles. Both typify the career leaver who gets stuck somewhere along the way and is unable to sufficiently free herself of the values of the career culture and from her own incompletely understood need to work in that environment.

Virginia represents the kind of career leaver who does not have sufficient motivation to leave her career in the first place and has not done enough second-stage self-exploration to understand why she works as she does. Moving to an isolated rural area was her husband's idea, not hers, she told me. Even though moving meant giving up her university faculty position, she agreed, first, because she valued the marriage and second, because she was recovering from cancer surgery and suspected that her fast-paced, harried lifestyle as a working mother had contributed to her illness. The family (Virginia, her husband, and two children under eight) moved into a beautiful old house. When I first heard from Virginia she told me that she planned to teach part-time, at a much slower, less frenetic pace, to write and to involve herself in community affairs. "I also plan to slow down and enjoy my lovely house, my wonderful husband and my terrific children," she said. When I asked her how she felt about this radical change in her life, she remarked candidly: "What occurs to me is that I miss the money and the power."

Now, three years later, Virginia has returned to full-time teaching, this time at a local community college—a more stressful work environment, she says, than the one she left. She speaks about her situation with some degree of insight:

> The shocking thing is that I have replicated my "old" life. I am sometimes afraid that I took this job because I can't structure my life any other way. My eye is on ten years from now when I plan to "drop out" for good—in a home by the ocean somewhere. Of course, I still wonder if I'll live that long.

Jessica's story opens a slightly different perspective. She was the high-salaried director of a state audit division in a northwestern state when she began to feel increasingly dissatisfied with her work and her personal life. She was physically and emotionally exhausted; she was concerned about the security of her political appointment; and she felt that she had no time to explore her own personal interests. When I asked about these interests, she was vague but planned to spend time trying to discover them. Seeking a less stressful work environment, she turned to college teaching—a temporary situation, she thought, until she could achieve the financial security that would enable her to quit work entirely and to do some kind of public service work, perhaps join the Peace Corps.

Jessica, however, was bitterly disappointed in teaching. She found the students ill-prepared and unmotivated, she did not enjoy playing faculty politics, and she was working just as hard as before but for much less pay. She tried volunteer work but found that she did not like it, and she could not seem to find the time to explore her own interests. It was no surprise to anyone that when her former boss asked her to return to her directorship, she agreed.

When I visited Jessica a year later, she confessed that she was back to working sixty-hour weeks. The money was, she said, superb—enough to support a luxurious apartment in an exclusive area of the city, elegantly furnished with white overstuffed sofas, glass-topped tables, and expensive art. Jessica looked worn and weary. She was chain-smoking. The basic problem, she told me, was that she had not been able to discover what she wanted to do instead of working. "Actually, I'm just trying to figure out what to do between now and the time I die," she said with a sad laugh. Later, she wrote to me: "I seriously question whether I'll be alive five years from now. If I am, I'll probably still be drifting, trying to figure out what I'm supposed to be doing with my life."

For Virginia, the search for a new way of working seems to have stalled on the twin issues of money and power. Although she identified ways in which she wanted to change (slow down, write, more fully enjoy her family and her home), the money and the status her position offered pulled her back into the career culture. Her work style remained unchanged.

For Jessica, the search for new work seems to have foundered on her inability to look into herself deeply enough to find an

150

answer to the question, What do I want to do? She, too, is hooked on power and money—or rather, feels afraid and powerless at the idea of not having a salary she considers adequate to meet all contingencies (including support for her two daughters, now in their thirties, who frequently ask for money). "I'm scared of becoming a bag lady under a bridge," she said to me, even though her financial resources at the present time are sufficient to support her at a modest level for the rest of her life.

For both Virginia and Jessica, the central issue, it seems to me, is that they were never able to fully dis-identify themselves with the values of the career culture, which are embodied so clearly in power and money and the security that both seem to represent. I have observed that those career leavers who continue to evaluate themselves by the standards of the career culture never feel free enough to choose what they want to do.

MONEY: IS THERE EVER ENOUGH?

Realistically and practically, the question of whether we can downscale our work depends almost entirely on whether we can downscale our appetites for the so-called good life. The good life, most of us now realize, comes at an enormous cost—of energy, time, money, resources—that is paid at both individual and national levels. Many are beginning to suspect that an investment of this scale is simply not worth the rewards. Many others are beginning to feel that the good life is not all that good anyway. They see that once a certain standard of living has been reached, the returns on their investment in time and energy to better it begin to diminish. When we take a close look at what a high income buys, we often find that the money does not make up for what we give up to get it. Even *Money* magazine, which usually fills its pages with advice on how to make money, now advises two-income readers to "reconsider whether earning more money really improves your life":

> If one of you is working for money rather than fulfillment, you may be able to improve your life by reducing spending and quitting the lower-paying job. That's usually the case if one of you earns two or more times as much as the other and child care and taxes consume fifty percent or more of the smaller salary.[4]

Over the next decade, many working women, and men, too, will reexamine the definition of fulfillment and discover that what they *thought* was fulfilling—career-culture success, status, and power—is not what they really need or want. At that point, the question of what is enough money is much more easily answered. Economist Warren Johnson, in his book *Muddling Toward Frugality,* argues that people willingly accept a modest income if they love what they are doing and the way of life they are creating. Whether they find viable alternatives for new kinds of work, he says,

> does not depend entirely on how much money can be made. More and more, the key to economic survival will be *to learn how to get by with less income.* . . . It takes a highly motivated and creative person or family to undertake the risk of developing [her or] his own work while getting by with less and learning how to become more self-sufficient. For the first pioneers, it can be lonely and difficult work in unfamiliar territory. The frequently heard criticism that says these people are 'dropouts,' and that they do not contribute their skills and energies to solving society's problems, is totally wrong. They are doing a task that is essential for our future, developing new skills and ways of living that will provide models for others as necessity pushes more of us in that direction. Nothing could be more important. The pioneers are opening up new economic territory where subsequent settlers can join them.[5]

Johnson is right. It is an enormous challenge to live modestly in a culture that barrages us moment by moment with the message that the only good living is high living, bought with the big dollars that come with success in the career culture. But it can be done. When we decide as individuals and families that enough is enough, modest living will become easier, not only for us but for our communities and our nation.

STAGE-SIX GROWTH

The task of adult growth is indeed a difficult one, for as we have seen, so much of the work involves letting go of attachments to the products and processes of earlier life stages. As young women, determined to be accepted as equals into the patriarchal world of the career culture, we passionately identify ourselves with our careers and our institutions, often to the point of having no other selves than the career selves we wear to work. If we are attempting to carry two careers—mothering and a professional career—we find ourselves anxiously split between our public and private lives, unable to give as much as we would like to either. In either case, as our idealistic dreams and visions about the career culture begin to fade and reality sets in, we often feel alienated and disaffiliated, disillusioned, and discontent with our positions and our roles.

At this point of disillusionment, paradoxically, growth begins, for not until we are ready to let go of our old illusions can our eyes open to new visions. Not until we are willing to release ourselves from the old affiliations that maintain us in a rigid role or persona are we free to try out new ones. Not until we have the courage to suffer the isolation and loneliness that inevitably comes when we separate ourselves from the central work culture of our time are we able to design new work—work that is collaborative, nurturing, sustaining, and mutually empowering for all who come together to do it. Only then can we see ourselves as selves-in-community, serving the needs of others as we serve our own.

There are, of course, many routes to growth. We grow by going to school, moving to a new culture, marrying into a new family. We grow through illness, through death, through grief and loss. In every major life change lie the seeds of growth.

For women in our culture during the present decade of critical change and challenge, perhaps the most significant area of growth is our work. We are likely to spend more hours in work than in any other area of our lives, and we give away far more of ourselves through our work than through any other activity. Through work, we are challenged or bored; pleased or frustrated; satisfied or made discontent; renewed or drained of energy. Through work, we are constantly called upon to establish our own authority or to yield to the authority of others. Through work, we are able to grow to our fullest potential or forced to stagnate.

It is no surprise, then, if women who disaffiliate themselves from the patriarchal authority structures of the career culture and establish a new kind of work find that their experience has helped them to reach a new level of freedom and psychological and physical health. It is also no surprise that they are not likely to duplicate their former salaries, or that they feel they are working on the margin, or that they sometimes feel panicked at the thought of buying their own health care and life insurance, which are offered as paid benefits by many employers. These are the risks and the costs of life on the outskirts of the career culture; it is a part of our growth to face them realistically and to compare them against the hidden costs of continuing to work as we are presently working.

Stage-six growth, then, involves the willingness to risk, to dream, to think new thoughts, to dare new deeds. At this level, growth means flexibility, receptivity, and an ability to accept things as they happen. It also involves the willingness to be responsible for ourselves, to learn self-reliance, to pay the price for true independence. It involves learning new habits of modest living, in the face of heightening demands from business and government for higher and higher levels of consumer spending. This kind of growth is active, in the sense that we must seek out what we passionately want; and it is passive, in the sense that we must wait patiently to see what comes. This growth is both intimately engaged with the world and quietly detached from it. Above all, it is as deeply committed to the good of others as it is to our own individual good.

Stage-six growth is fully realized when we have found and committed ourselves to our right livelihood.

Part

| 2 |

WORK
OF
THEIR OWN

The girl and the woman, in their new, their own unfolding, will but in passing be imitators of masculine ways, good and bad, and repeaters of masculine professions. After the uncertainty of such transitions it will become apparent that women were only going through the profusion and the vicissitude of those (often ridiculous) disguises in order to cleanse their most characteristic nature of the distorting influences of the other sex.

RAINER MARIA RILKE

INTRODUCTION:
THREE WOMEN

DOING THE RESEARCH FOR THIS BOOK, I BEGAN TO SEE MYSELF AS A collector of women's stories. I came to feel enormously privileged that the women I talked with were willing to share their histories openly and with so little reservation, even though their experiences were a radical counterpoint to the standard career-culture success story. I also came to understand how little we actually know about the pain and loneliness that successful women suffer every day behind the mask of their career selves. Although the media may be brimming over with so-called true-life coverage of the woman behind the desk, most of the stories we read are nothing but glossy make-believe that extols women's storybook successes in the career culture and obscures their real-life anguish. For the past decade, women's stories have climaxed with the big promotion, the pay raise, and the corner office with a window and an impressive glass-topped desk.

But the heroine's journey does not end in the executive suite: That is what career leavers want us to know; that is why they were so willing to tell me their stories and so anxious to hear how other career leavers were confronting the difficult task of shaping work of their own. "Somebody needs to tell women what success really costs," one woman told me. "We need to hear what's behind the glitz. We need to hear the truth about how women feel about their work."

In her book *Writing a Woman's Life,* Carolyn Heilbrun describes the difficulty of telling women's true stories. Writing about women's biography, she describes "how women's lives have been contrived" by the patriarchal culture in order to present them as something they are not. Even in the case of autobiography, she says, women have often been led to write untruthfully, casting themselves—at least in part—in the roles their

157

audiences and publishers expect them to play. Heilbrun is writing about accomplished women whose real achievements were often obscured by their biographers or by themselves, and whose pain is, "like the successes, muted, as though the women were certain of nothing but the necessity of denying both accomplishment and suffering." She comments: "Well into the twentieth century, it continued to be impossible for women to admit into their autobiographical narratives the claim of achievement, the admission of ambition, the recognition that accomplishment was neither luck nor the result of the efforts or generosity of others."[1]

In the last two decades, what has been written in the popular media falsifies women's lives just as Heilbrun suggests, but rather differently than she describes. The stories about women's individual and collective achievements in the career culture, impressive as they are, are what Phyllis Rose in *Writing on Women* calls partial biographies. They tell only a portion of the truth, and what they tell is not told impartially. Indeed, what is left out of these success stories may be far more important than what is included. Rarely do we hear of the physical cost of high-stress, high-powered competition; of the sacrifice of relationships; of the loss of the inner life. Because so much of the pain and sadness is omitted, the emphasis falls falsely—on the single theme of the great reward that comes from resourceful effort, sustained industry, and loyalty to the corporation. For American women, the Cinderella myth—the poor girl whose beauty and goodness earned her marriage with the prince and the privilege of living happily ever after—has been replaced by the Horatia Alger story: Use your wit and resourcefulness to earn a marriage to the corporation, and live happily ever after.

To confront such a myth as myth and to tell the truth are difficult tasks. In the preceding chapters, I attempted to get at the truth in an analytic way, reporting the experiences of career leavers according to a model of stages in the career-leaving process. In this section, I relate the myth narratively, through the stories of three women who abandoned successful careers because their work no longer met their deep needs for personal growth. Each story shows a woman working through a crisis of change in her life—one that emerges when compelling demands for a broader, more flexible, more creative work style begin to challenge a confining career pattern, requiring the woman to confront old issues, weigh new options, and reorient herself to her work. The three stories together invite us to witness the wide range of ways in which human beings reshape past selves to meet the new demands of the present and the unknown mysteries of the future.

During the three years that I did research for this book, I was privileged to witness women in the process of composing their lives, to use the graceful and hopeful term that Mary Catherine Bateson has given us. The art of composing a life, Bateson says, is an improvisational art. It involves combining known ways of living and being with unfamiliar ways and is "rich with the possibility of delicious surprise." As I watched these women making a new kind of sense of their lives, I was reminded of Bateson's remark and her description of her own life: a "sort of desperate improvisation in which I was constantly trying to make something coherent from conflicting elements to fit rapidly changing settings." As a reporter of the process of career leaving, it has been my privilege to know women as improvisational artists, creatively taking advantage of the odd twists and turns life offers, the chance openings, the dislocations. I agree with Bateson that we must explore the creative potential of lives like these, "interrupted and conflicted lives, where energies are not narrowly focused or permanently pointed toward a single ambition. These are not lives without commitment, but rather lives in which commitments are continually refocused and redefined."[2]

The work of reporting is a challenging task, for I must relate not only the outer events that make up the dynamic, dramatic course of the individual's life, but also the inner events, which are much less easily expressed or revealed. Writing about the inner life is difficult, because our private selves are often unknown to us and scarcely revealed to others—even to those with whom we are most intimate. We are often afraid of our inner lives or, at the least, tentative about them. There is so often a discontinuity between outer and inner. Contradictions abound between what we feel within ourselves and how those feelings are expressed in outer action.

It is a different, but no less daunting, challenge to report each woman's story in a context that preserves its basic essence while it is sufficiently disguised to protect her privacy. All three narratives in part 2 of this book have been altered in fundamental ways—in setting, in the facts of personal history, and so on. With some trepidation, I have not disguised the woman's career field, feeling that this choice reveals the basic nature of the choosing self and helps illuminate the meaning of the woman's life. I have designed a fictional setting for each of the three narrators, but the setting reflects very nearly the real one she designed for herself. Except for fictionalizing some elements of the narrators' identities, I have not fictionalized any events of their lives, outer or inner, and the words that are attributed to these women are their words. My chief aim in telling these stories has been truthfulness, in the sense of being true to the woman's life. It is a responsibility that has weighed heavily on me as I have edited and re-edited each story.

This editorial process included compressing hundreds of pages of typed transcripts and other written materials into brief narrative form. I have tried to arrange the material in a way that highlights the conflicts and changes in the narrator's outer experience and the private course of the inner journey to wholeness and peace with herself. I chose the first-person, present-tense narrative to help convey the sense of personal immediacy that I enjoyed as I got to know these women.

The reader has a no less demanding task than mine as a reporter. Each narrator exemplifies in a number of fundamental ways the process of career leaving as it is described in the earlier chapters of this book. Each also portrays the crises and challenges experienced by many other women: perhaps all women who have chosen to enter the career culture and then to abandon it. I hope that you will match these women's outer and inner experiences with your own and those of women you know. In this way we can develop a stronger sense of our collective experience—more precisely, our experiences as a collective. Only when we can begin to see the unique experiences and meanings of our lives against the background of the lives of other women can we see ourselves wholly, truly, and deeply.

8

MARGO:
PROFESSIONAL MOTHER

*M*argo Hammett wrote to me when she read about my research project in *Mothering*. "I had a very successful career in the airline industry for ten years before leaving to have children," her letter began. "I worked as a flight attendant for five years, then was promoted to a supervisory position and then to senior manager. I traveled a great deal as part of my job and although I wanted to start a family, I couldn't seem to get pregnant. So after a lot of soul-searching and discussion with my husband, Alex, about the huge loss in family income we'd suffer if I quit, I decided that we couldn't *buy* time or children. So I found a very low-paying local job as an exercise instructor and quit the airline. I was pregnant in about a month. That was nine years ago. Never for one moment have I regretted the decision."

Margo and I have talked several times on the phone, but this will be our first meeting. She and Alex live with their three daughters in a medium-size city about 125 miles from St. Louis. Their residential neighborhood is a shady oasis where the streets are named for the trees that line them: Willow, Maple, Oak. The small frame bungalows, built in the 1930s and 40s, are fronted by squares of green grass sliced neatly by flower-bordered concrete walks. Next door to the left, a wooden box sits on the curb, bearing a handprinted sign: Free Tracts. Take one and read. Ye do err not knowing the scriptures. The word *err* is printed in large red letters and underlined twice. A Harley-Davidson motorcycle is parked on the front porch of the house to the right.

On the Hammett's front porch is parked an orange-and-white plastic tricycle. A wooden baby swing hangs from the ceiling. It is late summer and hot, but when Margo opens the screen door and invites me in, the tree-shaded house seems cool. The living room is small, two walls lined with books, the third with shelves for the stereo and television set. There is a trampoline in the middle of the floor and a wicker basket of children's books in the corner. We are surrounded by a mob of children clamoring for my attention.

In the midst of the babble of children's voices, I find a chair to sit in—a comfortable oak rocker with curved wooden arms that reminds me of the one in my grandmother's front parlor— and Margo settles herself on the sofa. She is a petite, feminine-looking woman in her early forties with high cheekbones and a finely cut nose. She is fashion-model pretty even without makeup; her dark hair is casually loose to her shoulders. Her loose turquoise blouse is the same shade as her blue eyes. She is wearing faded jeans and sandals.

When I sort out the mob of children, I discover that there are only three: eight-year-old Karen, five-year-old Marjorie, and thirteen-month-old Victoria, who has just learned to walk. Almost without effort, Margo quiets the two older girls, dispatching them into the dining room to play with Barbie's ice-cream parlor and assuring them that they will make real ice cream later, after the company has gone. The girls move into the other room but are scarcely out of earshot. Margo holds out her arms to Victoria, who climbs onto her lap to nurse. Margo pulls up her blue blouse, and the baby snuggles close. While the baby nurses, Margo talks about the experience of mothering and about her own mother, who was a strong role model for her daughter.

"I always thought of Mom as a powerful woman," she says, "although she doesn't come across that way—intentionally, I mean, as if she wanted to use her power. She was a nurse for a family-practice doctor. When I was in kindergarten, my teacher sometimes dropped me off at the office after school. Later, when I was in high school, I sometimes worked there as a receptionist. I liked being around Mom at work, because she knew so much. People were always asking her questions, consulting her, and she always knew the answers. She was very competent, but in a warm, caring way. Maybe that was what made people come to her with their questions." She pauses and cocks her head to the girls' voices which have grown suddenly sharper. Then, deciding that her intervention is not necessary just now, she goes on talking about her mother.

"Somehow, I got the idea that there was never a big gap for Mom between what she did for the people at work and what she did for the three of us—me, my dad, and my older sister. At home, she was just as efficient as she was in the office. She did the laundry and cooked our meals. We almost never ate out."

Margo's mother had been a nurse before she was married. Her husband, faced with her firm intention to work and the undeniable usefulness of a second income, agreed that she should go on with her career after the children were born. Margo's father seems not to have been a man to stand up against determined opposition. He was reserved and not outwardly affectionate. At home, he did not talk about his work in the airplane factory. Now, Margo feels that her father might not have been happy in his job.

"He never seemed to want to move up the ladder. Looking back now, I wonder about that. He didn't seem to have much ambition to get ahead. He was a gentle-giant sort of person. He wasn't very competitive."

Margo slid into her career without giving a lot of thought to what she was doing. "The only thing I was sure of was that I wanted a career for myself. I didn't want to get married and have children. My older sister's marriage wasn't happy, and the guys I dated didn't measure up to my standards." She chuckles self-consciously. "I guess I was kind of choosy. I don't know, maybe I was snobby."

After high school, Margo lived at home for two years while she attended a local college, then moved to Kansas City and enrolled at the state university, majoring in sociology. Looking for a job that would pay living expenses, she went to the ticket counter at the airport and put in her application. She was surprised and enormously flattered when an airline offered her a job as a flight attendant at nineteen thousand dollars a year.

"The money seemed like a fortune," she says. She touches her baby's pink cheek, twists a dark curl of baby-girl hair around her finger. "It meant leaving school, but I jumped at the opportunity. I thought it was something I might not be offered again. And I loved the work. Every day was a fantastic adventure, getting on a plane, flying to exotic places, having fun. I had a great apartment in a yuppie suburb, terrific clothes, a new car." Victoria stops nursing and sits up. Margo pulls down her blouse as the baby climbs off her lap.

"I think I made a good choice under the circumstances," she says thoughtfully. "I'm easy with people; I adapt well to new situations; I'm usually cool in a crisis. So I had the kind of skills you need when you're handling large groups of people in an airplane. But sometimes I'm sorry I didn't stay in school and find out what other things I could do. I might have been good in a field like . . ." She waves her hand. "Oh, I don't know what. But I wish I had explored that side of things more. I guess maybe I was lucky to end up in a career that fit me so well, especially since I gave so little thought to what I was doing when I got into it."

Margo had been flying for three years when she met Alex. He was managing a record store and working toward a business degree at the university in the suburb where Margo lived. "I wasn't in a big rush to get into a relationship. Being gone a lot was my protection against getting involved. Any time I felt pressured, I'd say, 'Got to work now, got to fly a trip.'"

Despite Margo's hectic here-and-gone life, her relationship with Alex flourished. Within a year, they were married. "Of course, I was making a lot more money than he was," Margo remarks, in an offhand way.

"Was that a problem?" I ask. She frowns, reluctant to sound critical of her husband but wanting to face the issue honestly, wanting to remember how it was between them ten years ago. Her words come slowly.

"Back then, I didn't think it was. But now I look back and see some big, glaring things and I realize, yes, maybe it was a problem. I think he had the idea that a man should make more money than his wife. Also, maybe he had the idea that a wife should have more time at home."

They didn't have to confront the issue directly, because only two months after they were married, the airline moved its headquarters to St. Louis. Margo had to decide whether to commute or move. "Alex and I liked the suburb where we were living. It was more like a small town, really, not like a part of the city at all. But we finally decided, yes, we'd see what it was like. Neither of us had lived in a city before. We'd treat it like an adventure."

Margo and Alex lived in St. Louis for almost two years. Alex found a job in a large computer-software firm, a position he enjoyed. But both of them disliked the city, the freeway traffic, the noise, the absence of green spaces. "Alex was alone a lot," Margo says. "He and I really had separate lives. My life was focused on my work at the airline, his was focused on his work with computers. When we were together, things were good. But I was flying a lot of the time and there were long stretches—five or six days—when we didn't see one another."

Something in her voice makes me ask another question. Did Alex like that kind of life—being apart so much of the time? The answer, again, comes slowly. "I thought so, back then. I mean, he certainly knew what he was getting into when he married me. He knew I'd be gone a lot, which meant he'd be alone. When I was flying, he could do pretty much what he wanted, which meant that he had a lot of personal freedom. But I found out years later, when we could talk about it more easily, that the situation made him feel really insecure. By that time I'd gotten promoted to supervisor and was on my way up the corporate ladder. I was making even more money—more than I did before and more than he was. To him, it seemed like I led a glamorous life, managing all these people, doing all this exciting stuff."

After two years of living in the city, Margo and Alex decided it would be good to move to a quieter place. Alex had family ties in the small town where they now live, and when Margo was promoted to senior manager, they decided to move. "It seemed like the right thing to do," Margo says. "Alex wanted to finish school at the university here, and it was a lot nicer place to live than a big city."

The doorbell interrupts our conversation. I am introduced to Joannie, a pleasant woman who has brought her six-year-old daughter to play with Karen and Marjorie while she takes her son to the library. The three of us chat comfortably about children for a few minutes—mother-talk about toilet training and kids' books and measles. Then the little girls disappear into the bedroom to scavenge for more Barbies, and Joannie leaves, her son in tow. Perhaps feeling left out of the excitement, Victoria climbs up on Margo's lap and nuzzles her breast. Margo lifts her blue blouse once more.

Back to the subject. How, I ask, did her employer feel about her decision to live 125 miles away from the corporate offices? "It was easier for me to commute by plane than by freeway," Margo tells me. "I'd catch the first plane out and be at my desk in forty minutes. Anyway, I was beginning to make some choices for me." She emphasizes the word with a firm nod of her head. "I knew what was right for me and Alex. And I had this theory that what's good for the employee is also good for the employer. My VP agreed. She had also worked her way up through the ranks and she understood. If moving was what it took to make me happy, okay, because if I was happy, I'd do a good job."

At first, the new arrangement worked well. Margo's vice-president permitted her to work a flex-time schedule: longer hours and a shorter week. She gave Margo the freedom of managing her staff of eighty the way she wanted to. She also encouraged Margo to continue doing a substantial amount of in-flight supervision, which Margo believed improved customer service and enabled her to maintain a close relationship with her staff.

"But after a while," Margo says, "things got not so good. I was hardly ever home, which put me under a lot of pressure and wasn't good for Alex. And the airline—well, the whole industry was in trouble so there was a lot of anxiety around the main office, a lot of stress. I definitely didn't feel like a member of the corporate family." She frowns, shakes her head. "Customer service ought to be one of the most important concerns of an airline, wouldn't you think? But as far as corporate was concerned, the flight attendant management group was just 'the girls.' They were very condescending to us, very patronizing. For a long time, I had seen that attitude as a barrier, but I was willing to work around it because I saw my VP doing her best and helping the rest of us get ahead. Then she quit. That changed everything."

The story is one I have heard before. Under the sheltering wing of a sympathetic mentor who has already made it up the ladder, Margo had developed her own management style, including a willingness to let people take time off, when it was necessary, to deal with family responsibilities.

"It paid off," Margo says with clear pride in her creation of a productive, cooperative working group. "My people were always willing to stay late and do what had to be done because we were a team. We were all in it together." But the sympathetic VP resigned her job to start a family, and the new VP, a woman brought in from outside the company, did not approve of Margo's management style or the amount of time she spent out of the office doing in-flight supervision. She also did not approve of Margo's flexible work schedule or the fact that she lived so far away.

"She thought I was mothering the supervisors," Margo says, frowning. "But I didn't see it that way. I thought that if you wanted employees to be productive, you had to help them, give them suggestions. And you had to care about them. Not just say 'I care'—that's easy—but really care. You had to know the kids' names and the fact that somebody's husband's mother died last week. I cared, and my staff knew it. This new VP had no tolerance for a personal life. With her, it was all business and nothing else."

The nursing baby sighs and snuggles closer, almost asleep but determined not to give up a good thing. Margo's face softens as she looks down at her youngest daughter. "Something else was happening to me, too. I was beginning to want a child. When my boss left to have a family, that gave me something to think about. I was twenty-nine, and if I was going to get pregnant, it was time. I figured I'd have the baby and then go back to work, the way everybody else was doing it. Nothing to it."

To their friends, it must have looked like Margo and Alex had everything they wanted. They were living in a place they enjoyed. Margo was on her way up in her career—the next rung up the ladder was a corporate vice-presidency. With her salary and Alex's, they were making close to fifty thousand dollars a year. "But we were spending it all on good living," Margo says. "Every dime. My flying was usually free, but occasionally I wanted to be home on a weekend and the flights were full, so I'd buy a ticket. We had two expensive cars and season tickets to the Chiefs' games. We ate out a lot and went to movies and traveled. If we didn't have anything to do, we'd hop a plane to Vegas." She shakes her head with a wondering look, not quite believing that she and her husband had once been capable of spending so much money.

"But after a while, I began to rethink the way we were living, spending all that money with nothing to show for it. Especially, I reconsidered what I'd do if I had a child. Several of the women I supervised had babies. If I had an early meeting, I'd stay overnight with them. In the morning, I'd see them bundle up this precious baby and give him to somebody else. When they got home at night, they'd be too tired to play with him, just feed and bathe him and put him to bed. That bothered me. I began to think that if I had a child, maybe I couldn't do that. Maybe I couldn't give him up to a care giver just so I could go back to work."

Against the background of these considerations, Margo's conflict with her boss continued. Finally, after struggling with the situation for nine months, she decided that she simply could not take it anymore. She ticks off the items on her fingers: "The woman wanted me to move back to the city. She wanted me to stop flying and do desk work. She wanted me to distance myself from the people I supervised. She even told me to put her name on a complicated piece of research that I had done on federal regulations. That really rubbed me the wrong way." Still, there was not any particular event that pushed Margo to leave her management position. "It was," she says, "just a culmination of everything—the way she was, the way I was. We just didn't fit together. But I guess what really decided it for me was the sense that the energy I was spending on the job would be better spent at home. I'd get more rewards."

Given the state of the Hammetts' finances, the decision was difficult. They had few savings, and Alex had just started a new job in a security firm. If Margo quit, their income would be reduced to a fraction of what it had been.

"The decision was tough, really tough. Alex and I spent weeks talking, going back and forth, trying to decide. It wasn't just the money, either, although the idea of losing my paycheck was pretty scary. I felt terrible because I couldn't satisfy this woman, even though I thought she was wrong. Sometimes I felt like a failure because I couldn't do it her way. And I felt guilty, too, leaving the people I supervised." She makes a wry face. "I know I'm very good at guilt. But I cared about my people, and I knew their lives would be different when I wasn't there to fend for them. So I called them in and wrote evaluations for their permanent files—by hand, so the secretary wouldn't see them. I talked to them about their strengths. I tried to encourage them because I didn't want them to give up."

I feel compelled to break in. "But you were giving up, weren't you?" I ask. "How did you feel, encouraging your people to go on as if nothing had happened when you were leaving?"

Margo bites her lip. "It was an incredibly stressful conflict for me. I was a role model, I'd made it, and I was deserting them.

Sure, I felt guilty. Who wouldn't? But I couldn't make the choice for them, go or stay. It's something every woman has to decide for herself."

For the short run, Margo compromised. She resigned her management position, but to support the family finances, she stayed with the airline as a flight attendant. That gave her a paycheck, but her absences continued to be difficult for Alex. Most importantly, hard as she tried, she could not get pregnant.

"There wasn't a physical problem—I just wasn't home on the right days. Finally, I decided I had to do something. I made a choice. No more flying." She resigned from the airline and found a job in a local health spa, teaching aerobics. Her eight-hundred-dollar-a-month salary was one-quarter of her management salary. She was pregnant in a month.

The aerobics job lasted until her fifth month of pregnancy, when she was fired and went home to collect unemployment and wait for the baby. "Getting fired was a terrible shock, because we'd been counting on the money. But it turned out to be a blessing in disguise. I had time to read about birth and think about how I wanted to raise our child. I decided that I wasn't going to be a half-way parent. I became very interested in home birthing and breastfeeding and home schooling. But the most important thing was deciding that I wouldn't look for another job, never mind a career. I would stay home with the baby. I would become a *professional* mother. All that from four months of reading!" She laughs at herself but it is an affectionate laugh that lets me know she is proud of the choices she made.

When the unemployment checks stopped coming, financial realities closed in. Margo's joy in her new life turned to despair. "Alex had a job in a security firm, but it didn't pay very much. We knew our income would drop when I left the airline, but it was a matter of what was more important: the money or our lives. We talked about living on less and tried to figure out how to do it. To cut housing expenses, we bought a new mobile home with payments that turned out to be as high as rent." She chuckles, remembering their naiveté.

"We stopped eating out and gave up our season football tickets—big deal, right? We sold my Fiat and bought a small Chevy." She throws back her head and laughs outright. "It was brand-new, mind you, and we still figured we were saving. We

weren't smart. We should have bought a used car with no payments. But we were so hooked on credit." She stops laughing,
grows very serious. "That was our problem. When we wanted
something, we'd put it on a credit card. We never asked ourselves
how we were going to pay or how much interest they were charging. And we never once put a pencil to our total spending. It was
a bad time, a terrible time." She shakes her head. "Except for
Karen's birth, it was a really black time."

Margo had wanted a home birth, but Karen was born by
Caesarean. Margo was soon pregnant again. Although Alex had
found a better-paying management job working for the county,
with computers, they were still far behind with their payments.
Finally, in desperation, they sold the trailer for what they could
get and rented a small two-bedroom house.

"We cut back on everything we could," Margo says fiercely.
"Every single thing. Alex had a county car, so we sold the Chevy
and his truck. Then we got a really lucky break. The manager of
an apartment building offered us an apartment for practically
nothing because he wanted Alex to park the county car there as
security. That really turned the corner for us. We cleaned up our
bills and threw away all our credit cards. Now, we're on a cash-
only basis. If we don't have the cash, we don't buy. It's as simple as
that. We hand down clothes, trade with friends, buy used things.
We buy in quantity, in a food co-op. I'm constantly looking for
ways to do more with less money."

"Did you have any regrets?" I ask, thinking about the financial security of the management career she had left. But Margo is
not thinking of what she gave up. "You bet I had regrets," she
says firmly. "I wish we'd planned better. We were wearing rose-
colored glasses. We only thought about this wonderful life we
were going to lead, and we didn't think about paying the bills."

I ask the question a different way. "Did you consider going
back to flying when money got really tight?" She answers without hesitation.

"I couldn't leave my children. Karen was such a wonderful
first child, so bright and affectionate. She'd hug me and say: 'I'm
so proud of you, Mommy,' because that's what we'd say to her. I
was proud of us, too, even though we weren't managing well financially. I knew we were right not to leave the children, no matter what it cost. What you give them is theirs for life. If you don't

170

give it to them, they don't get it." She laughs. "You know that old saying, The hand that rocks the cradle rules the world? I really believe it. If you let somebody else rock the cradle, that's what you get—second-hand cradle rocking. But I did think about a few things I could do. I worked in the mall one Christmas during Alex's off-hours to bring in a little extra money." Her face becomes very still. "And then Helen was killed, and I had to deal with that."

Helen was Margo's older sister. She died in an automobile accident when Margo's second child was a year old. "It was a pivotal thing for me. I was living my new way of life, but I hadn't figured out how it all fit, how I was going to find meaning in it. After Helen died and I was struggling with the grief, I knew I needed to be doing something. Being home with my children was the most important thing I could do, yes—raising good people, good citizens, educating them, loving them. But I had to do something for other people. I was already involved with La Leche League, which encourages new moms to breastfeed. Then I went to a seminar for lactation consultants—people who teach breastfeeding. That's when it came to me what I could do."

Margo's voice rises, as if she has plugged herself into a new source of energy and enthusiasm. "I already knew that breastfeeding was really vital, because it had made such an enormous difference in my life. So I volunteered to teach. For a couple of years, I taught at the county prenatal clinic. Then the hospital asked me to teach as a paid consultant. It wasn't much money to start with, but it made me feel terrific, because I was doing something important. And it's developed into more things. They'll call me and say: 'We've got this mom who's having problems. Can you help?' I get paid at the nursing rate, which is really good. This year, they've also asked me to develop a parenting class and a childbirth education class."

Victoria is asleep by now, one arm flopped down, baby fingers curled into a vulnerable fist. There is a moment's silence. I ask, "What's ahead for you? What do you see yourself doing in the long term?"

"I love the breastfeeding work," Margo says. "It affects not only the babies, but also the moms. It symbolizes all the mothering they do. It makes their lives more full, and their bond with their children more real, more concrete. I think it can mean the difference in our society. To me, teaching breastfeeding is a way of teaching mothering. For the future, I want to take the lactation consultant's exam and have a practice."

This is a whole new area for me, one I have never heard of, and I am intrigued. I am also intrigued with the thought that Margo's at-home work as a professional mother is leading her toward a profession where she works with other mothers, helping them to become what she is. "Would a lactation practice provide you with enough to live on, if that were ever necessary?" I ask.

It is a question Margo has thought about already. "Yes, especially with the base I have now. I've been teaching at the hospital, working with different doctors and nurses. The longer I do that, the more credibility I have." She pauses, listening to the louder sounds of children's play coming from the direction of the bedrooms. "I want to have something ready for the time in my life when the girls' demands on me are different, so I can more easily let them go. I want to be ready for something that's satisfying to me. And I want to bring in some money so that Alex can do more of what he wants to do."

Margo had just started teaching at the hospital when Alex decided it was his turn to make a career change. He had a good position with the county, but he wanted more free time to develop and market a promising product he has invented. Alex quit his job, and the Hammetts decided to start a painting business that would give Alex more flexibility than an eight-to-five job. Alex had the experience and the painting equipment, and Margo knew what it took to weather a season of low income.

"This time, we planned better. We'd bought this house and we knew exactly how much money we had and how long we could hang on. If the painting business didn't work out, Alex knew he could get another job without a lot of trouble. We started out with several big contracts, but we had trouble with our employees so we scaled back and took over the work ourselves. We enjoyed it, the kids could go with us, and Alex got the free time he needed to work on the invention." She sighs. "But then I got pregnant again. We'd let our health insurance lapse—being self-employed, the cost was sky-high. So Alex had to give up the business and look for a job that paid benefits."

The Hammetts were lucky. Alex found a position as a programmer at just over thirty thousand a year, with insurance coverage for Margo's pregnancy. His employer lets him take flex-time, and he uses it to market the product he has developed. To date, he has made sales in the United States and Canada, and the market seems wide open.

"It would be nice if Alex's idea actually made some money," Margo says wistfully. "It's difficult sometimes. I especially wish we could put something away toward the kids' educations, but I'm not sure many people are doing that, even on two salaries."

I ask the question that I ask of everyone in the study. "Do people ever imply that you're not living up to your full potential because you don't have a career?"

"But I do have a career," Margo replies firmly. She lifts her chin. "I am raising my children. I am home schooling them. I am a mother." Then she relaxes. "But I know what you're asking." She laughs. "I hear it from family friends who think we've failed because we don't have stuff, who think I've blown it. I could've had the kids and gone back to work, and we'd have plenty of money. But I try not to let it get to me. I don't care about having a lot of stuff. I guess I'm the one who's pushed us toward non-material values. And because I'm the one who works at it, it's easier for Alex. He comes home to a house where everyone is content, the clothes are clean, and I've figured out something to cook even if we can't go to the grocery store until Saturday. But he's got to work, too. He's got to support this family. We're a team."

Karen comes in with a sack of salted chips, wanting to know if their teddy bears can have a picnic in the bedroom closet. Margo shakes her head to the chips, the first "no" I have heard from her since I arrived. "I think bears would rather have apples," she says, playing along with the game. "And there's some orange juice in the refrigerator." Karen goes happily off, and our conversation turns to lifestyle choices.

"I'm more interested in teaching the girls good eating habits than I am in every little thing that goes into their mouths," Margo says. "I want to teach them to read labels and make intelligent choices. We don't eat much meat, and this past year we eliminated most dairy products, although I occasionally buy cheese. We have a dozen chickens in the backyard for eggs. And I have a garden. I cook lots of tofu and beans, soyburgers, potatoes and grains, all sorts of pasta and vegetables." She laughs. "I try to get one simple, nourishing dish a day into them and not worry the rest of the time."

It strikes me that Margo gives more sustained thought to teaching her children than she does to feeding them. Home schooling is a subject on which she has passionate opinions, and she holds a volunteer position in the local county home-school association. She prepares a curriculum for the two older girls, designs their lessons and field trips, and takes courses to prepare herself as a teacher. The laundry room doubles as a schoolroom, with desks and a blackboard and maps on the wall. Even breakfast is an opportunity for teaching and learning.

"I pick out things to read from the newspaper at breakfast," she tells me, "and we go to the library several times a week." It was at the library recently that five-year-old Marjorie cornered a librarian and lectured her sternly on the virtues of home schooling. "When we got in the car, I tried to talk to Marjorie about how other people might feel when she criticizes that way. But the girls are proud of what we're doing. And so am I. Whether we send our kids to school or teach them at home, teaching is a big part of our responsibilities as parents. It's something that Alex and I put at the top of our list of things we need to do."

Margo has chosen for her work a complex and challenging task, made more challenging because she lives in a culture that fundamentally devalues mothers and children. But other people's attitudes are not what is important to her, nor does she count the high dollar-cost of leaving her career. What counts for her is the sleeping daughter at her breast and the two daughters picnicking with their teddy bears in the bedroom closet.

9

MARYALICE:
SIGNING OFF, CASHING IN

*M*aryAlice smiles easily, with a smile that lights her green-flecked hazel eyes. When she begins to talk about the career she left, however, her youthfully pixie face becomes intent and her eyes grow dark. MaryAlice shares her feelings readily, interlacing her story with analytic self-reflections that reveal the intense thought she has given to the events of her life and make her narrative seem multilayered. Talking with women, listening to them compose their lives, I often have the sense of looking into the past through the lens of the present and of hearing facts through the sometimes sharpening, sometimes softening filter of feeling. That sense is very strong as I listen to MaryAlice.

"After sixteen years in radio, I was making one hundred thousand dollars a year as general sales manager of a large station. I was cool and confident—why not? I had everything I'd aimed for. But that was on the outside. On the inside, I was afraid. I was worried that I couldn't stay on top. In sales, somebody's always judging, measuring, evaluating you by the bottom line—and you judge and measure yourself. You have to, and you have to be ruthless about it. If you don't force yourself to get better and better, you're automatically getting worse. And there's no such thing as job security. I was afraid that if I didn't stay ahead of my own past performance and ahead of the competition, I'd be out. I worked incredible hours, ignored family and friends, just to keep that fear—that terror—at bay."

MaryAlice pauses over the words, tasting the old anxiety, finding it bitter even in the recollection. Then she straightens her shoulders and goes on, pushing herself to an honesty that is clearly very painful. The pain shows in her eyes and in the tiny lines around her mouth.

"I was also scared of something else. If I lost my job and the income and prestige that went with it, I was afraid I'd lose my sense of self-worth and identity. Until just a couple of years ago, who I was depended entirely on what I did. What people thought of me depended on what I did. It was my career, my title, the money I made for the corporation and for myself. That was the source of my power."

Her mouth softens, her eyes lighten. "It's different now. I realize that I am exactly who I am, with or without a job. With or without money. I'm free of the old fears—well, most of them. I'd be lying if I didn't admit that there are days when I judge myself and feel that I'm falling short again." She looks down at her slim hands, knits the fingers together. "I got another rejection on a book in the mail today, and it made me doubt myself as a writer. I even fell back into the old fear that I'm not good enough as a person. But I'm not stuck with that fear, the way I used to be. It's just a feeling—it comes, it goes. My foundation as a human being is strong enough now to handle the fear. I'm strong enough, in myself. I don't have to have a career and a title to give me strength."

By the time she finishes her preamble, MaryAlice is smiling. We are sitting over coffee in the living room of her condo, in a neighborhood of elegant condos called Spicetree Village, located in a suburb of San Francisco. The room is tastefully decorated with an combination of antiques and contemporary furniture, and a large shaggy dog named Samson is uneasily asleep on the rug in front of the fire in the brick fireplace, his tail occasionally thumping in a doggy dream. MaryAlice is a slim, petite woman of forty-four, stylishly dressed in a silky beige jumpsuit and strappy heeled sandals, her makeup artistically subdued, her movements graceful. She has a quick, agile wit; her humor is dry; and the laughter that bubbles up freely is often ironic and self-deprecating. MaryAlice reminds me of the Debbie Reynolds I remember from the fifties. She might have been an actress. She was an actress, she tells me, mocking herself.

"All that time I was so successful, so cool, so confident, it was all an act. And I was very good. Nobody ever knew that I felt like a total phony."

MaryAlice grew up on the West Coast, wanting to be an actress because actresses were admired for their beauty, because they had power. "The women I knew had no power at all. They were housewives, secretaries, nuns. The men did all the exciting things, had all the fun, and that was what I admired. My father owned his own plastics business. He knew how to make things, make money. He was an alcoholic but I still admired him. There wasn't much to admire about Mom, as far as I was concerned. She got paid a two-bit salary as a sales clerk, and I didn't think she was very smart. Now, I think she hid her intelligence because she thought it would make other people—especially my father— uncomfortable. She wanted him to love her." She laughs a little, leans forward to pick up a package of cigarettes and lights one.

"I wanted Dad to love me, too. I wanted to look perfect, be perfect so he would approve. But I never got much approval or support from him. From the time I was nine and started acting, it was Mom who drove me to rehearsals and hung around to wait. Mom was the one who came to all my performances, the one who encouraged me." She leans back against the sofa and exhales smoke, remembering. "But I don't think Mom had much confidence in me, either—in what I could do on my own, I mean. I remember once when Elvis Presley came to town. She said: 'Go meet Elvis. Marry him and you can be anybody you want.' She was joking, but in a way she meant it. Southern California was like that, you know? We all had the crazy idea that somebody would marry us and we'd be rich and famous. Or we'd be discovered in a drugstore and voila!—we'd *be* somebody."

But MaryAlice had to make her own discoveries. After graduation, she moved to Los Angeles and got a job as a file clerk in a brokerage house. "That's when I saw where the power was," she says. "Power wasn't in being beautiful, or getting people to like you. Power was in *money*. Women didn't have power because they didn't have money—as simple as that. I decided I was going to have money. But then I got pregnant and married the baby's father, because that's what you did in those days."

She smiles, shrugs, taps her cigarette on the ashtray in wry unspoken comment on the irony of accident. "We moved to southern Oregon so David could work in his dad's store. After Tommy was born I saw an ad in the paper for a job in the local radio station. Next thing I know, I'm the receptionist and I'm also supposed to do a half-hour women's show. The trouble is, I don't know how to cook and I don't have any interest in crafts or sewing. So I improvised."

I think how much of MaryAlice's life has been a matter of

improvisation, making the best of difficult situations not of her deliberate choosing. I smile, thinking how readily adaptive she is. She answers my smile with one of her own, tacitly agreeing with my unspoken observation. "Over a couple of years, I changed the show into an in-depth news show. I took stuff off the [Associated Press] and [United Press] wire and wrote three- or four-minute background pieces on headline stories. And then I thought, well, maybe news is the way I want to go, so I applied for the vacant news director's job. But this was small-town America, remember?" She laughs outright, recalling the provincialism of the time. "Ralph, the station owner, said: 'MaryAlice, that's no job for a woman.' Then a sales position came open, and I told him: 'Okay, Ralph, it's your choice. I can leave, or you can let me sell.'

"So I got the sales job *and* I stayed on the air. By that time, I was writing and producing commercials and voicing them, too. I liked the job because I could be creative and flexible and I could do what I wanted without a lot of interference. And I had energy for other things, too, like writing a book. That was when I wrote my first novel. I stayed with that station for ten years, all during the marriage." She snubs her cigarette and picks up her coffee cup, a half-wistful look crossing her face. "I might still be there if the marriage had survived."

MaryAlice and David were divorced, and MaryAlice took Tommy to San Francisco, expecting to support herself doing radio commercials. But the work did not pay enough, so she looked for a sales job. She was hired as an account executive by a large radio station. "That's when I hit the fast track," she says. She leans forward, elbows on knees.

"The first year I was there, I made twenty-two thousand— no salary, totally commissions. The next year I doubled it. Then they put me on salary-plus, and it shot up into the seventies. After that, a hundred thousand. Part of the reason I did so well in the beginning was that I could write and produce commercials for my clients, which none of the other salespeople could do. But most of my success came from the fact that I wanted to impress the new owner, who had just added this station to his chain. He had a reputation for flying in like Superman to save a dying station." MaryAlice straightens up and does her imitation of Lois Lane, both hands to her breast, a starry-eyed gaze. "I took one look at this man and went, Gasp, my hero! I was inspired, totally inspired. I'd always wanted to please my father, now I wanted to please this man. But getting his approval was even harder than getting Dad's. He'd look impressed by my sales figures, but then he'd shrug and say: 'So what are you going to do next?' I'd laugh and say: 'Who knows? But I'll do something great.' And I'd go charging out the door to do it."

MaryAlice shakes her head in amused sympathy at her compulsion to get ahead, to be the best. "I was so totally driven. *Totally*. It was that need to please the boss, of course—the more he withheld his approval, the harder I'd drive myself to get it. But something else was pushing me, too—something I didn't think about at the time, but I see now. I was raised Catholic, and Catholics believe in original sin. You're born sinful, and you're baptized, and that makes you okay. But somewhere at the back of my head I had the idea that the priest screwed up and didn't get it right for me. I still had it. Original sin."

She smiles a little, raises one arm to lift her dark-blond hair with her fingers, lets it drop. "Or maybe my original sin was being a woman, like my mom. You know, second class. Not good enough. But I didn't cover it up by playing dumb or people pleasing, like my mom. I covered up by being better—better than I'd been the month before, better than the other account execs at the station, better than the account execs at the other stations, better than everybody. There were five guys on the sales staff, plus the house and the national accounts, and I was billing a third of the station's monthly income. I did three times as much as anybody else. I worked harder and smarter, and when I found a trick that succeeded, I'd repeat it. I was a bottom-line workaholic. I'd eat my lunch in the car on the freeway. I was always on the phone. I took clients to breakfast and dinner. I didn't get home until late. Those days, Tommy pretty much raised himself."

MaryAlice worked as an account exec for five years, staying pretty much to herself. "I was the Lone Ranger, which was the way I liked it. I didn't like playing politics with the guys at the station. When it came to in-fighting, they fought dirty, elbows and knees." She grins. "Politics takes too much energy away from making money, which was what I was there for. Five years after I came, there was a major corporate battle and the sales manager got fired."

She flips her hair again. "*I* was the one they promoted," she says proudly, "over five guys. And I'd earned it. But when it happened, there was a helluva lot of squawking. And in about four months, the station manager tried to fire me. He gave me a bunch of good-old-boy shit." She scowls, lowers her chin, purses her mouth to imitate a good old boy. "'In sales, MaryAlice, you're wonder woman, but you can't handle the guys on the sales staff worth a goddamn.'" She lifts her chin, her eyes suddenly fiery. "Well, I'm telling you, I wouldn't take that shit. I went to the president of the corporation and told him it wasn't fair. I had boosted sales in the few months I'd been on the job, but I wasn't getting any support from those yahoos at the station." She pauses, slows down, the energy momentarily dissipated. "I was very angry, but very rational, very straight, very clear. I got my job back and not one of the staff knew I'd been fired."

The success of MaryAlice's exertion of will is impressive, but I cannot help thinking what the effort must have cost—or how much she must have worried about one of the men on her sales staff finding out about her firing and seeing it as an indication of weakness. MaryAlice successfully defended her position as general sales manager for three years. Even though this was the mid-1980s and the economy was in a fast slide, the station's sales were increasing; MaryAlice could manage a confident exterior. Beneath that surface, she was running scared.

"Part of it was me, feeling second-class and phony. Part of it was the local economy, which was taking a nosedive. But a big part of it was the industry, the pressure it puts on you, the constant harping on performance. You did something good, it worked, it boosted the bottom line—but that was ten minutes ago. What are you going to do ten minutes from now? Even if I'd wanted to rest on my laurels, I couldn't. The business wouldn't let me. I could never breathe easy. It was nerve-wracking."

While MaryAlice was focusing most of her energy on keeping her professional life moving, her personal life was a shambles. She shakes her head, thinking back. "A holocaust, that's what it was. I got into this horrible relationship with a man who was alcoholic and verbally abusive, like my father. He was a prima donna and utterly charismatic. But the other side of the power coin was his ability to manipulate. To manipulate me." She picks up her coffee cup, cradles it in her hands, shakes her head.

"I can't believe I was so comfortable with that craziness. I can't believe I let him run my life, treat me the way he did. And it wasn't just me, either—it was my son. The thing I feel worst about is that Tommy was involved. He hated this man. He told me from the beginning, 'This is not going to work, Mom.' And then, when that relationship was finally over, I went out and found somebody else, several somebodies—all just like this guy, alcoholic, manipulative." She laughs sadly. "I guess I thought my mission in life was to get involved with every alcoholic jerk on the face of the earth."

During this time, money was never a problem for Mary-Alice. She shrugs when I ask about her financial situation. "People sometimes say that money is just a way of keeping score. That's how I felt. It wasn't the money I cared about, it was the power that the money symbolized. I was making a lot more than I had time to spend or time to manage. Tommy and I had a nice place to live, I drove a good car. I turned the rest of it over to other people: the bank, the accountant, the stockbroker. The stockbroker would call me with these fantastic tips—real estate partnerships, oil, junk bonds, investments that mostly went bad when the bubble burst." She laughs, but her eyes are narrow, her lips firm. "If I ever get rich again, I'll be smarter. I won't give it to an expert—it's going under my mattress!"

Before long, MaryAlice began to feel that she was no longer in control of the maelstrom that was her life. "Things were coming apart. My last relationship had disintegrated. My son was going to college. I felt tired all the time and frazzled. At the station, we were seventeen percent ahead of the year before, but I was barely keeping up the corporate facade. The competition was so absolutely crazy. It was like running in an endless race, no finish line, no time out to catch my breath, just running, running, running, while the stakes got higher and higher."

As she speaks, MaryAlice makes a spiraling motion with her hands, and her words come faster. "I was competing against every other radio station in town, of course—they all share billing figures. I was also competing against last year, because the CEO—the guy who always asked, So what are you going to do next time?—put me under enormous pressure. Our station was the star of his chain, so when we went to a management conference, we had to look the sharpest, be the brightest, have the best numbers, make the best presentation. I had to outdo, overdo everybody, all the time, on every level."

MaryAlice pauses, out of breath, and I break in with a question. "Is it possible to work in a different way in the environment you're describing?" I ask. MaryAlice thinks a while, shakes her head. "I don't know the answer to that," she says. "The whole industry is incredibly competitive, because you're fighting for dollars and you're fighting for audience. Sales figures and ratings don't lie, of course, so the station's performance is very clear. Our station manager tracked us a year ahead. It would be December and we'd be sold out for three months—and he'd say: 'July is looking soft.'" MaryAlice holds up her hands, makes a funny face. "What? It's *December*! Give me a break! And he'd say: 'I just want you to know, MaryAlice, July is looking soft.' There was always some vulnerability, somewhere. If you were smart, you found the soft spot and filled it before somebody spotted it. It's a helluva way to work." She grins ruefully. "No wonder everybody gets pickled at the end of the day."

As a child, MaryAlice had lived with an alcoholic father. As an adult, she surrounded herself with alcoholic men. She did not consider herself an alcoholic, because she says she wasn't physically capable of drinking as much as her drinking partners. But she sometimes worried about how much she drank and whether she could quit. When she became sales manager and began to drink with her staff after work, the drinking escalated.

"We used to joke about it being an alcohol culture," MaryAlice says, "but it was no joke. We'd have beer or cocktails with clients at lunch. When the staff and I knocked off for the day, we'd happy-hour. Lots of times, we'd hang around for dinner and drinks. Then there'd be parties." She shakes her head. "When you're dancing on a razor blade, you drink to dull the pain. You tell yourself you have to—if you don't, you'll go nuts. Anyway, it was the way everybody did business. To do business with these people, I thought I had to drink with them."

But for MaryAlice, doing business—at least in the old way—was about to come to an end. She gets up to put another log on the fire and speaks with her back to me, her voice muffled. "It was December. The general manager called me in and told me that the station was up for sale. Right away, I knew what that meant. When a station sells, the new owner cleans house. Normally, the sales manager stays, and I was outselling every other station in town." She turns around, warming her hands behind her back. She speaks matter-of-factly, but she has to stop to clear her throat. "I still figured I'd get the axe. I had a forty-thousand-dollar base salary and they could save some dollars by bringing in somebody below that. Also, the general manager was the same guy who had fired me three years before. The old CEO, who had protected me, was out of the picture." Her smile is crooked. "Merry Christmas, MaryAlice. You're fired."

"That must have been tough," I say inadequately. MaryAlice comes back to the sofa, sits down, pulls a cushion against her and begins to rock back and forth. "Tough? It was god-awful. If it hadn't been for Tommy, I might have sat in my Mercedes and sniffed diesel fumes. I refused to tell the staff until the end of the year. On New Year's Eve, when everybody was going out to get drunk, I said: 'Hey, guys, tomorrow is the New Year. I represent the old. I'm signing off.' And I went out the door, you know, this tragic figure, brave to the bitter end." She is mocking herself, but beneath the mockery her voice is brittle and she is still rocking back and forth, her arms wrapped around the cushion. "It was like dying, to be cut off from the work that had kept me going all that time. It was like losing a part of myself, both arms, maybe, both legs, my heart."

She pauses, clears her throat again. "But underneath the pain, there was something else, you know?" She tilts her head to look at me. "It sounds crazy, but I was relieved. The market was sliding fast, and I'd already done a budget projection that showed revenues down by fifteen percent. As it turned out, the drop was almost fifty percent. The market was going to give somebody a big fat black eye, and it wasn't going to be me. I had cashed out."

She puts the pillow back in its place and picks up our empty coffee cups. We stand and I follow her to the kitchen, where she pours coffee. Instead of going back into the living room, we sit down at the white formica kitchen counter. The kitchen is elegant and spotless, a picture out of *House Beautiful*. At the end of the counter, a tall vase of red tulips blooms bright against the white.

MaryAlice goes on. "Something else was happening in my life at the same time—something that helped me make sense, somehow, out of the whole sorry mess. A few months before the end, I'd hired a salesman who told us he was a recovering alcoholic. The guys at the station really got a laugh out of that. In our alcohol culture, this bozo would be off the wagon faster than you could say Jack Daniel's. But he wasn't. And when we went out to lunch together and he told me about himself, I could see a lot of me in him."

She twists her mouth. "Too much for comfort, actually. Things were going to hell in a handbasket. Even I could see that my life was out of control and that it was time to try to pull myself together. So I went to see a therapist. She wouldn't work with me unless I went to Al-Anon, so I started going to meetings. When I got fired, I'd been doing Al-Anon and private therapy for about a month." She shakes her head. "Getting fired was a real test. Would I fall apart or hang in there? I hung on and stayed sober. It was bad, very bad. But ironically, because it was so bad and I survived—I knew I'd be okay."

MaryAlice's first instinct was to get another job in the same industry, right away. She had about thirty thousand dollars in savings and a contract the station had to buy out at the rate of nine thousand dollars a month for several more months. "I figured I'd move to San Diego or Seattle and get a fat corporate position—you know, same deal, work hard, make big bucks. But two weeks after I was fired, I went to a therapy weekend, and I talked about my alcoholic family and all the shame I carried, and I figured out why I'd always believed I wasn't good enough—and it didn't have anything to do with original sin, either! I'd been thinking that right after this weekend, I'd start looking for a job, get on with the career. But during that weekend, I just stopped myself. I said, Wait a minute, MaryAlice. It's not what you do, but who you are. You don't have to be somebody you're not any longer. You don't have to pretend."

She rolls her eyes, grins. "Wow—talk about relief! So I told friends I was taking a vacation. When the contract expired, I applied for unemployment. I went for interviews, and I put my name in with a placement agency. But I wasn't really looking. What I wanted to do, I decided, was write."

MaryAlice had written one novel already, back in her twenties, and she had an idea for another one. She started sending out the first book and working on the second. Then she located an agent who read her work and encouraged her. "And ever since, I've been absolutely serious about the writing. In the three years since I left the job, I've written three novels. My agent's job is to send them out and collect the rejection slips." She lifts her chin, laughs. "There for a while, I was expecting any minute that my books would become best sellers and somebody would want to make a movie, and I'd say, Sure, as long as I get to play the lead. I lived on that fantasy for a while. But then I took myself in hand and decided, Whether you ever sell a book or make a movie, Mary-Alice, you're okay. I had to tell myself that three or four times before I believed me. Basically, I am okay now. But that wasn't a realization that came easily. I still compare myself to other people, especially other writers, and I sometimes get upset because my work is as good as theirs or better and it's not published yet. But eighty percent of the time, I know I'm okay as a person, regardless."

Two years after that conversation, MaryAlice and I meet again at her house for lunch. I bring two takeout seafood salads and she pours large icy glasses of raspberry tea. This is a different house, a two-story duplex that MaryAlice and shaggy Samson and a puppy named Delila share with her friend, Richard. I like this house better. It is more comfortable, more lived-in, more real. Out the window, I see a large hole the dogs have dug under the shrubbery, and next door, kids' toys are strewn around the yard.

MaryAlice has changed too: She looks older and thinner and she seems more subdued. She has lost some of her earlier elegance. She looks more lived-in, too. But her smile still comes readily, and the wry, self-ironic humor still sparks her words as she describes what she calls her patchwork—the combination of writing, teaching, doing commercials, and public speaking that earns her a living. The humor is most evident, and most painful, when she talks about her writing.

"I've finished five more novels since I saw you last, and not one has sold yet. Sometimes I wake up at night and think, maybe all these rejection slips mean that God is saying, You're not supposed to do this, MaryAlice. I think, maybe I should find a new agent who'll do multiple submissions, so I can get all the bad news at once, like the chorus in a Greek tragedy." Her mock-ironic laughter is underlaid with fierceness. "But I'm not ready to call it quits yet. In one of my books, one character tells another: 'The only reason you give up is when you don't want the goal any longer.' That's how I feel. I'm not quitting until I stop wanting to see my books in print. The rejections only make me more tenacious." The fierceness relaxes into light laughter again, and she reaches for a breadstick. "I'll probably drown Manhattan in manuscripts before some editor finally says, Okay, Okay, Mary-Alice, we'll publish your books—now, please go away."

While MaryAlice waits for her first big triumph, she's enjoyed a multitude of small ones, for she is still cashing in on the many skills she developed during her sales career. She does freelance work for local advertising agencies, writing advertising copy and brochures. She writes advertising material and product documentation for manufacturing firms. She wrote a playscript on the legislative process for a school district. She designed a curriculum and wrote a workbook for a course on communication skills, and now teaches the course. She writes commercials and voices them. She teaches actors how to make radio and television commercials, and teaches classes in communications skills at the local community college. Recently, she has been invited by several large corporations to offer training in communications.

"I try to be as creative as I can be about getting work," she tells me. "I contact old friends and say, Hey, you need help? I'm available, I write. I list myself in the creative directory. I call people and follow their leads. The process usually ends in an assignment of some kind." She shrugs and forks a piece of shrimp. "It may not pay much, but it's work. It's healthy work, sane work. Not like the old days, with all that competition."

What happened to her competitive drive? "I still compete with myself," she says. "But much less with other people. Somehow, it just doesn't feel good to me. Something happened lately that made me think about my old competitiveness. I write monthly articles for an employee magazine published by a big corporation. The other day, the editor suggested that I should teach my communications courses for this corporation. But I can't, because I know the woman who teaches there, and I couldn't push her aside. That's not the old MaryAlice at all." She puts down her fork, pushes her plate away.

"I guess I finally realized that the real bottom line is living with yourself. I walked away from the old life, the old career, the old way of doing business. And you know, you can't take it with you. I couldn't take the money. I couldn't take the power. I don't have those things today. I don't even have the condo—I gave it back to the bank. Back to the basics. All I have is me." She sips her tea. "I'd just as soon be somebody whose ethics I can live with, thank you very much. I feel healthier, even with all this change."

MaryAlice's relational life is healthier, too. The man she lives with is kind and thoughtful, a nondrinker. "The relationship is totally nontoxic," she says. "Richard has been in therapy, too, so we've both worked through our problems and understand them. We were going to get married last year, but both of us chickened out because the relationship is so good and we're afraid to jinx it. I was dragging my feet as hard as he was, but he was the one who finally decided we shouldn't do it." She wrinkles her nose comically. "So I was the one who had to deal with the abandonment." Then she laughs to let me know that she has recovered from a potentially painful rejection. "You grow from trauma, and I did a lot of growing."

MaryAlice and Richard split the bills, which has helped to ease MaryAlice's perennial financial difficulties. Always before, she was involved with men she could not depend on, who cost her money. "Now I'm afraid I'm the unreliable one," she confesses ruefully. "At this point, a lot of what I do is on spec and I usually have to wait for my money. Richard's awfully nice about it." She drops her voice to a near-whisper. "He'll say, very gently, Uh, MaryAlice, are you going to be able to pay rent this month?" She clowns, miming herself counting money out of a coinpurse. "I'll count my pennies and say, Uh, yes, I think so—maybe. For the last year and a half or two years, I've been expecting the situation to change. But it hasn't." She makes a face, not-so-comical, then relaxes and smiles. "But it will. It'll change. Things always do, don't they?"

Changes, changes. One more change. MaryAlice's son, whose college enrollment was one of the triggers for her decision to go into therapy, got married last summer. The marriage is a strong one, MaryAlice says. She adds, bemused, "I just found out that I'm going to be a grandmother in seven months." She shakes her head in wonderment at her own contentment in the midst of change and uncertainty.

"Which do you think will come first?" she asks. "The baby or a book contract?"

10

LYNN:
PERFECTLY ORDINARY WORK

*L*ynn Nelson and her herd of twenty-seven dairy goats live on a forty-five-acre farm called Briarwood in southern Indiana. The land is hilly, the open woods laced with sunny meadows. It is early November, and the air is crisp and chill, the leaves fired red and gold by the frost. As I drive down the narrow lane toward Lynn's house, I see an old red barn, newly roofed, a small yellow-painted frame house with green shutters and a large screened porch, a chicken house, a garden, a creek—and goats, lots of goats. They are Nubians, Lynn has told me, friendly goats with long flowing ears and aristocratic Roman noses. They are good milkers that yield, on an average, eight hundred pounds of milk a year, about a hundred gallons per goat. Lynn sells it to a nearby creamery. Milk is the chief cash crop of her small homestead, and tending to her goats keeps her busy.

A brown-and-black border collie greets me with an inquiring bark when I get out of the car. Lynn comes to the door, calls "It's okay, Patches," and walks down the path toward me. She is a tall, long-legged woman in faded jeans, a gray-plaid flannel shirt, and leather work boots. Followed by an entourage of four red hens and their flamboyant rooster, we walk to a fence and lean against it. I admire the goats.

"Those are the basis of my breeding program," Lynn says, pointing to a few with yellow tags in their ears. "They're all good goats, though," she adds, affectionately fondling the ears of a curious black Nubian that comes close to the fence to inspect me. "They're my friends. This one is Persephone. She dropped a pair of lovely kids last spring." The wind blows briskly, whipping Lynn's dark hair into her eyes and tugging at my scarf. Patches trots off busily on an errand and we go back to the house, where Lynn heats hot chocolate. Then we take our mugs and a plate of fresh-baked apple muffins to the porch and sit in the swing. Lynn is a person for whom words have so much value that they are not spent without reflection, and we sit in silence for a few minutes while she thinks where to begin. When she starts to talk, it is about the land.

"Even as a child," she says, "I loved plowed fields." Her reserve relaxes into a smile. "My mother tells me I called them beautiful mudpies. I couldn't understand why my father didn't just stop what he was doing so we could move to the country and be farmers. He tried to explain that some people are farmers and some people do other things. Once I remember spending a weekend on a farm in Michigan. There were kittens in the haymow and workhorses. The memory of the sunshine in the mow, the kitchen, good smells—it's still with me. It was like being in heaven. I dreamed of having my own place, maybe in Montana, with horses. I was obsessed with horses, and I wanted to be a horse trainer when I grew up." She drops her head back and laughs deeply. "I spent a lot of time drawing barn plans and house plans and deciding where to put the garden."

Lynn's father was a union official, on the road much of the time, dealing with labor-management conflicts. Lynn remembers that his homecomings were special occasions. "When he came home, it was like a holiday," she says. "Like Christmas. I remember once during the war, he brought me a whole box of bubblegum and made me the neighborhood hero. He was a generous person, and I admired that. Being a union man and Irish, he taught me that working people were decent people who deserved respect, and that the people with power and money weren't always the people who were right. I'm not sure I put it together that way when I was a child, but at some level I knew it, and it was important to me. I wanted to be like my father because he had so much integrity. He was a whole person. His life had consistency, it held together. He knew what his values were and he lived them."

She props her boots up on the porch rail and uses her knees to push the porch swing, setting us swaying. "But when Dad came home, the organizer in him came home with him, too. We had this terrible ongoing quarrel. I'd come home for dinner and hang my jacket on the doorknob on the theory that I'd go out again after dinner. He'd get angry and tell me to hang it in the closet, and around we would go. As a kid, I thought he was too organized, too structured. Looking back, I think he was worried that my sister and I weren't growing up to be thoughtful or useful people, that we didn't do enough work around the house, that sort of thing. But that changed when I was about sixteen and my mother had surgery. When my father came home that day, my sister and I had mowed the lawn, tidied up the house, done the laundry, and cooked dinner—and we kept things that way while Mother was in the hospital. Dad never nagged again. He knew we could do what had to be done. He didn't have to worry about it anymore."

Down by the creek, Patches barks sharply, and Lynn stands up to look. I feel in her the quiet, calm alertness that comes from years of watching and listening to animals, sensing when they are in trouble and need her to help or defend them. Satisfied that Patches has happened onto nothing more threatening than a rabbit, she sits down again and returns to her childhood, remembering her mother.

"Mother was small and mild, but as tough as Dad in her own way. She had her own kind of tempered resilience, her own inner steel. I lied to her once, and she took me downstairs by the scruff of my neck and washed my mouth out with Ivory soap. She made it very clear that there were principles. We weren't allowed to call people names, the way the other kids did. Mother just said, No. In her own quiet way, she managed and took care of things. But it wasn't easy for her, because she was very hard of hearing. Every night when my dad was gone, she had a ritual. She'd put my father's suit jacket over the dining-room chair, with his hat in front of it. Anyone who looked through the window would think he was home." She pauses and turns, as a marmalade-colored cat noses open the screen door and jumps up between us on the swing.

Absently, Lynn ruffles the cat's orange fur. It arches its back, stretches, then climbs into her lap and settles down, tail curled over nose. "I admired my mother's courage in dealing with her deafness. I remember once when she got a new hearing aid and we went out for a walk. There was a cardinal singing in a tree, and I said, 'Mom, listen and you can hear that cardinal.' She said, 'Oh, no, I can't hear birds.' I said, 'Listen.' We stood there and the cardinal sang, and she cried."

After high-school graduation, Lynn wanted to train horses, but her father insisted on college. She did not argue. She chose a small college near a stable where she could work with horses on weekends and enrolled in science courses. She smiles down at the tabby. "I thought maybe I'd be a vet. But I was young and much too noble to treat animals when people needed doctoring, so I planned for medical school. Then I took a required history course and got hooked on history, because it was about the way people thought and saw things. Over the next few years, I got caught up in learning and forgot about horses. In my senior year, the faculty nominated me for a Woodrow Wilson Fellowship, and I applied to graduate school in history. It seemed natural to go on. There was so much to know that it never occurred to me to stop learning."

Most people go to graduate school to pursue a professional specialty, and history majors usually wind up as college professors. But when Lynn entered graduate school, she was not thinking about a career. "I was driven by intellectual curiosity," she says. "I wanted to go on doing what I did as an undergraduate—discovering new worlds, new ways of thinking, new ways of looking at things. My major professor was a wonderful man, friendly and solicitous, and the other students were helpful too. It was a collaborative environment, at least in that department, in those years. I loved it."

The graduate program trained her to be a teacher of history, so when Lynn finished her dissertation, she found a position in American history at an elite private university and began teaching. As a junior faculty member, she found the atmosphere very different from the collaborative experience of graduate school. "It was highly competitive," she says, "and that troubled me. There was competition for students, for certain teaching assignments, for travel money, for recognition. I didn't like the personal ambition or the so-called professionalism of my colleagues. They were always trying to get ahead of one another by delivering another paper or publishing another book." She pulls her dark brows together in a scowl. "Whether the book or the paper said anything original was beside the point—the point was to lengthen your list of publications, because that's how you got recognized. I didn't enjoy my time in that place, but I learned from it. I left because I didn't belong in a university where I had to do a great deal

191

of research in a very narrow field and train graduate students. I'm a generalist, a connector. I belong in an institution that concerns itself with educating the whole person, not just the young professional." Her voice deepens, becomes more intent. It is clear that this idea is one to which she is passionately committed. "I deeply believed what I told my students—that a liberal arts education is not just about learning how to make a living, it's about learning how to live a meaningful, coherent life, a socially responsible life, a *moral* life. I can only pursue my own liberation, if you will, when I'm working with students who are pursuing their liberations."

Lynn looked for and found a position at a small liberal arts college in the heartland of the country that seemed to hold out the promise of a person-centered education. "It was good for me to be there. The college was full of ordinary kids and ordinary faculty who didn't have enormous ambition. I got involved in various experimental teaching projects. I was engaged in the life of the campus. I enjoyed teaching and learning. I felt at home."

Over the next few years, several events challenged Lynn's comfort and sense of security. Three years after she was hired, she became eligible for promotion to associate professor and tenure: the prized lifetime job security awarded to qualified college and university teachers. "I applied as a matter of course," Lynn says, looking out at the haze of reds and golds on the other side of the creek, where the trees climb out of a meadow and across a hill. "My chairman recommended me for both. But as the evaluation process got under way, I realized that I didn't like the feelings it was fostering in me. I didn't like the extended comparisons I had to make between my colleagues and myself. I didn't like the tallying and the weighing. I wanted to be held accountable for my work as a teacher, for my ability to communicate the love of ideas to my students. But the method of accounting seemed to me to be terribly skewed. I wasn't being judged on what kind of teacher I was. I was being judged on my pedigree—the degrees I earned, the prestige of the institutions I attended, the list of papers and articles and books I published."

Patches, tail and belly-fur dripping, emerges from the weeds behind the chicken house and trots up the gravel path. Lynn smiles as he shakes himself in a shower of droplets at the foot of the porch step. "Mind you," she says, "the people in charge of

192

tenure and promotion almost never look at, let alone read, the published material a candidate submits. For proof of professionalism, they look at the list of publications. It's the list that's supposed to be the product of my inquiring mind, my scholarly industry, my intellectual courage. It's the list I'd be evaluated on, not my actual performance."

There is a rising tone of marvel in her voice, as if she still cannot understand how people could so foolishly mistake the map for the territory. She sits up straight now, gesturing emphatically so that I will understand how important this is. Her hands carry part of her urgent message. "I was also bothered that the evaluation process gave so much weight to written work. For example, let's say I'm an English teacher interested in A. E. Housman. He was a British scholar and poet from around the turn of the century who wrote a collection of poetry called *A Shropshire Lad*. If I wanted to understand Housman better, I might go to Shropshire and look in various libraries for books that might have shaped his thinking. The research would be recognized as legitimate academic work. But what if I wanted to spend a year as a working shepherd in the Shropshire hills in order to better understand Housman's connection to nature? Would that be legitimate?"

She answers her own question with a negative shake of her head, her mouth drawn tight. "What counts is what's published, because it has become a public affair. Published work is valuable because of its association with the marketplace. Things that are private, on the other hand—my private thoughts, for instance, or the thoughts that I share orally with my students—are considered less valuable. But I resent having to measure my worth by counting things, and I refuse to have my private value calculated against public values. I decided that the tenure process was encouraging me to act according to values I didn't want to have.

"But by the time I had thought this through, here came the letter saying, 'Congratulations, you've been promoted and tenured.' I had to write back and say, Thanks, but no thanks. I asked to be relieved of both rank and tenure. My request, as it turns out, was highly unusual, and it took a while to get a response. But the administration finally agreed. The people in the department thought I was daft. No one in our college had ever turned down tenure."

In the meantime, another challenge had nudged Lynn to broaden and deepen her understanding of the world. For most of her life, she had been interested in Native Americans. "When I was a kid, I had this romantic stuff in my head. When we played cowboys and Indians, I was the Indian. I always admired Tonto more than the Lone Ranger." Early in her teaching career, she read Dorothy Lee's book *Freedom and Culture,* a collection of essays about the ways in which language shapes the way we perceive reality. Lee had studied Native American languages, and her book revived Lynn's childhood interest in Native American culture. Lynn applied for and received a federal grant to study Navajo (an oral language) on a reservation. Back at school after her study leave, she began incorporating Native American material in her classes and thinking about the life she had witnessed, so different from her own.

A few years later, she returned to the reservation to teach in a program that prepared Navajo and Hopi adults to take the high school equivalency examination. Two years after that, she spent a sabbatical semester high in the New Mexico mountains near Lukachukai, living with an old Navajo shepherd named Nesbah Tsosie. "Mama Tsosie was small and slim and aristocratic," she says. "She dressed in traditional Navajo velveteen blouses and tiered gingham skirts. She wore silver and turquoise always, whether she was bringing in her sheep or weaving, spinning, gardening, or cooking fried bread. She lived in a house built by her Hopi husband—unusual because it was built of stone—and her daughter lived in a nearby log house. Mama's sheep wandered every day through the trees and sagebrush into the mountains, an extraordinary landscape of red earth, blue sky, and the greens and textures of pines and sagebrush. At night they came back to a tall corral of Ponderosa pine logs, where Mama penned them to keep them safe from coyotes."

Lynn falls silent for a moment, captured, I think, by her own recollections. "It was a profound experience," she says finally. "In America, we're ignorant of what life was like—*is* like—for most of the people on the earth. Our science and technology cuts us off from the rest of humanity. We call this progress, and we're glad to have our conveniences. But progress comes at a price. To get it, we give up certain human experiences, emotions, feelings.

The Indians I lived with haven't given those things up. They are deeply rooted in the land, in touch with the universe of times and seasons and real human needs. They live in a natural world that helps them to frame human meaning, human value, human dignity. They know about hunger, about time, about darkness, and cold. A cup of cool spring water means something to them that it can't possibly mean to me, because I was raised with air-conditioning and ice cubes and popsicles. Being with them has helped me to see how technology has altered my experience of the world. It helped me reconnect with my humanity."

Lynn's sabbatical, which she hoped would give her a sense of the real world of work, effort, and survival, made her more sharply and painfully aware of the sheltered artificiality of college life. When she came back to school, she felt unconnected, out of sync, out of touch with the reality that her colleagues and the college administration seemed to assume. "It seemed like a foreign land," she recalls. "It was a culture whose language I had to relearn. But I didn't want to. I wanted to have more of what I had left behind in the mountains—more real life, life and work in touch with what's alive."

For a number of years, Lynn had been living with an older woman named Carol. "It was a relationship that started compli-cated," Lynn says with a sigh, "and in some ways was always complicated, which was something I didn't want to see for a very long time. I admired her wit, her energy, her fascinating range of interests and knowledge. She was interested in retiring early and living in the country, and I desperately wanted to be in touch with the natural world. So we bought a piece of land and started building a house. We put in a garden and a pond—the whole works." She looks toward the pasture, where one of the Nubians has both forefeet on the trunk of a small tree and is nipping a branch. "I added a few goats, partly to honor Mama and partly because I like goat milk and cheese. Carol liked animals, so she enjoyed the goats." She chuckles throatily, as if at a private joke, then adds, "Or at least, she enjoyed being an authority on them. I don't think she was as interested in farming—roll-up-your-sleeves, hands-dirty farming—as I was."

As time passed and a greater share of Lynn's effort went into creating a life centered on animals and growing things, she felt increasingly remote from the academic institution that paid her salary. "I still loved teaching, sharing with students, energizing them. But I was living in a world of personal experience, learning things by doing, by feeling. It was very different from my colleagues' world, where what is known is based on what's written down, on other people's authority. It wasn't that I didn't want to be an intellectual, or that I didn't like the people I worked with. They were kind and decent. And they liked me, too. They were even fond of me. But I think I baffled them. I didn't have the usual motives. I didn't want to be famous, or have a powerful position. I just wanted to understand—really, not just intellectually—my ordinariness. I wanted to accept mortality and death, to respect the lives of other creatures. I wanted to. . . ." She pauses, searching for words, her voice taut with the need to speak carefully, precisely. "I wanted to participate in the power that living beings have—simply by virtue of being alive. The academic world, as I knew it, didn't seem able to understand or respect or even tolerate my needs and wants."

Caught between the demands of her work at the college and her increasing interest in the farm, Lynn finally decided that she could no longer continue doing both. So she resigned her position, said farewell to her teaching career, and left the college. She and her partner bought a sizable piece of property in another part of the state. There, Lynn hoped, she could develop a real dairy herd and learn to live comfortably with a reality she could no longer ignore or deny: that her life's work was to be work with her hands, work with animals. She poured all her energy into building a quality herd, and her breeding experiments showed results. The herd grew, the fences went up, the house was renovated, the garden was rescued from weedy neglect, the fields were gradually improved. It was a good life, a strong life, the kind of life she had hoped for, but it only lasted four years.

Lynn's long-term relationship with Carol abruptly came apart. "It went to hell in a handbasket," she says in a wry tone that belies the anguish she must have felt at the wreck of years of living and working with someone she loved, toward goals she had thought they shared. The issue that divided them was the familiar issue of personal growth. As a result of her desire to choose work of her own, Lynn was growing; it was growth that

Carol was unwilling, or perhaps unable, to accept. "I think that as I came into my own more and more, Carol was increasingly threatened. The devoted, attentive young woman I had been was growing into a more autonomous adult—which from my point of view didn't mean separate or unconnected. Her reaction was to become more demanding. Things got ugly. I had to leave."

At the same time her relationship was going to pieces, Lynn discovered that her goats were infected with a deadly disease. She destroyed the herd, and she and Carol put the farm up for sale. Waiting to recover her real estate investment, she was alarmingly short of cash. "I left the place with nothing," she says quietly. "I started to scramble."

For three years, Lynn scrambled hard, sometimes desperately. She had only two goals—making ends meet and starting another herd—and she was willing to do almost anything to meet them. "I played salesperson for a while," she says, "but my spirit couldn't survive doing that, even though I was selling solar equipment. Then I got a part-time teaching job at a local college at slave-labor rates. That turned into a half-time position, and then I was named assistant to the academic dean."

The next year, enjoying the classroom and wanting to earn more money, she applied for a full-time teaching position in the history department. The chairman, however, made it clear that he would accept her application only if she would commit herself to research and writing and to the publication of her scholarly work. It was the same issue Lynn had confronted when she rejected tenure and promotion over a decade before, and she met it with the same passionate intensity. She delivered a talk at a department meeting.

"I argued that when God said, 'Let there be light,' he didn't write it down. I argued that the spoken word is action, and that our personal power comes from the degree to which we embody our words and our work in our lives—not just in print. But I was up against some very traditional academic mindsets. It was toe the line or move out."

So Lynn moved out. She did a stint as a writer in a local advertising agency. "I had quite a splendid time with the artists— the place was a hundred percent female, a lively and good-humored bunch. Then I began to talk with a friend in the women's studies department at the local university about the possibility of submitting a grant proposal." The proposal outlined a program that would help rural women prepare for school. Lynn helped write the grant. It was funded, and Lynn received the title of program director and a nineteen-thousand-dollar salary for a thirty-hour week. It is a self-designed position that allows her the freedom to teach as she teaches best. She smiles as she tells me about it.

"In some ways, teaching in the grant project reminds me of teaching on the Indian reservation. These women know what education can do for them, and they want it. They're interested, motivated, enthusiastic. I love watching them walk into the excitement of ideas and values and discover that words have meaning. I love watching them laugh and grow confident. I love teaching in this kind of setting, with no politics, no pressure to publish, no academic condescension, no competition, no easily bruised egos."

She pauses, reflects. "In other ways, the project reminds me of my father's concern for the working class. I think I'm very fortunate. My parents taught me to respect all people, not just people with money or degrees or fancy Brooks Brothers suits, or whatever. They encouraged me to go to school but they never urged me to do any social climbing. I didn't grow up thinking that it was especially wonderful to be a professional. I grew up knowing that it was just as wonderful to be the guy next door, who worked for a living. Maybe that's why I feel so much at home with these students. They're not in the project because they want to make a million on Wall Street. They just want to build the foundation for a solid, meaningful life for themselves and their children. I respect that desire, and I admire them for their courage."

The teaching, sustaining and rewarding as it is, is peripheral to Lynn's real work. After three years of saving and scrimping and looking for land, she stumbled on Briarwood and fell in love with it. "I badgered the bank that owned it and offered them far less than they were asking. I think the banker felt sorry for me because I wanted it so bad. He let me have it and somehow, miraculously, I came up with the money for a down payment. When I told my mother I was starting over with a dairy herd, she said: 'I don't know whether to admire you or have you committed.' I took it as a compliment."

198

Lynn looks around at the neatly kept barn and sheds and fences and paths, at the cat on her lap, the collie at her feet. She sighs with satisfaction and stretches her arms as if to encompass all of it. "So now I'm building the dairy herd, working on the house, and tending the fields and gardens. The old place finally sold, and I put the money into this farm, so the mortgage will be paid off next year. The herd is beginning to make a profit, so even if the grant isn't funded again, I'll be able to survive on what the herd brings in and what I can earn doing teaching and free-lance writing. It's good work. Perfectly ordinary work, work with my hands. It feels right."

Lynn's emotional life has found a new balance, too. "I moved here alone," she says. "I felt sad and lonely—and solid and good. I spent a lot of time thinking about what I wanted and whether I really wanted to farm if I had to do it alone. Whether I could. Whether I wanted to spend the rest of my life alone. And I said to myself: You bet, I can do it alone and it's okay. And I think that was an important recognition for me."

Then Katie came along—a successful sculptor and art teacher—and Lynn did not have to do it alone. "Katie's one of the reasons I feel good about what I'm doing," Lynn says. "We don't make much money, but we live richly. We've been together for almost seven years, and it seems simultaneously like all our lives and only a few months. The house is quite livable, although there's a lot of work to be done on it, and I'm always learning something. Next, I'm going to learn how to make drawers to hide all the bathroom things in. Then winter will be here, with plenty of quiet time for music and reading. In December, seed catalogs will come, and I'll start planning for the orchard and the gardens. In February, the sap will rise in the maples, and Katie and I will make maple syrup. Nubians breed year-round, but March always brings a good crop of kids. Then April and new green grass—"

She sighs again, shakes her head, as if she still does not quite believe her good fortune. "Every day seems a splendid gift. I don't know how I could be happier. I live in a most beautiful place. I share my life with a remarkable person. Just looking at my house gives me pleasure. I have been able to schedule my teaching so that most of the time I can live according to the needs of my farm and my herd—tending to them, I stay in touch with the earth. I don't know how I could be more blessed."

It is sunset when I go back to my car. I glance over my shoulder. Head up, shoulders back, strides certain, Lynn is headed to the barn to get on with the milking. She is followed by the dog and the cat, and on the other side of the fence, the goats push to get into line. Beyond the creek, the oaks and maples reflect the last red of the setting sun. Somewhere nearby, an owl calls, soft and plaintive in the dusk.

This place is Lynn's work, Lynn's life. A perfectly ordinary place.

Part

3

WORK OF YOUR OWN

*What does it mean to be a woman
in a man's world for those of us who
do not wish to stay home and become like our mothers or to strive
aggressively and become like men?
Why do some women express deep
disappointment with the reality of
career success and with the promises of feminism, so that they now
say that in some essential way they
have forgotten how to be a woman?
The answer can be found in a woman's longing to be authentically feminine, to experience herself fully as
a woman and, at the same time, to
be a strong, independent individual whose power and authority are
rooted within her.*

CONNIE ZWEIG

INTRODUCTION:
TRANSFORMING THE WAY YOU WORK

TRANSFORMING THE WAY YOU WORK IS A LONG-TERM PROCESS. THIS
is true whether you take the radical step of moving out of the career culture or simply make healthy adjustments in the way you
work each day. As a process, transforming your work involves a
deep inner change. Since you are reading this book, it is likely
that you have already begun to make some changes. At the very
least, you may be questioning the way you work and asking yourself whether you can keep on working that way for a long period
of time. In this part of the book, I will suggest some strategies you
can use to change your work into work of your own—work that
you design with your own needs and goals clearly in mind.

11

LEARNING ABOUT YOURSELF AND YOUR WORK

*F*or many of us, working is like breathing. We do it automatically, without thinking about it—until, for some reason or other, working starts to feel painful. Somewhere along the line, months or perhaps even years ago, we began to feel uncomfortable about the work we were doing. But the habits of automatic living—life on autopilot, as one woman put it—kept us working in a numbed state, unaware that something was wrong. Only when something awakens us out of that numbed, half-asleep state can we become conscious of the way we work. Only when we are conscious of our work choices can we begin to change them.

The first step toward transforming your work is to understand how and why you work. You need to reflect deliberately and thoughtfully on the goals of your work. You need to analyze or think through your work habits and skills, and you need to give yourself permission to feel your feelings about the work you do.

Reviewing Your Goals

If you have worked for a number of years in one industry or for one corporation, you probably have tailored your work goals to fit those of your employer. It is easier and more harmonious to work that way, of course: There is far less conflict when you and your employer are a team than when you are at odds with each other. In fact, your company probably puts you under a great deal of pressure, both subtle and direct, to adapt your goals to theirs. If you fail to do so, you are likely to be criticized for working at cross-purposes with your organization. You may be called a loose cannon, a poor team player. You may be seen as someone who cannot be trusted to act in acceptable ways or to make predictable decisions.

The truth, however, is that your goals and your employer's

are not the same. For instance, you may want to be creative in your work, to explore personal growth, and to develop your critical skills. Your employer, on the other hand, may expect you to produce the largest number of reports, sell more widgets than you sold the year before, or persuade the people you supervise that the corporation's new personnel policies are right for them.

Your situation may be even more complicated and tricky. You may be working for a supervisor who has an individual agenda, one that may or may not be recognized or approved by the organization. Your boss's on-the-job behavior may be shaped by a wish for recognition and advancement, or by the need to exert power over those lower down the ladder. Adjusting your work so that it meets your goals, fits your boss's agenda, and fulfills your employer's purposes can be a very complicated business. Employees working under such conflict-filled situations are subject to severe stress.

Perhaps you have already begun to give some tentative thought to your work goals; perhaps, as you read this book, you have been giving them a great deal of thought. In this section, you will find questions that are designed to help you explore and advance your thinking in an organized and focused way. As you read, you should write down your responses or tape-record them, so that you can come back later and review your thinking. If you keep a journal, these questions are fruitful topics for extended self-exploration. I have found that keeping a journal of my work experiences and my reactions and feelings has helped clarify what often seems hopelessly muddled.

The following questions are divided into two different groups: The first is for all readers; the second is for those who feel they are ready to modify their present working environment. Read quickly through all the questions in a group before you begin to answer them. On the surface, the questions are deceptively simple, but the answers can be soul-searing. It is not easy to tell ourselves the truth about what we want to do and what others want us to do.

For Everyone

- What are the most important goals that you have for your day-to-day work? For instance, your goal might be to work

four hours a day so you can have more time for
you consider your real work. It might be to
people. Most of us have multiple goals, but whe
clearly identified, they often fit into a pattern.

- Which of these goals are most important? Which are least
  important? Which fall somewhere in the middle? One way
  to answer this is to imagine which goals you could give up if
  you had to, and which you could never sacrifice. Your response to this question can be illuminating. If you say, for
  instance, that job security is your most important goal, then
  a goal that threatens your job security might have to be
  abandoned. If you are unwilling to do this, perhaps job
  security does not have the high priority you thought.

- What are your long-range goals for your entire career or
  work life? List these from most to least important. This can
  be another enlightening question. If, say, you are nearing
  early retirement and maximizing your retirement income is
  a major career goal, you would not be likely to consider a
  change that would jeopardize your benefits.

- How have your goals changed during the course of your
  work life? What goals were most important when you began
  your career? If you have worked or now work in more than
  one career field, it would be helpful to make a separate list-
  ing for each field. What goals have become irrelevant? When
  did you lose those goals, and under what circumstances?
  What new goals have appeared recently? Do you see a pattern in these changes?

- To what extent do your goals express your deepest needs
  and desires? Do any of your current goals express the needs
  and desires that others have for you (parents, lover/spouse,
  teachers, mentors and boss, therapist)? Do you feel any conflict between your goals and theirs?

- Which is a more important goal for you: making a good salary, or doing what you want to do? Do you see the answer to
  this question as temporary or permanent?

Now, take a few moments to look back over your written responses or to play them back on the tape recorder. Are there any

that surprise you? Are there any that seem particularly interesting? If so, you might want to spend more time thinking about those issues before you go on to the next group of questions— either those immediately following or those relating to skills and habits.

For People Ready to Modify Their Present Job or Career

If you have already made the decision to redesign your work environment totally, you may skip these questions and go to the section, Skills and Habits. If not, these questions may help you to clarify your feelings about your current situation.

■ What goals does your present employer have for your position? What goals does your employer have for you as a person? Most employers, like most people, have multiple goals. Can you see a basic pattern in your employer's goals?

■ What goals does your boss or supervisor have for your position? For you? Are these goals communicated directly or indirectly? Are all these goals acknowledged, or are some unacknowledged? Are they consistent or inconsistent with your employer's goals? Are there situations in which your supervisor's needs seem more urgent than your employer's goals? For example, a supervisor's personal goal of appearing competent may undercut the organization's goal of developing the best possible product.

■ What goals do your staff or your employees have for you? What are the similarities and differences between their goals and yours? Are there some behaviors they expect of you with which you feel uncomfortable?

■ What similarities and differences are there between your goals and those your employer or boss has for you? Is the fit excellent, acceptable, or poor?

■ If the fit is poor, what would you have to do to make it at least acceptable? What changes would your employer/boss have to make in order to create an acceptable fit? Is it realistic to expect them to make those changes? Is it realistic to expect that you can alter the fit to make it at least acceptable?

■ How can you better achieve your personal goals in your present work environment, and in your career as a whole? Put another way, how can you do work of your own where you are currently working? If you have thoughtfully worked through all of the above questions and you are forced to answer that you cannot achieve your goals in your present situation, you might consider a more radical change.

In *Do What You Love, the Money Will Follow*, Marsha Sinetar says: "The very best way to relate to our work is to choose it. Right Livelihood is predicated upon conscious choice." As long as we allow someone else's goals to structure our work lives, we are not choosing to do work of our own. It takes a great deal of honesty and courage to acknowledge the extent to which we have allowed others' agendas to shape our actions. Being clear about what we want to do and what others want us to do is the first step toward creating work that expresses our deepest selves.

REVIEWING YOUR SKILLS AND HABITS

We usually examine our skills when we are in the market for a new job. The rest of the time, skills are like tools—they are necessary and convenient, and we use them without thinking much about whether we like them or feel comfortable using them. But your career satisfaction is related to the conscious use you are able to make of your *preferred* skills. If your career does not permit you to do the things you enjoy and feel competent in doing, sooner or later you are likely to consider doing something else.

The following questions will give you a quick, overall assessment of your best skills and your preference for using them. Be forewarned, though, that personal inventories are challenging because we cannot always be objective about what we do well. When you have finished this inventory, if you feel that you have not been able to make a realistic assessment of your skills, you might ask a career counseling/planning service to administer a test, such as the *Strong-Campbell Interest Inventory* or the *Career Occupational Preference Evaluation (COPE)*. The results will give you clear indicators of your skill areas and be a useful supplement to your skill inventory. If you need help in thinking more generally about your skills, consult a career-change manual such as *What Color Is Your Parachute,* which provides a useful list of skills, as well as other helpful information.

- List *all* the things you do reasonably well *and* like to do. This can include job-related skills, such as managing, organizing, processing, in addition to noncareer skills, such as mountain climbing, playing the piano, caring for children, gardening.

- Go over your list, and give each item a number that represents its strength. For example, 10 means that you are expert; 9 means that you are very good, and so forth.

- Go over your list again, giving each item a number that represents your preference for doing that task. For example, 10 equals your favorite; 9 means that you really enjoy it, and so forth.

- Add the strength and the preference ratings for each item. Then recopy your list, putting the top-rated items at the top, the lowest-ranked items at the bottom.

Here are some questions to ask as you review your inventory:

- How many of your preferred skills are you using in your present career? How can you modify what you do so you can more often do what you like to do best? *Can* you modify your work to use these skills, or do you have to make a radical change?

- What skills do you want to develop? What resources do you need to do this (for example, training, time, family support, financial assistance)?

- Do you suspect that you have skills that you do not recognize? A skills-preference test may help unearth these. Or give your list of preferred skills to a friend and ask her to add to it any skills she thinks you have that you might not have listed.

When you have completed your skills analysis, give yourself time to mull over what you have written, to change your priorities, or to add items you might have forgotten. If you take time to think about what you enjoy doing and do well, your options for change will become more clear.

If analyzing your work skills is difficult, analyzing your work *habits* may be even harder. We may be so accustomed to our habitual patterns that they are often invisible to us. Here are some questions that may help you look with greater awareness at your work habits and how they affect the rest of your life. When you have completed this exercise, you might repeat it with a friend or coworker who is familiar with your work habits. You may be surprised to learn how someone else perceives your habits.

- Do you enjoy working alone, or do you prefer to work with others? When you work with others, are you comfortable being a member of the group or do your want to lead? What goal do you prefer your group to work toward: outcome, efficiency, or consensus?

- When you are given instructions on a project, do you follow them to the letter or modify them in order to do a better job? How often have you told your boss, It can't be done this way, or It can't be done at all! How often do you think, I'd rather be working for myself?

- Do you prefer to work with your office door open or shut? How much time to do you spend at your workplace's equivalent of the water cooler? How many of your colleagues do you consider friends?

- Has anyone ever called you a workaholic? Do people consider you (or do you consider yourself) a compulsive or driven worker? Do you go on binges, where you work straight through for days at a time? Do you conceal work from your friends or family so they will not know how much you are doing? Have you tried unsuccessfully to limit the number of hours you work?

- To be more specific about your habits, answer these questions: How many hours a week do you work? How do you spend your lunch hours and breaks? How often are you the first person in or the last person out of your workplace?

211

What percentage of your total waking hours is centered on your work—either doing it or thinking about it? How many vacation days have you earned in the past five years? How many have you taken? (Suggestion: Compute the days you have taken as a fraction of the days you have earned. Do not count *working* vacation days.)

■ How many sick days have you taken in the past five years? How frequently do you have to drag yourself to work? How often do you take medication or seek treatment for stress-related illnesses that you attribute to your work?

■ Off the job, how easy is it for you to unwind? Are you a compulsive get-it-done type? Or do you use your free time to relax or to work on creative projects that satisfy you in other ways?

■ Are you prone to compulsive or addictive behavior on or off the job? If so, are your compulsions related to your work in any way? Psychologists define compulsions as behaviors that we cannot control. These may include alcohol and drug abuse, eating disorders like binging and purging, relationship addiction, uncontrollable spending.

■ How often do you ask yourself, "Why am I doing this to myself?" or "Why do I let them do this to me?"

There is no single, simple way to interpret your answers. When you have read over what you have written, you might try to summarize your work habits by writing a concluding paragraph in response to the following questions: Are you satisfied with your work habits and attitudes? Do they seem generally healthy and productive, or are there some that cause you personal difficulty, on or off the job? If there are some that you need to change, how can you do that?

Our habits and attitudes toward work can lead to a constructive, productive work life that is healthily integrated with the other things we do. Or, as Diane Fassel points out in *Working Ourselves to Death*, they can draw us into a widening spiral of unmanageable activity that limits personal growth, destroys relationships, and damages health. No matter what the cause of our difficulties with work—whether the problems come from the work environment, from colleagues, from the nature of the work, or from within us—*we* are responsible for making ourselves healthier. It is *we* who must develop the kinds of habits and attitudes that contribute to a rich, full life and to stronger, more enabling relationships with others.

REVIEWING YOUR FEELINGS

Many employers act as if they believe that the ideal employee is one who leaves feelings at home. Our feelings are a significant component of the way we work, however. They have a strong influence over our successes and failures—in and out of the career culture.

Positive feelings about work are not hard to recognize and acknowledge. Pride in doing a good job, pleasure when we are praised for our achievements, confidence in our abilities, the sense of self-worth that comes when we know we are liked, respected, and admired—these are all feelings that we enjoy and look forward to reexperiencing.

Work brings us other feelings, too. It can make us feel angry, confused, helpless, powerless, guilty, inferior, mistrustful, aggressive, lonely, fearful. In our birth families and our early school environments, many of us were taught that these feelings were bad, and that we were bad when we allowed ourselves to feel this way. We may have been made to feel ashamed of our feelings, hence, we hide them from others and from ourselves. Hiding our feelings can become a habit—a valuable habit, at least where the career culture is concerned. Like our birth families and our schools, it rewards those who suppress bad feelings.

Negative feelings are especially difficult to acknowledge when we feel them in a situation where we are supposed to feel only good feelings: when we have just been promoted, for instance. Denial of our painful, negative feelings becomes a habit very quickly. When that happens, our feelings gain control of us, and we lose the ability to express them appropriately. We get angry when we are afraid, for instance, or we cry when we are angry. We may feel our emotions in our bodies and experience illness. We may feel through others in an inappropriately empathetic way.

Getting in touch with your feelings has become a popular phrase in psychology over the past decade, and with good reason. Although experiencing your feelings is not the only route to wholeness and health, it is one of the major routes. Unless you acknowledge and experience your feelings about work, you are likely to be imprisoned by them and forever unable to change the way you work.

The following questions are designed to help you explore the way you feel about your career and the day-to-day work you do. They will be helpful to you only to the extent that you respond to them as honestly and as deeply as possible. Again, it will be useful to read all the questions before you respond to any of them because they are arranged in a series that takes you from one aspect of your work and your career to another.

■ How do you feel about the work you do? Do you enjoy it deeply? moderately? not at all? Always, sometimes, never? All of it, some of it, none of it? Does your work more often bring you satisfaction or disappointment? What are the most positive feelings you have about your work? What are the most negative?

■ How do you feel about the people you work with and for, and those who work for you? Are they interesting and challenging or boring? Do they inspire your respect, admiration, affection—or do they make you feel frustrated, angry, resentful? What are the most positive feelings you have toward them? What are the most negative? Are your feelings about them in any way similar to your feelings toward other people in your life?

■ How do you feel about the organizational environment in which you work? What feeling words would you use to describe it? Are you a member of the corporate family, or do you often feel like an uninvited guest or a taken-for-granted fixture?

■ How does your organization feel about you? Does it show that it values and respects your work? Do you feel that you are adequately recognized through promotion? Do you feel that your work is adequately compensated? Do you feel optimistic or pessimistic about future advancement?

- How do you feel about your physical working environment? Do your surroundings make you feel comfortable, uncomfortable; secure, anxious; cheerful, depressed?

- How do you feel about the present balance between your work, your career, and the rest of your life? Is it comfortable or conflictual? How do others with whom you share your life feel about your work and your career? Are their feelings a source of comfort for you or a source of conflict?

- What do you do with your feelings about work, positive and negative? Do you hide them, reveal them, stew over them, lose sleep over them? Do you work them out, play them out, run them out, dance them out? Do you keep them to yourself or share them? With whom?

- If you continue to work as you are working now, where will you be in five years, ten years, twenty-five years? How do you feel about that prospect?

The career culture does not encourage us to have negative feelings about our work or to explore those feelings, alone or with others. In fact, most professionals experience a deeply ingrained prohibition against talking about feelings. Although we all spout off to our coworkers from time to time or open up with a member of our staff, it usually seems inappropriate to make more than a few superficial remarks about how we feel.

There may be good, practical reasons for holding our feelings inside. If you tell your boss that you resent being asked to work three Saturdays in a row, you may fear that your resentment will be remembered at salary-review time. If you tell a coworker how you feel, the word may get back to your boss. Worse yet, the coworker may be promoted over you and become your boss. If you share your feelings with a subordinate, you may put that person in a difficult situation. There are many sound reasons why you may feel that you cannot share your resentment except with those outside the work environment—and they often do not understand enough about the situation to respond helpfully. Given these difficulties, you will probably bury your feelings and behave as if you cannot wait to work the next weekend. Douglas LaBier, the author of *Modern Madness*, has a name for the millions of people who hide their anger, fear, and resentment about their jobs and their careers. He calls them the working wounded: people who are deeply hurt by what happens on the job but act as if nothing is the matter. If you do not acknowledge your feelings of anger, guilt, betrayal, anxiety, or fear, you are likely at some point to become permanently injured by them. If, LaBier says, you view life as one big career, you may wake up one day and discover that for years you have been stifling your very worst fear: the fear that you have betrayed yourself into spending this precious life doing something you never really wanted to do. Or worse, you may not wake up to this truth at all—or until it is too late to do much about it.

If the preceding questions have given you a good start toward exploring your positive and negative feelings about work, you may want to continue this exploration on a more regular and consistent basis. A work journal is a good way to do this. At its simplest level, a work journal is a record of the things you do and the events that happen at work—a diary. More than a log, it includes your feelings, your thoughts, and your interpretation of what is happening. A good work journal prods you to respond to such questions as, What is really happening here? How do I feel about what is going on? What is at stake in this? What can I learn from what is happening?

At first, a work journal may be only a place for you to express the feelings you can't easily talk about, a place to write out your anger, your frustration, your fear. As people through the centuries have discovered, a journal is worth keeping even if that is its only purpose. Once you have expressed your feelings, however, you have captured them for your continuing examination. Several weeks later, you can return to a situation you have recorded in your journal and review what happened and how you responded. Were your feelings confused, exaggerated, or inappropriate to the situation? If so, you may be able to explore the root causes for the way you felt. If you feel that your response was appropriate, it may be the situation that needs to be altered. Such examinations can reveal important patterns that the day-to-day flow of events often obscures.

Furthermore, a work journal may turn out to be a very significant help in assisting you to deal with sticky problems involving coworkers and supervisors, such as sexual harassment. A

216

clear record of the words and actions, the circumstances, and possible witnesses is invaluable documentation in the event you find it necessary to seek a remedy. I am not advising you to note down every little nuance you catch or to use your work journal to develop problems. I am suggesting that the ongoing practice of keeping a journal may help you to see emerging problems and to deal with difficult situations in a rational, objective way. If the idea of keeping a journal is new to you, you might look at Tristine Rainer's book, *The New Diary: How to Use a Journal for Self-Guidance and Expanded Creativity.* Rainer offers a perceptive, readable introduction to the personal art of journaling.

There is no question that where work is concerned, we *must* be fully in touch with the way we feel. If we are not, we may find ourselves unwitting, unwilling victims of our stifled feelings, incapable of meeting the challenge of personal growth and development. If we are in touch, we can respond to the signals our feelings send us and allow those feelings to motivate us to make constructive change in ourselves and our environment. In order for constructive change to occur, however, we have to be able to see ourselves as change-makers.

VISUALIZING TRANSFORMATION

*I*n the preceding chapter, you used your analytic abilities— what is sometimes called your left brain—to examine your work goals, your skills and habits, and your feelings. This kind of conscious understanding of ourselves is vital to responding flexibly and creatively to our changing place in the changing world around us.

Important changes in habitual responses, however, are not made solely on the basis of analytic understanding. Imagination also plays a role in the process. This phenomenon has been demonstrated by highly trained athletes who are committed to improving their performance. In *Peak Performance: Mental Training Techniques of the World's Greatest Athletes,* Dr. Charles A. Garfield has written that the use of mental images—three-dimensional blueprints for physical activity—can substantially enhance and accelerate our physical learning. He reports an experiment that took place during the 1980 Winter Games at Lake Placid, New York, where athletes followed controlled training programs. These programs involved varying amounts of visualization: In their mind's eye, the athletes rehearsed every single movement of their performance, seeing themselves moving flawlessly, effortlessly, without fear or anxiety. Athletes whose regimens involved 25 percent physical training and 75 percent mental training showed significantly greater improvement than athletes whose regimens involved lesser amounts of mental training.

The technique of mental imaging is also being used in medicine. A psychologist at Pennsylvania State University tested the claim that creative imagery can help to combat cancer. Dr. Howard Hall determined the white blood cell count of a number of cancer patients. Then he taught the patients some techniques of progressive physical and mental relaxation. He asked the adults in his study group to imagine their white blood cells as hungry sharks devouring their cancer cells; he asked children to visualize Pac Man gobbling up the bad cells. The blood cell count was repeated at the end of the experiment, and the patients were asked to practice the visualization twice daily for the next week. The results showed a significant increase in white blood cells, the body's defense against invasion. The experiment suggests, Dr. Hall says, that "the mind can influence the body by changing the biochemistry of the blood."[1] Other similar experiments have created the new science of psychoimmunology, which studies the mind-body relationship, including the effect of the controlled use of imagery on the human body.

Over the past several decades, science has shown us that the age-old concept of mind over matter is more than just an intriguing idea. We know that we can use our minds and our feelings to make important changes in our physical selves. We also know that a person's general self-image has a powerful influence on that person's appearance, emotions, health, relationships, and ability to plan and to carry out plans.

It is logical to assume, then, that the concepts we have about ourselves in the contexts of our jobs and our careers also have a powerful effect on us. This already has been demonstrated by the contributors to this book, whose stories have shown us how our early interactions with mother and father program us to respond in certain ways to our later work environments. In a very real sense, we may spend our lives rehearsing other people's scripts for the way we work.

We *can* rewrite the script, however. Throughout this book, I have shown career leavers in the process of transforming their work. Their stories are intended to serve as transformative models, for when we see that a major life change can be made and we understand how someone else did it, change in our own lives seems more possible. Although you may agree that other women's stories are interesting and enlightening, you may not be able to see how you could make a substantial change in your work life. Those women's lives are a lot simpler than mine, you may be saying to yourself. There's too much at stake in my career—I can't leave it, no matter how much I'd like to!

If you are truly motivated to change, you can—just as the Olympic athletes were able to improve the quality of their physical performance and the cancer patients were able to raise their white blood cell count. The following visualization exercises are designed to help you to write a new script for your work life, one in which you are cast in the starring role. This role is entirely yours to choose. As scriptwriter and actress in your own drama, you can imagine any kind of work you would like. *You* are the one who decides what the limits are. Perhaps, in the process of this imaginative work, you will even decide to change those limits.

BASIC TECHNIQUES

Before you begin, you need to know something about basic relaxation and visualization techniques. The first goal is to relax your mind and your body so that you are receptive to your new script. Here are three easy relaxation techniques that are frequently taught in stress management courses. You might try all three, then choose the one you like best.

Muscle Relaxation

The first technique is progressive muscle relaxation. Choose a time and place where you will not be disturbed. Sit in a comfortable chair or, if you are sure you will not fall asleep, lie down. Take a deep breath and let it out, then alternately tense and relax each major muscle group three times, breathing deeply and rhythmically. Begin with your toes and move upward: feet and calves (carefully, since they are prone to cramp), thighs, stomach, hands, upper arms, shoulders, neck, face, eyes. When you are finished, relax with your eyes closed. You are ready to begin your visualization.

Breathing

Another often-used relaxation technique is the breath technique. Again, be sure you will not be disturbed. Then sit or lie down. Loosen your clothing. Close your eyes and focus on your breath, breathing in through your nose, out through your mouth. Let your diaphragm muscles rise and fall with your breath and feel the sensation of the air as it moves in and out. Listen to the slight sound and sense the rhythm without trying to change it. When your breathing is even and you feel calm and relaxed, you are ready to begin your visualizations.

Focused Attention

Sit comfortably. Choose a spot in front of you—simply a spot, or an object—and look at it. Your eyelids will begin to seem heavy. Let them close naturally. They will feel relaxed, and this relaxation will spread pleasantly through your body. You are ready to begin.

Visualizing

Numerous visualization techniques are available, several of which are described in Shakti Gawain's book *Creative Visualization*. The technique I suggest here is one we can call making a movie. Eyes closed, feeling relaxed and calm, create for yourself an imaginary vacation retreat away from the distractions of your work life—a cabin in the woods, a studio overlooking the ocean, a primitive camp in the high country. It should be a safe place, secluded, and as comfortable and beautiful as you wish to make it. The only requirement is that your space includes a screen of some kind on which you can watch the movie you are about to make. At the end of each visualization, you will want to make some kind of record of what you imagined—either in your notebook or on a tape recorder, so have your equipment with you when you begin.

A PREVIEW

Each of the three following visualization exercises represents a specific stage in the process of transforming your work: creating work of your own, integrating that work into your life, and saying good-bye to your old ways of working. The exercises are arranged in a sequential order, but doing all three exercises in one sitting is tiring. Probably the most effective way of working is to space the exercises over a three-day period. Do the first visualization, write down or tape record the results, and give yourself a day to let it soak in. The next day, reread or listen to your record of the first exercise and do the second exercise. The third day, review both the first and second exercises and do the third. By spacing the exercises in this way, you will have time to assimilate the new images. You may also find during your review that you would like to change something: Feel free—after all, it is *your* life you are envisioning!

Before you begin the exercises, note that the instructions for each visualization ask you to imagine yourself as a scriptwriter who has written a movie. You will view your movie twice. The first time, you will see yourself as the scriptwriter, seated in front of the screen, watching yourself act out the role you have written and suggesting necessary revisions as the scene progresses. The second time, you will see yourself as the star on the screen, acting out the lead role, seeing the scene through the eyes of the actress. I suggest this strategy because it is useful for us to understand that in a real sense, we *can* write our own scripts. We *can* remake our lives if we choose to do so. But we also play the lead role in our lives, and it is useful for us to visualize ourselves in the process of acting the role, not just creating it. Further, psychologists have found that people who visualize themselves from the performer's point of view—that is, mentally rehearse the motions as if they were actually carrying them out, feeling the muscle reactions, the timing, and so on—gain a stronger and longer-lasting effect from their mental imagery than do people who simply watch themselves doing something from the audience's point of view.

Perhaps, by the time you have gotten this far in our preview, you are feeling uncomfortable with the idea of visualization. I'm not very good at conjuring up images, you may be saying. I'm a word person, not a picture person. If this is true for you, and if you cannot persuade yourself to experiment with mental imaging, you might try a different strategy. If you are a word person, write the exercise instead of imagining it. You might use the familiar unsent-letter format: Write the descriptions asked for in exercises one and two in a letter to a friend or family member. In your letter, give as many concrete details as possible about your new situation, in the most vivid language you can summon. Another strategy is to write the descriptions in your journal, dating them at some date in the future. What is important in these exercises is to put down some sort of plan, whether it comes to you in the process of visualizing images or writing words.

Perhaps you are intending to skim through the following section, get the gist of it and go on, without actually doing the exercises. I don't have a lot of patience with exercises, you might be saying. I'd rather just read, if you don't mind. Of course, as a reader, you are completely in charge of the way you deal with a book: You can open it, close it, skip a chapter, or stop in the middle. If you are planning to skim-read or skip the next few pages, let me make an observation: Change is a difficult, ego-wrenching process, and many of us have a great deal of psychological resistance to it. It might be useful for you to spend a moment examining your reasons for not doing the exercises. Are you resisting the possibility of change in your life? What might actually happen if you were to choose an alternative way to work? What is frightening about that possibility? Why? If you are still planning to just read rather than do the exercises, please read with a pencil in your hand. Something might come to you that is worth writing down.

Exercise One: Creating Work of Your Own

After you have completely relaxed, imagine yourself taking time off from work and going to your vacation retreat. There are no reports to hand in, no quotas to meet, no meetings to attend, no calls to return. Give yourself time to appreciate your imaginary environment, tune into your calm breathing, and let your body loosen further.

When you are ready, think back over what you wrote in response to the questions of chapter 12. Now, imagine yourself as a screenwriter, developing a scene in which you are doing *work of your own*—the way you would be working if you were pursuing your *own* goals, using the skills and competencies you enjoy most, and feeling good about your work. In your scene, you may choose to modify the position you presently have, or you may imagine a completely new kind of work. If you can think of several kinds of work, narrow your choice to just one, for the purposes of this exercise. You can repeat the visualization later, with a different script.

When you are ready, project your scene onto your screen and watch it, making necessary changes as you go along. Then, when the scene is exactly the way you want it, play it again. This time, cast yourself in the main role, carrying out the work as if you were actually doing it, looking out of your own eyes. Spend as long as you like with this scene, replaying it several times, if that seems interesting and useful.

When you have played the scene at least twice, once from the point of view of the scriptwriter and once from the point of view of the star, turn off the movie. You can continue to spend some time exploring your vacation retreat, or you can decide that it is time to end the visualization session. When you are finished, take several deep breaths, open your eyes, and stretch.

Now it is time to record what you have imagined. Using your notebook or your tape recorder, note down the elements of the scene you constructed and in which your starred. As you write, use the present tense to answer questions, such as the following: In what setting are you working? What kind of work schedule are you keeping? Are you working alone or with others? If you are working with others, what kind of relationships do you have with them? Are there certain work habits that you no longer have? Have you developed new work habits? How do you feel about what you are doing, about your colleagues, about your environment, about yourself? What salary are you earning from your new work?

Here is an example of a report written by Helen, who saw herself doing something very different from her normal administrative work in the personnel office of the insurance corporation where she had been for ten years. For the past five years, she has gardened for a hobby. In her visualization, Helen imagined herself raising plants for a living.

> I am the owner of a nursery called Gardens Galore, which I financed by cashing in my retirement fund. Today, I am setting out a new landscape display, with a small stone fountain surrounded by some lovely blooming shrubs: hydrangeas, fuchsias, crepe myr-

tles. The two older women who work as my helpers are watering the new shipment of summer annuals. We smile at one another as we work because we are sharing something we deeply enjoy. I feel grateful that I can be outdoors all day, not cooped up behind the desk, buried by mounds of paperwork. I feel relaxed about my work, not driven to please other people. I actually *enjoy* pleasing my customers, because they share with me my love for growing things. I put the finishing touches on the new fountain display and find, to my surprise, that it's closing time. I check out the cash register and find that we've had a super day. I'm pleased—the business is doing much better than my initial projections. I decide to treat myself to a celebration dinner.

As you record your impressions of your visualization, or perhaps as you were doing the visualization itself, you may find yourself raising what seem like very logical objections to what you have visualized. For instance, Helen might have objected, "I don't know enough about plants yet to risk going into the nursery business."

It is useful to note down the objections that occur to you, because they can help you anticipate practical problems you may encounter if you decide to make this change. Helen's concern about having sufficient knowledge is certainly legitimate. Somebody who goes into the nursery business needs to understand plants! Helen's objective, however, may arise out of psychological resistance rather than practical business sense. Our egos have invested heavily in the old career, and they can come up with plenty of solid-sounding reasons not to make a change. As you look back over your objections, try to decide which ones raise practical questions and which ones are evidence of resistance to change. Both can be useful to you, for practical objections can almost always be resolved with the right kind of planning, and resistance objections are evidence of unconscious psychological issues that can be resolved.

Exercise Two: Integrating Work of Your Own into Your Life

Changing your work in significant ways is likely to change your life outside work. In this exercise, you will enlarge the context of your imagining and visualize the way your new work fits into the rest of your life. You may imagine that you have moved to a different residence, perhaps even a different part of the country. You may imagine that your income level has changed. Perhaps you have made important changes in your relational life: You are married, or divorced, or have children, or are more closely related to your parents. Whatever changes you have made, imagine yourself joyfully alive, finding pleasure in your new choices. See yourself in recreation that truly re-creates you: art, dance, sports, hiking, gardening. See yourself keeping a healthy schedule, getting plenty of sleep, eating and exercising prudently, shedding compulsive behaviors, enjoying new levels of physical and psychological health and energy. Visualize yourself exploring your spirituality in new and deeper ways, alone or with others. Imagine giving the gift of time to yourself, to those you love, and to your community.

After your initial relaxation, go to your private vacation retreat. As screenwriter, imagine that you are writing a scene that takes place on Friday afternoon. It is the end of your working week—your *new* work—and you are coming home. If you are working at home, you are winding up your work for the week. Imagine the events of Friday evening as they would be if you could do anything you would like. Then think of Saturday and Sunday and imagine scenes for each day. Then, as you did in the first exercise, switch roles. See yourself acting out the scenes you have just imagined, actually going through the motions. When you have played your scenes at least once from each point of view, turn off the movie. You are back in your private vacation place, where you can linger as long as you like. When you are finished with your visualization, take a few deep breaths, relax, and stretch.

It's time to make a record, in the present tense. Now that you have made changes in your work, how have those changes affected your life? Where are you living? Alone? With whom? What does your home look like? What changes have you made in your personal habits? If your new income level is lower than the old, in what ways have you (and your family) accommodated this reduction? What kinds of activities do you choose for relaxation, recreation, personal enrichment? How do you feel about these activities, about the people you share them with, about yourself? How do you feel physically?

Here is the report of Margo, a nurse-administrator who lives in an apartment in Chicago and visualizes herself moving back to the small city in Iowa where she grew up. In the first exercise, Margo saw herself developing an elder-care business in which she provided trained staff to care for elders in their homes, on a regular or part-time basis. Now, she imagines how this work fits into a new life that also includes her ill mother.

> The office for my business is the small house I have bought several miles out of town. This afternoon when I finish my work, I drive quickly to Mother's to make sure she has a hot meal. I usually eat dinner with her, but tonight I am going out to dinner with some friends from the church, and then we're going square-dancing. On Saturday, I get up early to do the laundry (including Mother's). After an hour's yard work, I'm off on a special errand. I've always wanted a dog, and today I bring Honey home, a wiggly golden cocker spaniel with huge brown eyes. On the way back, I pick up Mother, and she and I spend the afternoon getting acquainted with Honey. Saturday evening, I start a sewing project—new drapes for the living room I'm slowly redecorating. On Sunday, there's church, and afterward a friend comes home with me for dinner. He grills chicken on the barbecue, while I make salad and Honey runs circles around us. Later, I visit with Mother, then make a quick check on an elderly woman who lives in her block and whose regular nurse is ill. Home again for more work on my drapes, a good mystery, a hot bath, and Honey curled up on my feet when I go to bed.

As you record your visualization, you may sense some of the same kinds of objections that you did earlier. If so, note them as well. They can be useful in helping you resolve practical issues and in exploring your psychological resistance to change.

TRANSFORMATION AT WORK

*P*sychologists say that the practice of visualization is useful because it helps us to see ourselves making the right moves. In the experiments with Olympic athletes, however, visualizing the right moves led to actually *performing* those moves. Although thinking through the athletic performance might have been an enjoyable process, the mental imagery was not useful until the athlete actually put it into practice on the ski slopes or the ice or the gym floor. In the same way, you cannot transform your work just by visualizing transformation, although that is a helpful first step. Going for the gold involves putting your dreams into action, giving them a real-world trial.

Finding work of your own—work that reflects your interests and competencies and leaves room for other activities in your life—is a complex process and requires many skills. Before anything else, however, it requires your commitment. You are the one who has to commit yourself to doing your own work, in your own way. You are the one who has to make plans for the change and carry out those plans. No one but you can make the commitment. Once you have made it, no one but you can decide how to get from where you are to where you want to be. No one but you knows what you are willing to give up in order to get to that new place.

So let us assume that you have been in stage one for some time—that you have been questioning your career commitment and feel a compelling need to make a change in the way you work. Let us further assume that your doubts have escalated to the point where you are willing to make a commitment to transforming your work. This may not be the case. People often read books because they want to find out about the subject, not necessarily because they want to follow the prescriptions the book offers for change. For the purposes of this chapter, let us assume that you are so deeply committed to change that you are willing

to see the change process through from beginning
is not true for you, you are invited to read just to se
to suggest, and on the chance that reading more a
cess may help you decide to become committed.

Planning Transformation

In the preceding two chapters, you constructed two different
kinds of understandings of what you have and what you want: a
logical, left brain understanding of your goals, skills, habits, and
feelings; and an intuitive, right brain picture of what you would
rather be doing. The next exercise is stage-three work—weighing
options and thinking through the steps that are required in order
to make a change. It will result in a well-ordered plan that will
help you through the actual change process. For the purpose of
this next exercise, look back over your answers to the questions
presented in chapter 11 and your reports on the visualizations
that you did while reading chapter 12. These are the starting points
from which you will begin to take significant steps toward change.

Step One

Look at the report you wrote of your first visualization and think
for a moment about the work you saw yourself doing. Then take
a separate sheet of paper for each of the relevant questions that
follow here. (Not all the questions may fit your situation.) Write
out the answers to these questions in as much detail as you can.
The more specific you are, the easier it will be to see what is
ahead. But please do not feel confined or pinned down by your
answers. A good plan is always open to change and modification
as the need arises. Some of the questions may require some research before you can answer them. If so, jot them down so you
can look for the answers.

MY GOAL—WORK OF MY OWN. What specifically is your new work,
in terms of goals, duties, structures, work organization, and so
forth? Who are you working for? Where is your new work located? What does it pay? A complete description here constitutes
the goal for your overall plan.

κ OF MY OWN—SKILLS AND ABILITIES. If your new work requires new or modified skills and abilities, what are they specifically? Where will you acquire them? What will they cost, in terms
of time and money? How will you finance their acquisition?

WORK OF MY OWN—CREDENTIAL. If your new work requires a credential you do not have, how long will it take to obtain it? Where
can you obtain it? What will it cost? Where will you find the
money? (Be careful here. Sometimes a credential only *appears* to
be necessary, when you can get along perfectly well without it.)

SEEKING WORK OF MY OWN. If your new work involves working
for someone else, you will probably need to seek it out. As
Richard Bolles remarks in *What Color Is Your Parachute*, many
work seekers simply sit at home, waiting for God to send them
the right job. Of course, it can happen that way. Assuming, however, that you would rather conduct your own search than wait
for a job to happen to you, where will you look? What strategies
will you use? When will you start your search, and when do you
hope to end it? What level of effort will you put into it? What resources will you need for your search? Where will you get them?
(Hint: *What Color Is Your Parachute* is probably the most invaluable job seeker's manual ever compiled. It is full of tips, suggestions, instructions, and good common sense, regularly revised to
fit the changing job market. If you are looking for a job in somebody else's organization, small or large, Bolles' book can help you
organize your search.)

WORK OF MY OWN—BEING MY OWN BOSS. If you want to work for
yourself, what financial resources will you need for start-up?
Where will you get the money? What kinds of business knowledge will you need? Where will you obtain this knowledge? A
good resource here is the magazine *The Entrepreneurial Woman.*
There are numerous listings of valuable free or low-cost resources to help you develop your business idea. If you are going
free-lance with your own professional service, such as accounting or public relations work, the professional organization in
your area is a helpful source of information and assistance, as is
your local women's network.

WORK OF MY OWN—EMOTIONAL SUPPORT. Make a list of the friends and family you can depend on to support you and to provide the emotional help you may need. You might want to specifically note the kind of support you will be asking from the individual. For instance, if you have a partner or spouse, you will need that person's understanding, acceptance, and *active* support. If you think you may need more help than you can obtain from the people on your list, you might want to seek out a support group. If you have not done stage-two work, or if you need professional help in sorting out the issues you encountered in your stage-two self-analysis, you may want to look for a competent therapist.

DISENGAGING FROM MY CURRENT/OLD WORK. Finding new work necessarily involves saying good-bye to the old. That is not always easy, for we are often deeply embedded in what we are presently doing and feel we have obligations there. On this sheet, list the steps you will have to go through in order to disengage yourself as smoothly as possible from what you are currently doing. Will you ask for a leave of absence to explore new possibilities, or will you simply resign? What preparations will you make for someone else to assume your responsibilities? What difficulties are you likely to encounter in the process of disengagement? How will you resolve those difficulties?

Step Two

Now, take the first sheet that you filled out after your general work description. Looking at your answers to the questions, write down the steps you would have to take, in the proper sequence, in order to carry out your plan. For example, this sheet might be the sheet headed Skills. If you listed new or modified skills that you need to obtain, write down the steps you will have to take, in the order you will take them, to obtain those skills.

Consider, for instance, Helen's decision to start her own nursery business: Gardens Galore. Among the various skills she needs to acquire, Helen might have listed managing a large greenhouse. To acquire such a skill, Helen might choose to take a course in greenhouse management at a university. Or she might design her own self-directed study project. Or she might ask a local greenhouse owner if she can work Saturdays during the busy season in order to get hands-on experience in greenhouse management. Helen decided to take the second option. Her self-directed study of greenhouse management contained the following steps:

1. compile a reading list on the subject of greenhouse management and study as many of the books as possible

2. find out if there is a professional organization of greenhouse managers and contact them for information

3. make a list of large greenhouses within driving distance

4. contact owners and ask for permission to visit

5. spend some lunch hours and weekends observing greenhouse operations and talking to owners and employees

If you are planning to go into business for yourself, like Helen, be sure to familiarize yourself with all the costs. You may not know, for instance, that self-employed people pay twice as much social security tax as employees. They also have to make quarterly estimated tax payments to the IRS, and they have to pay 100 percent of the cost of health insurance and retirement benefits. These overhead costs are not always obvious to the person who is dreaming about being her own boss.

Now, repeat the process of defining steps for the different activities listed on the other sheets you filled out. When you have finished, you will have the outline of a step-by-step plan that is aimed specifically at achieving your goal: finding or creating the work you described on sheet one. This outline, of course, is not necessarily your final plan, for you will be modifying it as you go along.

Step Three

When you have listed the necessary steps for each activity on each of the relevant sheets, make a realistic timetable for yourself. This timetable will allow you to change your work within a reasonable, comfortable time frame that depends on where you are now in the career-leaving process, where you plan to go in terms of new work, and how committed you are to making that change. Remember Crystal, who left her work as the director of a career-counseling program to become the director of a women's spirituality network? That change, which involved the slow maturation of Crystal's interests and commitment, required ten to twelve years. If your change is a radical one, or if it requires the creation of new work, it may be a long-term project. If you are simply modifying your present work, however, you may be able to make a significant change in much less time. You are the only one who can decide the right pace and the right timing for the changes that you are committed to make.

Step Four

Your work is not the only thing that will change, for when we make significant changes in our work, our lives change, too. Look back over your report of the second exercise in chapter 12, where you visualized the kind of life you are likely to be leading after you have changed your work. When you have read that report, take another sheet of paper and head it *Integrating My Work and My Life*. On the sheet, make a list of the various things you would have to do in order to make that dream a reality.

For an example, think about Margo, the nurse administrator who returned to her home town to open an elder-care business. If Margo had made a list of the substantial changes she would be making in her life, it might have looked something like this:

1. Change in my location—sell house in the city, rent or buy a small house in the country close to my home town, where I can have an office, living space, and space for a garden

2. Change in my income level—accommodate myself to a 50 percent income reduction, at least for the next three to four years, until the business has built up

3. Change in the way I spend my time—stop spending fourteen hours a day working! Plan my business so I am on the job six hours a day and have time for myself, Mother, friends

4. Change in my relationship with my family—assume responsibility for Mother's care, find her an in-home care giver for four to five hours a day, spend at least two hours a day with her. Connect with aunts, cousins

5. Change in friends—make time for friends, join a church, become active in community, be open to a new relationship

6. Change in taking care of myself—make time for myself. Take up gardening, sewing, crafts, reading, exercise. Find the right pet. Pay attention to my diet.

Now that you have your list of significant changes, construct a timetable for change, setting dates wherever possible. Some of your change items may be difficult to plan, because they depend on others. For instance, Margo cannot accomplish any of the other changes she wants to make, either in her work life or her personal life, until she has located a place to live and work. Her relocation plan will have to dovetail with her plan to establish her elder-care business. If your new work involves relocation, research and careful planning will be necessary to coordinate the various aspects of your change.

Step Five

Another major feature of your life-change plan is likely to be a reduction in income, at least in the beginning. Margo puts this change close to the top of her list because she knows that income reduction will make a big impact on her life. It will be useful to her to do some special cash planning. She must be able to estimate not only net income from her business but also her personal expenditures. If there is no income for a few months, as is true in some start-up operations, she will need sufficient financial reserves to cover the difference between what she brings in and what she must spend.

If your change will result in a reduced income, either short- or long-term, you will also want to make a financial plan. Here is a simple way of figuring your financial reserves. You can do this on a sheet of paper called *My Financial Picture.*

1. Start by adding all your liquid assets—your checking account balance, savings, stocks, bonds, your retirement account (minus early-withdrawal penalties), the cash value in your life insurance. For the moment, leave out real estate and other nonliquid assets.

2. Add up all your liabilities—the amount you owe on everything except real estate.

3. Subtract your liabilities from your assets.

4. Add the real estate and other nonliquid assets you plan to sell or cash in. Use only the actual amount you will realize from the sale after the mortgage balance and sale costs are paid. Be realistic about what you will realize and the length of time it will take to sell. Get a market analysis on real estate, so that you do not trick yourself into overestimating your reserves.

5. The final figure, cash assets added to the proceeds from the sale of nonliquid assets, is your total financial reserve.

Some people, when they subtract liabilities from assets at step three, will come up with a negative number: their liabilities are greater than their assets. If this is true for you, you need to get yourself on solid financial footing *before* you leave your work. Figure out how many months it will take to get your finances in order—pay off your car, eliminate your credit card balances, finish paying medical expenses, and so on. That is the earliest possible target date for leaving your work. An alternative is to use your equity in real estate and other nonliquid assets to reduce your debts. It may be wiser, however, to treat those assets as a reserve against an uncertain financial future and concentrate now on reducing your liabilities.

In addition to figuring out how much money you have, you may also need to plan to reduce your expenditures. This may mean selling your big house and moving into something smaller and less expensive, perhaps even something that is paid for. For instance, when Bill and I moved to his land, which was paid for, we bought a used mobile home for forty-five hundred dollars cash. The writing life has its financial ups and downs, and we were not willing to saddle ourselves with mortgage payments.

We have had many occasions to be grateful for the fact that we have no mortgage.

The standard of spending that you have grown accustomed to will affect your plans. Reducing your expenditures may well mean changing the way you live, drive, dress, entertain yourself, feed yourself. For some people, this kind of change is a welcome challenge, for it represents freedom from the compulsions of the consumer society and the media's constant drumming of *buy-buy-buy*. For others, the challenge is deadly. If you already know it will be deadly and there is simply no way you and/or your family can give up the material things for which you trade your work, perhaps you should not consider a change that will reduce your income.

If you are committed to making a change and the income reduction is the only thing holding you back, you might make a serious study of the meaning of money in your life. In our culture there is a very high premium on conspicuous consumption, which is considered the standard of success and authority. If you and your family have adopted that standard, you may need help in releasing yourself from it. A resource I have found useful is Joe Dominguez' seminar called "Transforming Your Relationship with Money and Achieving Financial Independence" (available on audio tape from The New Road Map Foundation, Box 15981, Seattle, Washington 98115). The seminar includes a workbook that helps you to examine your financial attitudes and habits and to develop a more mindful approach to personal money management.

Transforming Your Work, Transforming Yourself

Transforming your work is a wonderful concept. It remains just that—an intriguing concept, a thing of the mind and the imagination—until you put your strength, your ability, and your commitment into action. You have read about many women who did it, some of them the hard way. You have followed them through the six phases of career leaving, and you have seen how the change process took place in the lives of three women who actively reshaped their work. You have read about how you can do this for yourself. Some of you have done the exercises that can strengthen both your commitment and your ability to make a change.

Change will not happen, however, unless you put down this book and pick up your life, determined to take control of your work, to own it for yourself, to work the way you choose to work. Others can wish you all the luck in the world, they can cross their fingers, can promise to say a prayer. But unless you commit yourself to change, it will not happen. Getting there from here, under your own power, depends entirely on you.

Getting there under your own power is, of course, exactly the point. Women have become successful in the career culture under somebody else's power—under masculine, not feminine power. In order to succeed and be accepted as powerful, authoritative people, we have adopted a model of success, power, and authority that does not belong to us. Releasing that model—giving up the masculine-adapted career self and the definition of success that comes with it—is the first major step along the way to transforming our work and transforming our *selves*.

These transformations are not easy; they may be the hardest changes we have ever made in our lives—much harder than climbing the career ladder in the first place. Giving birth to a new self that is uniquely our own requires courage and commitment and the willingness to risk all that we presently have, all that we presently are. Whatever work we do, our ability to be ourselves is our greatest goal, our greatest asset. It is an asset that does not come cheaply.

Once we allow ourselves to *be* truly ourselves, what will we do? What grand, important world-changing work will we choose, create, perform? I have come to believe that what we do, in the long run, may be far less important than the way we do it, that the attention and love and devotion that we give to our work, whatever that work is, makes that work important. I believe that it is not our world-changing work that will eventually reshape our culture, but our world-changing feminine *selves*, dedicated to work that honors us, honors others, and honors our planet, however unglamorous it may be. I believe that when we bring to any work our mindful focus, our focused mind, we work in the spirit of right consciousness. In that spirit, the question of right livelihood resolves itself.

AFTERWORD

$\mathcal{T}$his book is an ending and a beginning. It is a piece of work, a substantial piece, which has taken me over four years of research and writing. It marks the close of a major period of my life: that time when my life's circle was narrowed to the limiting circumference of what I did for a living. Writing about my compulsive work habits and the effort it took to change those habits has brought me a sense of clarity: I believe I understand now the private demons that drove me to work as I did. It also has been enormously freeing, for the finished book puts a kind of period to the paragraph of myself that closed when I left the career. I can go on now, to new work, new thoughts, new explorations.

Writing this book has been liberating in a different way, too, for meeting and talking with other women who shared my experiences has given me a far broader perspective than I had when I began. I was not alone in my compulsions or in my needs: My demons, as it turns out, are not private demons after all. I belonged to a large group of women who received something totally new in the history of human work, so new that we yet barely comprehend its meaning: the opportunity to establish our citizenship in a part of our culture—the career culture—that had previously been closed to us. Given the difficult circumstances of our admission and the strenuous effort required to make ourselves over into model citizens of this culture, it is no wonder that some of us, many of us, perhaps, became its slaves. Witnessing the emancipation of the women who have chosen to leave this culture has been wonderfully liberating for me. I salute and celebrate them, for theirs was a difficult, wrenching choice. To give up the achievement of women's success in the corporate workplace for the creation of women's own work is not an easy thing. To give up the corporate workplace, and the hope that perhaps women can change it from within, is not an easy thing.

That, perhaps, is the ultimate question: can the workplace, as we know it in the last decade of the twentieth century, be made over into a human and humane place? My own answer to that question is a deeply qualified yes. The workplace, even the corporate workplace, *can* be changed. More flexible schedules, more attention to the needs of care givers, less mindless competition, more worker input into personnel policies and practices—these changes can be made, little by little. The larger the corporation and the more rigid its bureaucracy (the two are paired), however, the smaller the chance for anything but cosmetic change. Institutional structures (which include government, education, the church, and business) have a life of their own. They resist change, particularly liberalizing change. Meanwhile, forces that work for the status quo—market forces, competitive factors, and profit margins—will be operating against change. Which will win? Where corporations are concerned, I feel that large-scale change across the country will be so slow as to be practically imperceptible.

The American workplace and the American imagination are dominated by big corporations, but the corporation is not the only place to work. We are beginning to see in this country a revitalization of independent business, small-scale manufacturing and distribution, home businesses. In my view, these are the places where change in our work habits and attitudes is truly possible. Jobs in small businesses may lack the glitz that spangles corporate careers, and they certainly lack the financial rewards. But small workplaces, human-scale workplaces, can be shaped by humans working together for their common benefit and with the belief that we are capable of something more than the mere creation of material wealth and the maintenance of a certain standard of material consumption. To my mind, these are the workplaces where we need to put our energy for change, for it is from these that our models for large-scale change, if change is possible, will come.

If this is so, then we need a radically changed view of work in our society and a new understanding of the word career. This new understanding is most likely to come from women and men—career leavers—who dare to challenge the career culture's vested interests in controlling our work and our lives. They are the ones who can bring us to a new perception of how we use work, how we are used by it, and what we have to do to transform it. Theirs are the new voices to which we must listen.

239

NOTES

CHAPTER 1. CAREER LEAVING: TRAGEDY OR TRIUMPH?

1. Juliet B. Schor, *The Overworked American* (New York: Basic Books, 1992), 29.

2. Deborah L. Arron, *Running from the Law* (Seattle: Niche Press, 1989), 20.

3. Judith Bardwich, *In Transition: How Feminism, Sexual Liberation, and the Search for Self-Fulfillment Have Altered America* (New York: Holt Rinehart and Winston, 1979), 50.

4. Barbra Bools and Lydia Swan, *Power Failure: Why Some Women Short Circuit Their Careers and How to Avoid It* (New York: St. Martin's Press, 1989), 153.

5. Quoted in Bools and Swan, 174.

6. Bools and Swan, 44.

7. Sarah Hardesty and Nehama Jacobs, *Success and Betrayal: The Crisis of Women in Corporate America* (New York: Franklin Watts, 1986), 6.

8. Karen Horney's view of adult development is laid out in *Neurosis and Human Growth* (New York: W.W. Norton, 1950).

9. See Charlotte Buhler, "The Curve of Life as Studied in Biographies," *Journal of Applied Psychology* 19 (1955): 405–409.

10. Jung translated his own traumatic experience of separation from his mentor, Sigmund Freud, into a psychological theory describing the holistic growth and development of the personality across the life-span. His concept of adult growth is described in *The Adult Development of C.G. Jung*, by John-Raphael Staude (Boston: Routledge & Kegan Paul, 1981). Two works of Jung that are relevant to this concept are *Man and His Symbols* (New York: Doubleday, 1964) and *Memories, Dreams, Reflections* (New York: Pantheon Books, 1962).

11. Carol Gilligan, *In a Different Voice* (Cambridge: Harvard University Press, 1982).

12. Robert Kegan, *The Evolving Self: Problem and Process in Human Development* (Cambridge: Harvard University Press, 1982).

13. Maureen Murdock, *The Heroine's Journey: Woman's Quest for Wholeness* (Boston: Shambhala, 1990), 79.

14. Murdock, 84.

CHAPTER 2. THE FIRST STAGE: DOUBTING

1. Douglas LaBier, *Modern Madness: The Emotional Fallout of Success* (Reading, Mass.: Addison-Wesley, 1986), 9.

2. Helen Rose Fuchs Ebaugh, *Becoming an Ex: The Process of Role Exit* (Chicago: University of Chicago Press, 1968), 41.

3. June Singer, "The Sadness of the Successful Woman," in *The Goddess Re-Awakening*, edited by Shirley Nicholson (Wheaton, Ill.: Quest Books, 1989), 117.

4. Hilary Cosell, *Woman on a Seesaw: The Ups and Downs of Making It* (New York: G. P. Putnam's Sons, 1985), 74–75.

5. Nancy W. Collins, Susan K. Gilbert, Susan H. Nycum, *Women Leading: Making Tough Choices on the Fast Track* (Lexington, Mass.: Stephen Greene Press, 1988), 173.

6. Tom Peters and Nancy Austin, *A Passion for Excellence: The Leadership Difference* (New York: Random House, 1985), 419.

7. Margery D. Rosen, "All Alone: The New Loneliness of American Women," in *Ladies' Home Journal*, April 1991: 140, 216, 218.

8. Ebaugh, 69–74.

CHAPTER 3. THE SECOND STAGE: REFLECTING ON THE SELF

1. Patricia McBroom, *The Third Sex: The New Professional Woman* (New York: William Morrow, 1986), 115.

2. Margaret Hennig and Anne Jardim, *The Managerial Woman* (New York: Pocket Books, 1977), 100, 104.

3. Polly Young-Eisendrath and Florence L. Wiedemann, *Female Authority: Empowering Women through Psychotherapy* (New York: Guilford Press, 1987), 92.

4. Young-Eisendrath and Wiedemann, 90.

5. Marion Woodman, *The Ravaged Bridegroom: Masculinity in Women* (Toronto, Canada: Inner City Books, 1990), 74.

6. Arleigh Hochschild, *The Second Shift: Working Parents and the Revolution at Home* (New York: Viking, 1989), x.

7. Arlene Rossen Cardozo, *Sequencing* (New York: Atheneum, 1986).

8. McBroom, 92.

9. Paula Bernstein, *Family Ties, Corporate Bonds* (Garden City, N.J.: Doubleday, 1985), 10.

10. Anne Wilson Schaef and Diane Fassel, *The Addictive Organization* (San Francisco: Harper and Row, 1988), 47.

11. Schaef and Fassel, 132.

12. Communication, quoted in Schaef and Fassel, 29.

13. Schaef and Fassel, 30.

14. Of the eighty women in the group of career leavers I studied, seventy-three (91 percent) say they undertook serious self-examination sometime during the career-leaving process. For 62 percent, this self-examination involved individual or group therapy.

CHAPTER 4. THE THIRD STAGE: WEIGHING OPTIONS

1. Anne Wilson Schaef and Diane Fassel write that the organization's benefits and bonuses often become a controlling factor in the lives of employees, preventing them from "moving on and doing what they need to do." In a time of spiraling health insurance costs, insurance may even be perceived as a benefit almost as great as the salary. Further, certain companies arrange the vesting schedule of their retirement and benefit packages to entice employees to remain with the company. In February 1992, a *New York Times* poll reported that 38 percent of American workers were staying on the job because of their benefits. Schaef and

Fassel quote one of their clients who commented that he and his friends planned to work in the same company until retirement, not because they enjoyed the work, but because they "needed the benefits; they lived for them; and they could not afford to leave the organization if it meant losing them." *The Addictive Organization*, 126.

2. Ebaugh, 111–117.

3. Sinetar, 121.

CHAPTER 5. THE FOURTH STAGE:
THE CAREER CRISIS

1. In my study, about 40 percent of the women made the change to their new work over a period of two to twelve years.

2. Ebaugh, 125.

3. Ebaugh, 128.

4. Kathleen Gerson, *Hard Choices: How Women Decide about Work, Career, and Motherhood* (Berkeley: University of California Press, 1985), 103.

5. Ebaugh, 130–132.

6. Among the women I studied, 26 percent cited health problems as a significant reason for leaving.

7. Arron, 20–21.

8. Hochschild, 57.

9. Of the eighty women in my study sample, 22 percent returned home to work as caretakers for their children or for elderly parents. Thirty-one percent became self-employed, usually converting their career skills into some sort of free-lance work. Another 31 percent stayed in the workplace but sought less stressful work that they did not consider as a career; half of this group worked only part-time. Nine percent chose to return to formal education for retraining in professional fields in which they felt they would have control over their work. Seven percent had put together enough money to live without being employed and chose to leave the workplace altogether. For those women who returned to the workplace during the course of the study, the average temporary

length of self-imposed absence was two years and three months. Several are considering returning but remain absent at the time of this writing.

10. Carl Jung, *Two Essays in Analytic Psychology, Collected Works,* vol. 7, paragraphs 155–156 (Princeton: Princeton University Press, 1954).

11. Jane Wheelwright, "The Breakdown of Animus Identification in Finding the Feminine," in *To Be a Woman,* edited by Connie Zweig (Los Angeles: Jeremy P. Tarcher, 1990), 153, 155. For a full discussion of the "animus problem," see Young-Eisendrath and Wiedemann, chapter 6, "Animus as Father, God, or King," 88–111.

12. Young-Eisendrath and Wiedemann: "Adapting to male dictates for validation is actually a healthy transition from fusion with Mother to greater independence in a patriarchal society," 90.

13. June Singer, *Boundaries of the Soul: The Practice of Jung's Psychology* (New York: Doubleday, 1972), 215.

CHAPTER 6. THE FIFTH STAGE: THE BLACK HOLE

1. Adrienne Rich, *Of Woman Born: Motherhood as Experience and Institution* (New York: W.W. Norton, 1976), 53.

2. Jung, *The Development of Personality,* in *Collected Works,* vol. 17 (Princeton: Princeton University Press, 1954), paragraphs 289, 294.

CHAPTER 7. THE SIXTH STAGE: WORK OF HER OWN

1. Sinetar, 162.

2. Duane Elgin, *Voluntary Simplicity: Toward a Way of Life That Is Outwardly Simple, Inwardly Rich* (New York: William Morrow and Company, 1981), 79–80.

3. Arron, 95.

4. *Money Magazine,* December 1981: 75.

5. Warren Johnson, *Muddling Toward Frugality: A Blueprint for Survival in the 1980s* (Boston: Shambhala, 1979), 191–92.

PART TWO. INTRODUCTION: THREE WOMEN

1. Carolyn G. Heilbrun, *Writing a Woman's Life* (New York, Ballantine Books, 1988), 24.
2. Mary Catherine Bateson, *Composing a Life* (New York: Atlantic Monthly Press, 1989), 9.

CHAPTER 12. VISUALIZING TRANSFORMATION

1. Dr. Hall's research experiment is cited in *Omni*, vol. 5, no. 5 (February 1983), 87.

INDEX

ABOUT THE AUTHOR

A former university professor and vice-president, Susan Wittig Albert is now a full-time writer. She is the author of numerous articles and books about literature and writing, over fifty novels for middle-grade and teen readers, and The China Bayles mystery series. She and her husband, William Albert, also a writer, frequently collaborate on writing projects. They live on three acres in the Hill Country of Central Texas, together with a varying number of cats, chickens, geese, ducks, and peafowl. Dr. Albert has three children and three grandchildren.